to have
and
to
hold

to have and to hold

WALTER MIKAC
WITH LINDSAY SIMPSON

MACMILLAN
Pan Macmillan Australia

The authors and publisher wish to thank all those who have granted permission to reproduce correspondence in this book.

They would also like to thank EMI Publishing and Mushroom Records for permission to reproduce lyrics from the following songs:

'Heaven Help my Heart' (D. Tyson/T. Arena/D. McTaggart)
© Into Wishin'/EMI Blackwood Music (Canada) Ltd. For
Australasia EMI Songs Australia Pty Ltd. All rights reserved.
(D. Tyson/T. Arena/D. McTaggart) Mushroom Group of Companies

'That's the Way a Woman Feels' (Arena/Reswick/Werfel)
Mushroom Group of Companies. All rights reserved.

First published 1997 in Macmillan by Pan Macmillan Australia Pty Limited
St Martins Tower, 31 Market Street, Sydney

National Library of Australia
cataloguing-in-publication data:
Mikac, Walter.
To have and to hold.

ISBN 0 7329 0910 4.

1. Mikac, Walter. 2. Mikac family.
3. Mass murder - Tasmania - Port Arthur. I. Simpson, Lindsay.
II. Title.

364.1523099464

Typeset in 12/15pt Times by Midland Typesetters, Victoria
Printed in Australia by McPherson's Printing Group

'Grandpa and I went for a walk and he told me when he saw Gran in the coffin she looked so peaceful and beautiful that he fell in love with her all over again. I started crying. I hope someone will say that about me one day.'

NANETTE IN A LETTER TO WALTER WHEN HE WAS IN AMSTERDAM, 22/8/84.

Netty, when I found this letter recently, I felt a chill run down my spine. In writing this book and becoming submerged in our memories, I am falling in love with you all over again. I've written an entire book dedicated to you, Lani and Maddie. You are the inspiration that makes my life worth continuing. The love, fun times and laughter that we were fortunate enough to share together has made me a better person.

Lani and Maddie, you are both parts of me that I can never replace and you have a place in my soul that can never be taken. I am proud to be your dad. I hope this book will be a lasting tribute to you all. It's my hope that enshrining your memory in this way makes everyone appreciate the fragility and preciousness of life.

I miss you and always will.

AUTHORS' NOTE

A conscious decision has been made in this book not to print the name of the gunman who perpetrated the dreadful acts of 28 April 1996 – a campaign begun by the Dunblane parents in a book published in Great Britain in 1997 called *Our Year of Tears*.

As we prepared the book for publication, we were determined to continue the crusade. This is a story of love and hope with no place for either of these creatures. They do not have a place in history, alongside their victims.

W. M. & L. S.
1997

FOREWORD
by the Hon. John Howard, Prime Minister

Walter Mikac's story is one of tremendous courage and hope, and his book, *To Have and To Hold*, is a moving tribute to his wife Nanette and his two daughters Alannah and Madeline. I am honoured and delighted to have been invited to contribute this foreword to it.

Like all Australians, I have been deeply moved by the strength and grace shown by Walter, other victims of the tragedy at Port Arthur and their families. While few of us can begin to understand the enormity of the loss they have suffered and the sorrow they have endured, we can all be inspired by their courage, their hope and their determination.

I can only describe Walter Mikac's determination in working to see good come out of tragedy as heroic. In the wake of Port Arthur, Walter showed immense courage in speaking out in favour of tighter controls on firearms. Walter's contribution to the debate helped the Commonwealth government achieve agreement with the States on national controls which, as I write, have reduced the number of the most dangerous weapons in Australia by half a million.

In February 1997, Walter established the Alannah and Madeline Foundation, which aims to provide financial and other support to child victims of violent crime or the sudden loss of family. As its patron, I commend the aims of the Foundation and ask you to be generous in your support.

Those two achievements alone are remarkable tributes to the memory of Nanette, Alannah and Madeline. To those tributes, Walter Mikac has added this book which celebrates his love for his family. Walter's love, and the decency, generosity and empathy of his fellow

Australians that have sprung from it, are a wonderful reminder of the central role of the family in Australian society. The family is our society's moral and social anchor, providing us with strength and hope. Those of us who might be tempted to take for granted the comfort and joy provided by our families cannot help but reflect upon what is truly important in our lives as a result of Port Arthur.

In many respects the greatest memorial we as a nation can create to the victims of 28 April 1996 is a renewed determination to rid our society of violence. I would ask all Australians to reflect on that, and recognise that violence is not the answer to any problem or to any difference of opinion.

I commend Walter's book to all Australians. I believe it will help bring comfort and strength to the lives of those touched by tragedy, and provide inspiration to us all.

(John Howard)

Contents

Prologue

*L*ight filtered through my eyelids, interrupting a dark, fitful sleep. At first, when I opened my eyes, I saw what was familiar and reassuring. The antique walnut wardrobe, the full-length pastel curtains, the soft Monet prints on the wall. Then my eyes focused on the photograph on the bedside table: my daughters, Alannah and Madeline, smiling in their usual carefree way. Alannah's shoulder-length, wavy brown hair tied with a pink scrunchie, her six-year-old grin revealing the two missing front teeth. Her long eyelashes and piercing blue eyes dominate her rounded face. She is lovingly holding my arm. Maddie is sitting on my lap smiling with her usual cheesy grin. With her curly golden hair and plump three-year-old body in between infant and child, she looks like an angel.

Then I realised I was clutching something. Why was I lying alone in the bed? And on Nanette's side?

All sorts of thoughts crammed into my mind, competing for attention. Nanette's new perfume Poême floated towards me. What was I holding? Where were they? Why was it so quiet? But the perfume *belied my thoughts. Closing my eyes, I could see her so clearly. 'They must be hiding behind the door or by the bed.'*

All of this in perhaps twenty seconds, but a vague sense of unease was clammering behind. I looked at the scrunched-up bundle in my arms. Nanette's red-and-blue tartan pyjamas. Then, further down the bed, Alannah's flowing white cotton nightie with navy blue spots and the words 'Hello good morning', and in a heap next to that the tiny baby pair with pink and yellow hearts that belonged to my Maddie, affectionately called 'Chubby'.

'Are you awake, Walter?' The voice belonged to Keith Moulton, my father-in-law, who lived only a few kilometres away from our house at the seaside resort of White Beach.

As I walked out of our bedroom I remembered it was my birthday. Today was 29 April. I was thirty-four years old.

The house was silent. There was no laughter or dogs barking, no cartoons on the television and no sound of Nanette's familiar voice. If this was a nightmare, why wasn't I waking up? Why was Keith here? I could see him, his face pale in the light of the fire he was stoking.

'It really has happened, hasn't it?' I must have walked or stumbled through to Alannah's bedroom. I was screaming.

Now I was running back to our bedroom, tugging at the bedside drawer next to Nanette's side of the bed. On top of the clutter, where I knew I would find it, was an Anne Geddes birthday card. Two tiny babies asleep in the crevice between a man's arms and his chest. They are naked. The tranquillity of the scene brought tears to my eyes.

I opened the card. Nanette had not written in it. I began sobbing uncontrollably. Keith was standing behind me. He put his arm around my shoulder.

'It's just you and me now, Walter. Nanette and the girls are gone!'

I slumped puppet-like on the bed crying until my vision clouded.

I was kneeling now and yelling for the world to hear.

'Couldn't he have just left me one, just one?'

My Last Goodbye

*P*eople came and went that morning. Among the first to arrive at 7.30 a.m. were Eddie and Pam Halton, who owned the Nubeena Riteway supermarket and post office on the Tasman Peninsula. They had also been nearly the last to leave the previous evening. But this morning Eddie's usual effervescent smile was non-existent. He, too, was caught up in this nightmare. We had been playing golf together the previous afternoon at Tasman Golf Club when we heard the gunshots. Thinking back to what seemed like days ago, we had no idea the popping sounds had been the sound of shots from a gun. Red-haired Eddie, my golfing partner and amateur actor in our local revues, was now wrapping his arms around me and hugging me like a brother.

Steve and Pam Ireland, our friends and the two doctors on the peninsula who had been the first medicos to enter the devastation of the Broad Arrow Cafe, also arrived. Kerrie Shoobridge, another close friend, was there making cup after cup of coffee.

I sat in the lounge-room gazing blankly over the blue water of Parsons Bay, over the garden I had planted and landscaped in my time off from the pharmacy, creating this dream house for all of us. The house stood on the hill, above the town of Nubeena, an ordinary weatherboard sixties' house which had been neglected after being rented for years. I had painted and carefully transformed it into the house we had always longed for. Once the wattles and eucalypts and pittosporum hedges were chopped down, the view was breathtaking. Even now, as I stared out of the window across the lawn, I was affected by it.

Just before 9 a.m., a news flash update finally gave us the news we had been waiting for.

'The man who has been holding police at bay for nearly eighteen hours after the multiple shooting at the Port Arthur Historic Site has been apprehended after an all-night siege at Seascape Guesthouse.'

The coffee in my mouth made me feel nauseous. The voice of the broadcaster was so matter-of-fact – as if he was talking about the weather.

How could one person create all this carnage? What did Nanette and my two innocent darlings ever do to deserve a death like this? Why wasn't I there? Why was I still here when I wanted so much to be with them? These questions were relentless, reverberating in my mind. They still plague me now and will plague me for the rest of my life.

I closed my eyes, placing my cup on the table. Yesterday morning they were on the back verandah in their pyjamas, waving me goodbye as I left for golf. As I thought of them in their pyjamas, the early morning light on the verandah capturing the smiles on their faces, an overwhelming desire to feel their bodies for the last time consumed me. They were still on the road in the grounds of the Port Arthur Historic Site where they had been all night and I hadn't even seen them. I had been told not to go there until the gunman had been caught. Police had ordered everybody at the site to stay indoors because there were radio reports the gunman had returned. A longing to touch the softness of their skins, their hair, to hold their bodies, was a deeper urge than any I had experienced before.

Pam Ireland had been the one who told me of their fate – six hours after the shooting, as I searched desperately for them at the site. She was the one who identified her friend Nanette, and Alannah and Madeline, after working among the dead bodies and the injured inside the Broad Arrow Cafe. Then having to inform me of the news would be the most difficult moment in anyone's life. She deserves the utmost respect for her incredible courage.

'It's time to go, Walter,' she said to me now. 'I've spoken to Ian Matterson [the coroner]. They're going to let us through the roadblocks.'

I sat next to my father-in-law in the front seat of his green-blue Toyota Corolla. Pam's husband, Steve, sat in the back. Eddie had departed just minutes before in his Pajero to meet my parents and brothers off their flight from Melbourne. We followed Pam's car past my pharmacy with the 'Closed' sign on the door. Only twenty months ago, I had opened up in this little village, off the beaten track about an hour and a half's drive from Hobart, with such dreams for the future. Most tourists who make the 100-kilometre drive south-east of Hobart don't come to Nubeena. They head straight for Tasmania's premier attraction, the Port Arthur Historic Site.

At the Tasmanian Devil Park, where Nanette and the girls used to visit, the honeyeaters were on the prominent green sign out the front and the sheep grazed leisurely behind a barbed-wire fence as if this was any other day.

My eyes were swelling and becoming puffy from crying. My hands didn't want to leave my forehead in some kind of bid to shield the reality from entering my brain. As I focused on the people in front of the park, I saw a huge contingent of vehicles, police milling around and people standing behind an impromptu barricade. Interim police headquarters and a media base had been set up outside the park. It was not until we had become stationary in the carpark that I realised they were news crews. Scores of them gazing in our direction with TV cameras pointing and long-range lenses at the ready. It then became clear that we were the focus of their attention. Not being quite sure how to react, I held my hands up over my face as tears streamed down my face. I was totally unprepared for this.

'Can't they leave me in peace? I haven't even had a chance to say goodbye to my family yet,' I cried.

Pam Ireland was outside jousting with the powers-that-be. Her dogged ability to steamroll where necessary meant that, although it would be difficult, she would get the required permission.

During this brief period the media edged closer towards the three of us waiting in Keith's car until we felt like caged animals being thrown to a sea of unknown, ravenous faces. More media congregated up to the barricade. Keith's face was totally expressionless, as though all life had been drained from it. His wife and Nanette's mother, Grace, had died just three months before from a long-standing illness.

Steve Ireland could feel I was uncomfortable. Propped on the edge of the back seat, he placed his hand on my shoulder to ease my anxiety.

'How pathetic are the press. They're bloodhounds,' he said, unable to contain his aggravation.

I desperately wanted to escape to the refuge of a dark cave somewhere far away.

Then, Steve jumped out the rear door. Moving just a few steps towards the barrage of lenses, he yelled, 'Have some bloody consideration. This guy has just lost his entire family. Give him some privacy.'

This had the effect of a 44-gallon drum of berley being dumped into a shark cage. The media line acted like a starting line rather than a barricade. Bodies with microphones and cameras surged towards our vehicle. I didn't want to be photographed like this, but then again I wanted the world to see the tears that were welling up in every cell of my body. I could hear the shutters flickering. At that moment I knew that I was no longer just a husband and father mourning the loss of his life's essence – whether I liked it or not, I had become one of the living casualties, the walking wounded from Port Arthur. The image of my distressed, slumped body trying to deny the inevitable would be splashed all over the newspapers the following day.

Thankfully, at this stage, Pam completed her negotiations and returned to the car. We left the pack behind as we headed the

10 kilometres south to Port Arthur, driving through the first roadblock. I looked at the road ahead. It was strangely quiet after all the commotion. Two and a half kilometres before the historic site I could see Seascape, the pink guesthouse which had been burned to the ground. It was here that the gunman had held police at bay for eighteen hours.

As we approached it, I saw thick, black smoke billowing, the finer wispy bits dissipating into the azure blue of the sky. Despite knowing it to be a fact, I was deeply moved when I saw the guesthouse, a charred heap of rubble that was still smouldering with the smell of death. The fruit trees, positioned between the house and the water's edge, were all that was left standing. We drew to a halt as dozens of police vehicles were erratically positioned on both sides of the road.

I could see figures, like ants disturbed from their nest. Then a dozen black-fatigue-clad Special Operations Squad officers charged past our car, their faces blackened with what looked like war paint. Each of them clutched a military-style assault rifle, radios and other paraphernalia. In a strange way, it matched my sense of disbelief, as if I belonged to the set of a movie and this was part of a dream.

Steve echoed my sentiments. 'This is like being in a war zone.'

Yes, I thought. This is what people might expect in Bosnia, Somalia or the Middle East, pictures that flash up on a television screen, but this is Australia in 1996. War doesn't happen here – and yet, what was to be revealed just minutes down the road at Port Arthur could only be described as the most one-sided warfare I have ever seen on this planet.

An ambulance wailed past as I watched Pam, in the front car, get the final go-ahead to proceed to Port Arthur. About 300 metres from Seascape, we passed an aqua-coloured 4WD with its front doors wide open and its windscreen shot out.

I took in the surroundings as we approached the historic site, drawing a small amount of comfort from their familiarity. I could see the Fox and Hounds Hotel, the Tudor-style accommodation only two kilometres from the site where we met for our weekly Rotary meetings. The worst moment of my life was drawing ever closer.

There was the 'Welcome' sign for the Port Arthur Historic Site, looking incongruous near the three tourist information boards. I stepped out of the car in front of the local cemetery. We gathered in tight formation as if huddled for protection and set out, clinging together for solace.

Within a couple of strides, I saw the chilling sight of four white body bags on the right-hand side of the road 100 metres away, near the speed hump in front of the toll booth. They were almost stacked one on top of the other. Just a few metres further on I saw the yellow Volvo sedan with the surfboard on the roof racks, described on numerous news reports as belonging to the gunman.

We walked towards the toll booth with its teepee-like roof and large terracotta flowerpot in front of it. My body was trembling uncontrollably, my legs wobbling like jelly. Pam clutched me firmly to keep me upright. The piercing silence was only disturbed by my sobs. These are the most difficult steps of my life, these are the most difficult steps of my life – the words kept running through my mind. I had run three marathons over the years, but the agony I felt now would make the hundreds of blisters and unbearable cramps insignificant.

'I owe this to my beautiful girls', I vowed. This, and the thought of Nanette's loving smile, kept my feet stepping one in front of the other. From the toll booth, I began walking into the historic site as the road descended gradually through a tall canopy of eucalyptus trees. Suddenly visible ahead of me was the sight of uncovered bodies lying on the bitumen. There were a number of police standing very close by and two or three people dressed in full white boiler suits from the coroner's department. They pulled back slightly from the bodies as our entourage approached.

Having almost ground to a halt, I began to run towards Nanette's body on the pavement and knelt as if praying to God above that what I was seeing was an apparition. I gazed at my gorgeous Netty, lying on her back, her head pointing down the hill, and it became apparent to me that no prayer was going to remove the hole through her temple. Her life-giving blood had poured from the exit and run some ten metres down the bitumen road. Seeing this was one of the greatest blows a human being could be dealt. The person whom I was sure I would grow old with was no longer with me. I let out a horrible, animal-like shriek – I did not remember this until I was told months later – that pierced sharply through the hearts of each person present.

I studied Nanette's figure with such intensity as if trying to absorb the last little morsel of life from her peaceful body. Satisfied that every minute detail was indelibly etched in my memory, my brain released the physical part of my body to hold my beloved wife. Nanette's ringlets of reddish hair still glistened and her make-up was, as always, intact. Her left hand was perched upon her stomach as if she was showing to the world for one last time the ruby and gold engagement ring I had given her.

I kissed the soft skin of her hand, but could only feel the dankness of the night air she had been in. She wore a burgundy velvet-like top with blue denim jeans that were, in fact, mine. We frequently shared clothes and this served to accentuate the oneness that we had together. On Nanette's feet were the tried and true Blundstone boots that had been worn more often than her slippers. I knelt closer, wrapping my arms around the stiffness of her body, trying to induce just one final cuddle. I told her how much I loved her between tears and sobbing, and that my love for her would never die.

I was dimly aware of detectives and others on the other side of the road looking aghast at my outpouring of grief. Two detectives in suits moved to as close as two metres away from me, clearly worried about me disturbing the evidence of the crime scene. Pam Ireland had positioned herself between me and their line of vision. They wanted to get on with their jobs, but my final goodbye had to be said.

Looking just slightly up the hill some two or three metres away in the ditch, I saw the tiny torso of my Maddie. A raging shout of disbelief, 'No, Maddie, not Maddie. She's only a baby,' echoed through the historic site. My cry would surely have reached even the most distant of spirits from the old penal settlement.

Her long, dark eyelashes, that we had often marvelled at, were curled outwards. She was lying on her stomach, slightly to one side, her tiny hands joined together and the petite fingers curled as if slumber was in progress. The blue checked dress still flowed down her body to white lacy socks and black patent leather shoes. 'Immaculately angelic' was the only record my mind could make of what my eyes were seeing. There was no fear or horror in her face, no disturbance of her clothes and, most importantly, absolutely no sign of trauma. My hands gently surveyed her three-year-old body without really wanting to uncover the source of her injury. With arms gently embracing my baby, I placed my lips by her serene face and my mind began recounting precious moments of touching. The bony bottom jumping up on my lap, probing fingers playing with my face and the tremendous sense of bonding when holding her as she slept.

Staring at her golden locks, I noticed something was different. Her hair had become amazingly frizzy, the moistness of the Tasmanian night air had turned her hair even curlier. My own flesh and blood had been ripped away as if from my own body.

One final everlasting kiss on Madeline's cheek gave me the impetus to scan around for Alannah. From where I was kneeling on the ground, I could not see her anywhere around me. Jumping up in panic, I could see a glimpse of clothing behind a one-metre-wide gum tree some three metres away. I set off along the road. A distraught cry of 'Oh, Lani! Oh, Lani!' rang out simultaneously with each step that I took towards the rear of the tree. Lunging desperately in the hope that there was an iota of life left in my young beauty proved similarly futile. Lani was curled up on her left side, in foetal position, as if contouring to the shape of the tree. She was wearing a superb tartan Esprit dress that came down over her knees and was obviously worn for the first time. I had not seen it before and I admired the contrast it gave to her dark, flowing hair. As with Maddie there was no evidence of trauma and her position on the ground spoke of peace.

I still thank God to this day that such was the case. It is my truthful belief that had I seen the injuries to my babies that I would not at this moment be writing these words. The hands I held so often when going to sleep were now joined as if making one final request. My first child, my daughter, my friend and my pride was lying coldly stark before me.

I began to think about how Alannah had come to be dead in this position, behind a tree, and this filled me with intense, soul-destroying remorse.

'Why wasn't I here to protect my wonderful child? Could she have departed this world as helpless as a rabbit?'

Momentarily, I felt incredibly angry with myself, but I remembered the entry in her diary that I had read but days before: 'My dad is the best dad in all the world. I want to eat him all up in my tummy. I love him and no [sic] that he loves me.'

Upon letting the spirit of Alannah's words flow through me, I clutched the gentle contours of her body with every ounce of passion left in me.

'Lani, I love you with all my heart and I will never forget you!' bellowed out proudly for all the world to hear. Getting up, I strode back to Nanette, kissed her for the final time and told her I would meet her again in heaven. As I did likewise to Maddie, the detectives were clearly getting agitated and extremely uncomfortable.

'I'll just be a minute,' I implored as I rushed back to Alannah. Grasping her for the very last time, my tears totally blurred my vision. I vaguely remember hands gently being placed under my arms and being helped away. The reality could be denied no more; I had seen it and touched it with my fingers. After some eighteen hours of uncertainty, every sensory part of my body was confirming what I had hoped it would deny.

My three beautiful angels were now in heaven.

TWO

The Girl with the Bright Red Lipstick

I remember the days when I used to be Walter Mikac, the local pharmacist, involved in local theatre productions, who sat on the school council, who played golf with the town's shopkeeper, whose wife and children were part of a small community in an idyllic setting in Tasmania.

These days I find it hard to go into the supermarket without being recognised. I am now Walter Mikac, the man who so tragically lost his wife and children when they were shot and killed at Port Arthur. The public face of tragedy. Mothers with children in pushers sometimes cry when they see me in the aisle at the supermarket. No words are spoken.

I was in the Wrest Point Casino in Hobart recently, watching a blackjack game, when a woman approached me.

'Haven't I seen you on television?'

I shrugged my shoulders. 'You may have.' I didn't want to talk to this woman. I didn't want my privacy shattered again. I wanted to be left alone.

'I know. I know where I've seen you. "Perfect Match", that was it. You were on "Perfect Match".'

I didn't know whether to laugh or cry.

Crying has been part of my life now. I cry most days, watching videos of my family, seeing a mother with a child Madeline's age holding her mother's hand walking down the street. At a nightclub, looking through the crowd for the face of my wife. Crying on the footpath outside in the early hours of the morning. On my first New Year's Eve alone at the Koonya Hotel in Sorrento, Victoria, near where I proposed to Nanette so long ago. In the minutes leading up to midnight, being comforted by my brothers Steve and John and their girlfriends Justine and Mary, then other friends joining in until we formed a rugby-style pack in the beergarden. Everyone sharing my grief.

Three weeks after they were killed, my first social visit to the outside world was a 21st birthday party for a girl who was a friend of my brothers. I was standing in the marquee when the disc jockey played the first song. It was ABBA's 'Dancing Queen', the song I played at their funeral. Alannah was my dancing queen.

Memories are always with me. When I receive a letter from a mother whose six-year-old son was shot dead in the Dunblane massacre, I think of how Scotland was the one country Nanette always wanted to visit. She had tartan pyjamas. The ones I was holding the day after she died.

I am alone now. I have sold our house on the peninsula and my pharmacy. I don't need to work for the moment and nor do I feel I can. I have bought another house, back in Melbourne – the house Nanette and I dreamt of buying. I am starting another life. I have freedom to come and go. I could climb Mt Everest if I wanted to.

But the one thing I don't have is the thing I want the most. My family.

   Regrets. If we hadn't come to Tasmania, if I hadn't been playing golf that day, if they hadn't gone to the Port Arthur Historic Site, but then what if I hadn't ever met this wonderful girl who shared thirteen years of my life, who gave me my two extraordinary children. If I hadn't been at the Pharmacy department at the Austin Hospital that day she walked through the door.

Tuesday, 17 November 1983 was one of those mundane afternoons. I couldn't tell you what the weather was like as I was in the pharmacy in the Harold Stokes building of the Austin Hospital in Heidelberg, a north-eastern suburb of Melbourne. Inside, it was new with bright white walls, no windows, strong fluorescent lighting and a sterility typical of hospitals. I was industriously counting and dispensing my inpatient drug orders on the work bench, staring at a stock box of Serepax, daydreaming about going to Europe the following year, where I would be free to travel and leave all this hard work behind me. The 'S' section of the dispensary was directly at eye level. Various long-worded drug names like *sulphasalazine* whizzed past my eyes as I scanned along the shelf. Glancing underneath this shelf, I could see Angelo helping someone at the drugs-of-addiction cabinet. Angelo Tonietto was already qualified and was one year ahead of me. It was the words he used that stopped me in my tracks:

'Walter does your ward and he loves giving flowers.'

I crouched down and peered between the shelves.

The naturally curly brown ringlets, unusually attractive blue eyes and captivating smile belonged to – I looked at the badge – 'Sister Nanette Moulton'. I smiled cautiously, but from my covert position behind the shelves was able to continue watching her. Her eyes had slightly different shapes and were as animated as her hand movements. Her make-up was very natural, except for the bright red lipstick. The knee-length white uniform had a pink rose pinned to the lapel – the reason behind the comment about the flowers. She was wearing a silky red scarf tied in a flamboyant bow amongst the curls.

All of this I took in in a matter of seconds. We looked straight at each other as Angelo introduced us.

'Hello. How are you?' I said fairly sheepishly.

'Well, when do I get my flowers then?' was the unexpected reply.

My first thought was: Wow, she's really nice, but why would she possibly be interested in me. I was only a trainee pharmacist and she was a deputy charge nurse.

Then she was gone, drugs in a bag in her hand, head down as if she had forgotten the earlier conversation. But at the last minute, as she passed me going towards the door, her hand gave me what I was later to discover was a characteristic dismissive wave.

We discussed this first meeting many times, Netty. You thought I was good-looking. Maybe it was those blue eyes of mine that I inherited from my Croatian parents. At twenty-one years old I had a lot to learn. I was selfish and my experience with girls was fleeting and non-committal like most young men of my age and, I admit, I was a little shy. I didn't really understand girls.

But you persisted with that request for flowers, Netty, and drove me mad until I finally presented you with a rose. I had you floored that day, when I finally presented you with it in the middle of the Pharmacy department. You were speechless. It was worth it just for the look on your face. I was beginning to like you. You were different. You told funny stories about the patients on the ward, like old Sid in bed 12, who had a bit of dementia setting in. He'd worked on the railways all his life and used to watch the trains out of the hospital windows. One day he was found at the train station without his clothes on. The two nurses who were listening to you tell the story said after you left:

'She's such a wag.' 'Isn't she just an absolute classic?'

I had to admit you had a great way of telling a story. I had an urge to find out more about you.

I finally asked you out on a date – to a basketball game – and when we bumped into one of your ex-boyfriends I got jealous and couldn't understand what was wrong with me. The feeling was already there, Netty, at that first date. You had an effect on me which lasted through ten years of marriage. By then, I was more in love with you than ever.

At the time Nanette was living in an Edwardian house – No. 37 Sherwood Road, Ivanhoe, a quiet, affable suburb about a kilometre from the hospital, with beautiful tree-lined streets and majestic period houses. Nanette had described No. 37 as the Amityville Horror House and, I had to admit when I pulled up to take her out on that first date, it did bear a striking resemblance. It had an alcoved front verandah with eight concrete steps leading up to it. This verandah was to become the scene for our first kiss and many intimate moments, although I did not realise that at the time. The fronds of a large Kentia palm swayed gently in front of the verandah and pink, perfumed roses lined the driveway. A staggered white picket fence contrasted markedly with the white weatherboards of the house. The room on the front corner overlooking the street and the railway line was Nanette's. 'Surf's up' was one of Nanette's favourite expressions when a train roared past.

The house, I was to discover, belonged to Bruce Johnson, a registrar at the Austin Hospital, whose aim was to become a plastic surgeon. He was a tall, skinny fellow with neatly trimmed hair and a moustache. He was particularly fastidious in labelling things all over the house, identifying the stations on his radio by sticking tape on it, labelling onions, potatoes and anything else that was his in the pantry. The other two occupants were women – a social worker called Rosemary and a Finnish nurses' aid called Maikki. They were such great fun, I could see why Nanette enjoyed the atmosphere of the house.

You didn't give up, Netty, even after that first date when I refused to come in for a coffee at the end of the evening. I was still smarting over seeing your ex-boyfriend. One of my old girlfriends, Denise, had come along to a dress rehearsal for the hospital revue in which I was starring and you turned up. You weren't impressed when you met Denise. But, on the night of our first performance, you hung out of the windows of Ward 5 and gave me that exuberant smile and I asked you out to the cast party on Saturday night after the show. Remember how I blew kisses into your cleavage? As I close my eyes, I still remember the look on your face.

The band that played in the revue doubled up at the party. Boy, was that place going wild. Early in the evening, beer cans, wine glasses and bottles of champagne covered the tables, window ledges and every spare inch of horizontal space. There were a number of old, floral club lounges pushed to the outer walls of the huge room which managed to lend it charm. People were smiling and laughing. Alcohol was being consumed at a frenzied rate, but everybody was just out to dance and enjoy themselves.

We danced together a few times and I soon realised Nanette's manic personality extended to her behaviour on the dance floor. It was getting terribly hot with so many bodies expending so much energy boogeying. Nanette was wearing a knee-length pinafore dress and was fanning the bust region to cool herself down. I blew gently in her direction to cool her down as her face was becoming quite red. Upon getting closer to her, it became very obvious that she wasn't wearing a bra. I then blew downwards, which amused Nanette immensely as the cool air passed between her dress and her cleavage. She smiled in a different way than I had seen before. There was a look of mutual admiration as I slowly kissed her on the lips. It was certainly more of an inquisitive, touching kiss than a passionate kiss. At this point I knew that something was going to happen between us. I kept drinking beer at a rapid rate to compensate for sweating on the dance floor. As I joked and nattered with everyone, I hadn't noticed that Nanette was getting tired after her stint of night shift.

'I think I'd like to go home.' She had moved closer to me when we sat down to have a drink.

Being so caught up in the whole buzz of the party and revue, I said without thinking: 'I'll take you home and then come back.'

Nanette looked astonished. She stood up and began walking off.

'Where are you going? I said I would take you home,' I jumped up and followed her.

'I want to go now,' Nanette said.

'Fine, I'll take you.'

So we drove back to Amityville Horror and I walked up the steps to the front door.

'Are you really going back to the party?' she asked.

'Yeah!'

She later revealed to me how shocked she was that here was a guy who wasn't making a move on her. Especially when she wanted him to. This called for drastic action on her behalf.

'Would you like to stay with me tonight?' she asked.

I wasn't quite sure how to respond to this, although I did know she had a special effect on me. I leaned over to kiss her. Not much else had to be said from this point.

Slowly, she extracted herself and began opening the door of her bedroom, only a few steps away. Slipping under the doona of her double bed, our skins touched for the first time. It was exhilarating, yet I felt anxious. The bed was really comfortable with a high, slatted wooden bedhead. There was some awkwardness on both our behalfs, but we did end up making love. We must have both been near exhaustion by this time as it is hard to say whether or not it was a mind-blowing experience.

The most wonderful thing as far as I was concerned was that I woke up with Nanette in my arms. Her skin was incredibly soft and warm. The alarm rang out at about 6.15 a.m. as Nanette was on a morning shift. We both agreed that it had been an excellent party and a lovely night. The smiles said it all.

At about 6.45 there was a mouseish knock at the front door. It was Glenice Lee, Nanette's best friend, dropping in to offer her a lift to work. Nanette introduced us casually, even though I was sitting up in her bed.

'Glenny, this is Walter. He's just brought the morning paper around for me.'

Glenice, who had straight black hair and olive skin, chuckled in an amused kind of way. She'd obviously heard that line before.

People have told me how you and Glenice were inseparable after the first year of your nursing course. Remember how you used to say you could put a bomb under Glenny and it wouldn't hurry her? How you hung her lacy bra and underpants outside the nursing home which faced onto the main road. And how she pinched your clothes and your towel when you were in the communal shower and you had to run back to your room stark naked. She tells me how you would place buckets of cold water above each other's door and how you both drank port and Bailey's Irish Cream while listening to bursts of Cold Chisel. She cried at the funeral, Netty, when she spoke about you. She found it too hard to recount the times you had together. She can't believe you're gone.

Nanette never had to study for exams, breezing through with consummate ease. Her reputation inside the Austin Hospital and beyond was legendary. If you wanted to know where there was a party on, you'd contact Nanette. If you wanted to advertise a party, invitations weren't necessary. Inform Nanette and the word would spread like an infectious disease.

Her antics on the ward included taping up the telephone with sticky tape, then ringing that phone from somewhere else in the department and watching the frustration of the person answering the phone through the window of the nurses' station. Then there was the old vaseline on the ear/mouthpiece trick. The *pièce de résistance* involved sewing the arms of the doctors' white coats together. The doctors were easy prey, and although they sometimes tried for revenge they were repaid with dire consequences.

Another prank was telling the young interns to 'Go to the nurses' station and speak to the nurse with the red lipstick and a pink carnation in her buttonhole'. The unsuspecting intern would arrive at the nurses' station only to find three or four nurses all fitting the description. Sometimes, Nanette would carry out patient observations in the neurological ward dressed in full scuba gear.

Soon after our first night together, I went away on a houseboat trip for a week. I sent Nanette a postcard while I was gone and on the Tuesday I returned, I dropped round to see her in my lunchbreak.

She was still working night shift, so I knew she would be home and probably asleep. The back door was open and I crept into her room, sat on the bed, gave her a gentle peck on the cheek. She slowly roused, then her eyes widened as she saw my face. Having been in a very deep sleep, she smiled warmly and extended her hands to me. She looked so snug curled under the covers, I decided to hop in with my clothes on.

'How was your trip?' she asked, sleepily.

'I had a great time, did lots of fishing ... but I missed you. How about you?'

'I've been slaving over a hot patient.'

My clothes did end up coming off and making love this time was really gentle and intimate. In some ways, it was just as if it was the night before that we had been together. I felt so incredibly at ease with her that it scared me. I had never encountered this situation before and wasn't sure what to do. This confusion filled my consciousness over the following days. We spoke frequently on the phone, but couldn't wait till we'd actually see each other.

Christmas with my family that year, unlike most years, was boring. Nanette had gone to spend Christmas with her family at her parents' place in Romsey, sixty kilometres north of Melbourne, near Hanging Rock. Not being able to see Nanette that day made me feel empty and a little agitated.

What was wrong with me? I wondered. Then the answer struck me. *I really feel different about this person.* It was something I had never experienced before.

Meeting Nanette's parents in February 1984 was a turning point in our relationship. On the way to their ranch-style house on five acres at Romsey, Nanette spoke about her father, attempting to be light-hearted in her usual way. 'My father used to be a choir master at the Shepparton Baptist Church,' she said as we drove through flat grass plains with cattle and sheep grazing.

'Oh?' I said, not quite sure how to respond.

'When we were living at Shepparton, we used to have to go to the services twice on Sundays, morning and night.'

'So, was it strict ... what was it like?'

'We weren't allowed to wear jeans – they were "worldly". We weren't allowed to do anything that was "worldly". We couldn't go to the pictures.'

'Why not? What do you mean – worldly?'

'Well, anything the church considered worldly. Other kids did those things, but we couldn't.'

'So is he still involved with the church?' I was beginning to wonder what I was getting myself into. I had gone out with another girl whose dad was a Presbyterian minister and I had memories of being summoned into the lounge-room. Her father had inspected me as if I was a contender for an episode of 'Gladiators'.

She seemed to sense my discomfort.

'No, he gave it up a while ago. My brothers used to have a joke about speaking in tongues. They'd say: "Yabba dabba doo. Diddyundi".'

I laughed out loud.

'Maybe I should sprout some Croatian for them.'

This idea appealed to Nanette. 'Yep, that would really get them going. Hey, we're nearly there,' she said as we turned into Knox Road on the edge of Romsey.

'What about your mum?'

'Old Gracie, she's an old bag.'

'Charming.'

'Oh, don't worry, she *loves* entertaining. Visitors give her a chance to have a glass of wine. Dad's never had a drink in his life. During the time Dad was with the church, Gracie missed out on lots of things. After a while, she got sick of it – oh, turn in here – it's that one with the two big gums at the front of the driveway. Wait till you meet Dad. I always tell him he's got a haircut with a hole in it.'

I smiled. She really was irrepressible.

Dinner was lamb roast with lots of vegetables and gravy. Grace revelled in the fact that there was a special guest in the house. She was the perfect host and I was struck by her warmth and acceptance. It was as if there was a natural affinity between us from the start. I could see where Nanette got her vitality and outgoing nature.

'Mikac is an unusual name. Where do your parents come from?' she asked as we finished dinner.

'They're from Yugoslavia up near the Italian border.'

'So were you born here?'

'Gracie,' Nanette interjected. 'What's this? The Spanish Inquisition?'

'I don't mind, Nanette,' I interrupted. 'Yes, I was born in Carlton.'

'Oh, I remember when Netty was only about four –' Grace started, laughing heartily.

'Not that story, Mum,' Nanette said from her position on the wicker couch, her face flushing red. 'Why don't you stick to taking your lollies.' This was Nanette's word for Grace's numerous prescription pills.

But Grace, who'd had a couple of glasses of wine, was unstoppable.

'Net took some sequins out of my sewing box. I was working as a milliner at the time and I had a lot of bric-a-brac in my sewing box. Netty thought these sequins were a valuable commodity and she proceeded to smuggle them into church on Sunday and deposited them in the collection plate. The look on the collector's face when he saw what she'd put there ...'

After dinner, we sat around in the spacious lounge-room and chatted about their early days with five young children. Graeme was the eldest, then Bronwyn and Peter, the twins, Rodney and finally Nanette.

It was on this visit that I discovered that Nanette's family affectionately called her Netty. It had a much softer feel to it than the normal 'Nan' or 'No No' to which Nanette was often jovially referred to around the hospital. From that point, Netty became my choice of name for Nanette.

After a cup of tea, Grace put her feet back into her black leather slippers. Nanette, in contrast, was wearing purple slippers with elephant heads, ears at the side, trunks waving from the toes. Nanette yawned, indicating that she was ready to turn in for the night.

The guest bedroom was at the far end of the house, the room most distant from the master bedroom. As we carried our overnight bags along to the room, I said to Nanette, 'Are you sure this is okay? I don't feel quite right about this.'

I hadn't expected to be sharing a bed with her on our first night at her parents' house. We lay in bed like naughty children expecting to be sprung, while Nanette talked about her mother.

'She would have thought of this to make me happy,' she said. 'She's always thinking of other people. Gracie's had a tough life, you know. She was brought up in an orphanage from the age of nine – after her mother died. Then she had us five in the space of four years. She always tried to do her best for us, but sometimes it just got too hard ... She was away a lot when I was little as she was often sick. It must be hard being a mother.'

I ran my fingers through her hair and she nuzzled into my neck and sighed.

We held hands and cuddled. The bed was warm and soft and soon I could hear from Nanette's breathing that she was sleep. Voices floated up from the dining room and I could smell the new paint from the cream walls where three flamboyant ceramic flying pigs were placed diagonally down the wall. From the paddock, across the front yard, I could hear the faint braying from one of the donkeys, either Dolly, or Nanette's donkey, Duffy.

When Gracie died only three months before you, Netty, you had such vivid, horrific dreams about her lying under the ground that you would wake up suddenly and I would need to comfort you. Gracie meant so much to you. Your only sister, Bronwyn, says you inherited some of Grace's insecurities, which wasn't helped by having four older siblings. Those of us who knew you knew why you liked to make people laugh but we also knew how insecure you were deep down.

'Netty Petty' – that's what you used to call yourself when you were at school. Growing up in the country with so much freedom. You used to run around in bare feet, feeding lambs with the bottle. When you lived at Shepparton in a small State Electricity Commission home, the five of you would swim in the channel and have competitions to see who could get the most leeches on them. They would be lined up and counted.

Your brothers were sometimes tough on you. Like the time when they tied you up, put a For Sale sign on you and put you out on the roadside in front of the house. True brotherly love.

Bronwyn says you developed your sense of the ridiculous when Grace was breeding corgies. You were six and you would attend dog shows with her at many rural towns in Victoria.

Sometimes, after her strict convent upbringing and marrying so young, Grace would disappear for varying periods of time, unable to cope with the responsibilities of family life. As you were the youngest, you probably felt Grace's absences the most. Perhaps this made you reflect on your own ability at mothering. I watch one of our earliest home videotapes where you are cradling Alannah in your arms. The look on your face is one of disbelief and fierce possession. This is your very own baby to have and to hold.

You were the proverbial 'earth mother'. You took our children everywhere. Maddie went with you to writing classes, the school canteen when you were on duty, delivering the prescriptions to the nursing home and she was always there at the pharmacy getting the mail and doing her 'wrk' as she called it. Our life then seemed so perfect.

Looking back, I know sometimes I did things I shouldn't have. Remember how upset you were when I left you for four months and went overseas? How you told me, never to leave you like that again. We'd only been going out for eight months. At least when I came home, I was here to stay.

In spite of our blossoming relationship, I decided in March that I would still carry on with a trip to Europe I had planned with a couple of old pharmacy friends, David and Lou. Travelling overseas was a goal I had set years before while an impoverished student of pharmacy. I knew, deep down, I had to go alone. Nanette and I were becoming more serious and I felt I needed time on my own to analyse where my life was heading. It was all part of growing up and I didn't want to slip into any further commitment without consideration.

At about the same time I decided to go to Europe, I began work in Reservoir, a working-class northern suburb of Melbourne, managing a pharmacy, my first position of responsibility. David and Lou were departing in late July. It seemed like the right time for me to go, too.

I knew that telling Nanette would be a major obstacle and I was dreading telling her the news. I waited until we were at a party, surrounded by lots of people.

'You know how I always wanted to go to Europe. Well, I've got the ticket. I'm going in July.'

Her face dropped like a sack of potatoes.

'What will I do at home by myself?'

The barrage continued incessantly with only the words 'Can I come too?' not being voiced out loud.

Sometimes, I must admit, I wondered if I was doing the right thing, especially when we seemed to be getting on so well. It felt so natural being together.

In the early months of 1984, Netty suggested we do a scuba-diving course together. Nanette's idea of leisure involved sitting down with a good book, so her idea to do something physical, like carrying around heavy diving gear, was a trifle out of character. That's not to say that she wasn't adventurous, as she often did an about-face when you least expected – it was this unpredictability that excited me. It was impossible to be bored with Nanette. I was becoming infatuated with her complexity and uniqueness.

On 27 July 1984, with tears streaming down her face, Nanette's last words to me as I was heading for the departure lounge at Tullamarine Airport were, 'I'll be here when you get back.'

THREE

Postcards From Europe

To: Walter Mikac, c/o American Express Office,
DA MRAK 66,
AMSTERDAM, HOLLAND, EUROPE.   5.11.84

*Sometimes I pretend that I have a crystal ball and I look into it and I
see you and I want to reach out and touch you, but it would spoil it as
then you would know that I was watching. All I want to do is to touch
you, smell you, caress you. I want to look at your body and feel you
against me. I hope that's how you feel about me because if it's not, I've
just made an idiot of myself. When you get back I am going to have a
bath in scented oils so you will be able to smell my skin and it will be
so soft, and you can put your head on my bosom and I can play with
your hair and we can talk. Won't that be terrific? I've got goosebumps
thinking about it. I love you, my darling boy and I want to be with you.
Always yours. Netty xxxx*

I am looking for an old pair of sunglasses. The letters are in the top drawer of the old bedside table in my parents' house, in the bedroom that I had slept in as a boy. Rummaging through, I find them tied with an elastic band – the letters Netty sent me when I went to Europe. I thought I'd thrown them out. As I read through them, it's as if I am looking back on a life I hardly recognise. Have I changed? How can I not have changed? I was so young then, knew so little about life's responsibilities. I wanted to see the world. I wanted to go back to the place where my parents were born. So much of my future lay before me then. I wished I had your crystal ball then, Netty. But, I really wish I had it now. Am I doing the right thing, Netty? Are you proud of your boy now? I had to do that trip, honey. I had to realise how much I loved you. And I always wanted to take you back to those places. I saved the Eiffel Tower for you, you know. I always wanted to take you there.

Paris was magical. It was summertime. I had landed in London with David and Lou, and then headed for the Continent. Artists were sprawled on the footpath up and down the Seine and barges slunk lazily past as the city baked in the heat. At every turn, I would see another sight out of the picture book. The magnificent architecture and art of the Louvre, Notre Dame, the Eiffel Tower and the Arc de Triomphe I viewed from all angles. Wandering down the Champs Elysée a multitude of coffee aromas wafted by. People prepared to pay $10 for a coffee and croissant sat under umbrellas near the kerb of such a famous place. Still, it's not every day you visit Paris and I wanted to experience this first-hand. With the traffic whizzing by and the sun shining warmly, I enjoyed the last mouthfuls of my coffee. The shops here were very exclusive, with immaculately attired women strutting up and down with bags of newly acquired accessories. Gazing through a brief break in the traffic, I glimpsed a lingerie store on the adjacent corner. Well, if Nanette couldn't be here, why not send some of Paris back to her? By the time I reached the front of the store, I wondered how I was going to explain what I wanted as my knowledge of French was poor. The shop was on the corner of a busy intersection with displays of underwear lined across the large windows. I felt self-conscious, convinced all eyes were on this man entering a woman's domain. As I walked in, the counter at the far end seemed to be miles away. Dragging my eyes away from my feet, I lifted my head and made for where I could see a few bras hanging. With body language I explained to the young assistant what I wanted to buy. She seemed very amused, but remained exceptionally helpful.

She cupped her bust in an effort to ascertain whether the person I was buying this for was smaller or larger than herself.

'Oui, oui, oui,' I kept repeating, becoming more animated as her hands expanded to the right size. She laughed, appreciating my dilemma. With size and cup size worked out by various demonstrations of my hands, it was time to select colour. The silk material was so delicately smooth that it reminded me of Nanette's skin and I longed to put my arms around her. I settled on cream for colour, ensuring there was ample lace on the bra and matching knickers. After having it beautifully gift boxed, I posted it off feeling very satisfied with my efforts for the day.

After getting the parcel from Paris, the X-ray department at the Austin Hospital turned into a catwalk where the Paris lingerie and tantalising bits of the lace were shown to friends and even interested patients.

Nanette was in love. I was sure of it. Every letter I received from her stated this at least three times on a page. She kept my letters down her bra and took them to work. She was teaching her two-year-old nephew, Daniel, Bronwyn's child, how to say 'Walter'. Daniel would call Nanette 'Dit Dit' as he struggled with her name. She sent me his scribbles through the post. One letter was stained with his Vegemite sandwich. I even received an invitation to Daniel's second birthday party.

4.10.84

I am sitting at work watching an angiogram. I brought your letter to read and everyone was laughing at me. Les Oliver (the cardiologist

I was telling you about) was saying he'll be glad when you're back.
I hate to tell you but this letter had just been irradiated.

I responded with declarations of love and reassurance.

18.10.84
'Geez, we're good for each other', as you would say. I just don't feel
complete without you and I'm sure you feel the same way. Whenever I
see something extremely beautiful like when walking through the Black
Forest yesterday, I think how much more I'd enjoy it if you were with
me. But I think that being by myself has done a lot for my growing up.
I'm certainly able to do things for myself now and have lost lots of
inhibitions . . . In a way my leaving has made me realize just how much
I love you and how I depend on you for my total happiness.

From Edinburgh, after visiting the castle, I wrote:

It's raining outside at the moment and so this morning when the others
wanted to leave, I said I was staying in bed. I wanted to write this
letter to you and go into town and buy you those bagpipes for your
charm bracelet.

Back home in Melbourne, Netty's friend Glenice became her confi-
dante. Netty would turn up at her flat with a packet of cigarettes –
it didn't matter that neither of them smoked. As long as Nanette got
to talk about how much she loved me and she wasn't reduced to
staying at home. They would go for 'adventures' all over Melbourne.
One weekend, they got drunk in a seedy motel in Queenscliff, on the
coast west of Melbourne.

We booked into the 'Riptide Holiday Flats'. Real doozies. Well, the
guy at the office was really rude and had food coming out his mouth.
We sat there and watched the Grand Final and got drunk. When it
was time to go to bed there were no sheets on the bed. We both just
sat there and laughed.

Glenice became an important release for Nanette who was plagued with her old enemy, insecurity, particularly in the first of the twelve letters she sent me in four and a half months. She was worried our relationship wouldn't last the distance.

I hope you are being faithful. I am. There have been a couple of guys who have asked me out, so to speak, but I just tell them about you. But then they laugh and say what he doesn't know won't hurt him. But don't worry nothing happens.

But I *was* faithful. At the beginning of the trip, I was walking through the red light district in Amsterdam with David and Lou. We walked down a back street full of mean-looking black guys. Even with the safety of two other males I felt mighty scared and was ready to hand over my wallet as soon as any demand was made. Drugs were everywhere and we walked down the streets like moths drawn towards a light, marvelling at what we saw, a melting pot from Europe and Africa where the two cultures fused to create a curious blend of exciting intrigue. The women bathed in the red glow from the shop windows postured and preened and displayed their wares like moveable mannequins.

I did go in to one of those places, Netty, to spite those unadventurous guys I was travelling with, but nothing *happened. I felt so claustrophobic and the women took pity on me. My mates never got to know that I never did the deed. That wasn't sex the way we knew it.*

After Amsterdam, I headed for the Scandinavian countries, leaving David and Lou in Amsterdam. Norway was my favourite. I met an American backpacker and we were invited by two Norwegian girls to stay with their parents in a house in the hills above Oslo near the Olympic ski jump. Each morning, I was fed grain bread and honey and jams. Nanette's letters continued to follow me to American Express offices across Europe.

25.9.84

Darling, I have just got back from your parents' place. Gosh your mum cooks a mean meal. I think I'll have to take half a packet of lasix and twenty laxettes. It is so hard going over there and you not being there. I keep looking up at the doorway waiting for you to come in. We sat around and watched home movies. Gee whiz, you were a thickhead. I really got the giggles. There was one where you were sulking. It was so funny. I kept sitting there picturing you naked, not when you were a little boy, though. I saw the film of your 21st and I heard the joke about the axe handle and oil. I watched you and I thought to myself, what is it about this guy who puts pieces of rubber on his head? Why am I hanging around waiting for him?

Chemistry, I suppose, Netty. That's what we had. Who knows why we felt this way about each other. Perhaps, it was not as unique as we thought it was. Other people fell in love. But our love felt different. Our love was going to last.

I headed back towards Central Europe after Scandinavia: Germany, Italy, Greece and then up to Yugoslavia, where my real destination awaited. I boarded the train at Thessaloníki after eating a big Greek salad in an open-air cafe for the twenty-four-hour trip to Ljubljana, the capital of Slovenia, lugging my dark-blue backpack and camera, the familiar bumbag around my waist. From there, I took a bus to Umag on the Adriatic coast, a town of red roofs and tenements.

Near the bus terminal, I recognised my cousin Idanela, whom I had not seen for thirteen years.

I first visited my parents' homeland, the Istrian peninsula, in 1971 when I was nine years old. It was then the Croatian part of Yugoslavia. My parents had migrated separately to Australia in 1958, faced with a depleted post-war economy and grim employment opportunities in Yugoslavia. My mother, Milka, had endured a childhood few people could contemplate. Her father, Andrej, was shot by the Germans en route to fight in the Second World War when she was only three years old. Her mother, along with two sisters and a brother, had died shortly after the war due to meningitis.

Now I was back as a young man, visiting the tiny village of Crveni Vrh ('Red Hill'), where my mother spent her teenage years with her older sister, Maria. At eighteen, she left this village and headed off from Trieste with one suitcase for a better life. She boarded the *Aurelia* for Australia, where her uncle and brother had migrated years before. They had sent her letters and parcels of clothes telling her of all the opportunities to be had and how much work there was.

My father, Danny, was born in Brest, 30 kilometres away from my mother's village. At the age of twelve, his parents separated and he was living with his father in Rijeka. Dad considered America where he had relatives and even Argentina. He was also looking for better prospects for the future, but never imagined he would have to travel across the world to meet his bride.

As I arrived in the village of Crveni Vrh, with its handful of houses at the top of the hill, I was amazed to find it had hardly changed. There were the same views of the sea, the vineyards and valleys studded with cherry trees. Outside my Teta Marija's (Aunt Maria's) house were dry stone walls which ran beside the road and across the fields. After thirteen years, the green shutters were more weathered but had not been repainted. Chickens scattered as I walked to the front door.

I remembered arriving as a nine-year-old in the communal courtyard at the front of her stone house, watching the bare-chested children playing the game of bocce with wooden balls. And soon I was joining in. The stone walls of the village houses were from a world gone by. Shepherds, walking with stick in hand, would lead their goats or cattle up the main street. We followed behind them, laughing at the steaming turds the livestock deposited in the street.

Old ladies dressed in black from head to toe would slowly limp by with vegetables that they'd collected from the fields. We had other adventures, so unlike those we had in our suburban home in Melbourne – like rock climbing, frog hunting and hay cutting.

Grape harvesting time was also an experience. The ripe grapes were deposited in a huge wooden vat. Having had our feet first dipped in a little clean water, we were helped over the top edge of the vat onto the grapes. My brother, Steven, was six at the time and thought Christmas had come early when, standing nearly chest deep in grapes, he was told to start jumping. The squelching between our toes was marvellous as we soon became covered in sweet, red grape juice. It was as if we had been told to do something that felt instinctively wrong, but we were having immense fun and we were helping.

I remembered Teta Marija preparing for dinner by grabbing the nearest chicken in the yard, taking it to the woodpile, lifting the axe and chopping off its head. Once, her aim was slightly askew and the chicken, its head hanging by a thread, ran around the yard several times and she couldn't catch it. So, she went for another unsuspecting victim.

For my return visit Maria had prepared a feast. She had baked her own bread, there were potatoes, salad, roast chicken and piles of prosciutto. Red wine arrived from the pantry where glasses were filled from a big barrel as high as the ceiling.

A week after my arrival, my cousins took me to a local fiesta in the next town. In the darkened hall as I watched the mirror ball rotate, Chris Rea's song 'I Can Hear Your Heartbeat' played. It was Nanette's favourite. My earlier happy spirits dissipated and, in spite of being back with my relatives, I wished I was already home.

Could I book to get back early? Was I missing her? Nanette's voice always had such a dejected and low tone to it when I spoke to her now. This was so un-Nanette. I didn't like talking that much on the phone about my feelings but, boy, did I let them flow in the letters. I look at them now and wonder what sick, romantic fool wrote some of this twaddle. But back then I know what I was saying was coming from the bottom of my heart. One of the postcards I sent her was filled with the words I LOVE YOU. But even though Netty asked incessantly *when* was I coming home, I knew I had to finish my trip.

After Crveni Vrh, I visited my father's village. It was on the side of one of the highest mountains in Istria. I stayed in the house opposite my grandmother, who was suffering from tinnitus and seemed to have given up on life. I spent a long time thinking about my father's life and the contrast he and my mother must have experienced when they first arrived in Australia. Croatia was my homeland, too, but my life was in Australia and I knew I could never fit into this sort of life, even though I had been brought up with Croatian traditions, eating the same sort of food they ate in these peasant villages, keeping the Catholic faith and speaking the same regional dialect. It made me wonder how different my life would have been if my parents had never left Istria.

It always intrigued me that it took a trip across the world to Australia before my parents met. They met the day after my father arrived in Melbourne. He was living in a house in Clifton Hill, an inner northern suburb, and my mother was working in a confectionery factory on the production line. She had come to visit some friends who lived in Dad's house. That same day, as well as finding a job as a painter, Dad also found himself a wife. He had been looking for a partner for a while and had distributed signed photos of himself to possible contenders. Two years later, after a courtship which involved dances at the local town halls, they were married at St John's Church in Clifton Hill. They chose to make their home in the then leafy outer suburb of Macleod. By the time I was born in 1962, Dad was working for himself, seven days a week, while Mum stayed at home. She felt quite isolated because she did not understand English. Simple tasks like going to the butcher would involve much pointing and inevitably ended with the same order, the only one she knew how to give – one pound of veal chops for two shillings.

Reading a timetable and working out where buses left from meant public transport was difficult for my mother, so she went everywhere on foot, wheeling me in the wonky second-hand pusher in front of her.

When I was two, I fell into a twenty-litre drum of white, oil-based paint. My mother couldn't read the instructions on the can and had no idea that mineral turpentine was the only solvent capable of properly cleaning me. So she put me in a bath of water, wielding a big scrubbing brush. As the redness of my body increased, the tears flowed and the screaming got louder. Somehow, I survived the scrubbing.

At three and four years of age, bored with staying at home, I began going to work with Dad. By the age of five, my enterprising skills had developed and I set about collecting all the redeemable bottles lying around the building site. This kept me going for a couple of hours and, if it was a lucrative day, I bought Redskins, Wagon Wheels and aircraft models with the money the bottles fetched. Not having attended kindergarten, my grasp of English was non-existent on my first day of school. But now that I was in a situation where I had to speak I picked it up very quickly. Soon, I was just another average kid at St Martin of Tours Catholic Primary School.

Being brought up a Catholic gave me a good moral upbringing, even though I was naughty in my first years at school with the dreaded 'D' for behaviour in Grade Three. By Grade Five, I had a reason to be bad. It was about then I realised my father was an alcoholic. My mother would send me out to the garage to call him for dinner and he was always surrounded by boxes filled with empty beer bottles. Early one morning I saw him stop the car in the driveway on the way to work to take a swig of Johnny Walker. I knew then his drinking was worse than I'd ever imagined. But it was our family secret. I didn't want my school friends to know. Once, Mum started walking down the footpath away from the house, telling us we were leaving Dad. There was no money in the bank – he'd drunk it all. I remember being acutely aware that people driving past or, worse still, the neighbours might know our family was falling apart. I remember saying, 'Where will we go? Don't leave Dad. I want us to be with him.'

He somehow found his way to AA. After quite a battle he did succeed in getting on the wagon and to this day he has not had a drink. As alcohol was such an important part of the European culture, it must have taken phenomenal strength and will-power for Dad to stay sober. His ability to do this has been a huge inspiration in my life. His inner strength and humility have a soothing effect on me. He is always there for me like a rock on which I can depend. Perhaps I have inherited some of his doggedness and inner confidence. My mother is far more emotional. She has a warm heart and looks after and loves me as only a mother can. They both love each other and they have each provided me with an upbringing I can be proud of.

During my trip to Europe, I found I missed them all terribly as this was the longest I had been separated from them.

It's funny, Netty, without my family I don't know how I would have coped with all of this. My brothers are my closest friends as well as my family. Steve and John both still live at home. Steven has always been so loyal. Even as a toddler he used to cry in sympathy for me when I got a smack. He took all the rough-house tactics I threw his way and came back for more. He came to the court case with me, leaving his job, and has been by my side since. With his tall frame and tied-back long hair, he is my protector, looking hauntingly over my shoulder, ever ready to defend me. Similarly John, although he is ten years younger than myself, has maturity well beyond his years. With the body of a triathlete and that long blond hair, he is a good-looking bloke. I have watched him grow up and we have spent lots of time together. I am so proud of them both.

Perhaps it was this strong bond for my family that made me realise how important the value of the family is. I am so glad I didn't get swallowed up somewhere in Europe on that trip and that I came back to claim my bride and to have a family of my own.

* * *

On 29 November 1984 I arrived back at Melbourne's Tullamarine Airport. There were a few butterflies in my stomach. Did I look different? I'd probably lost a little weight from lugging a heavy pack across Europe.

The automatic doors opened in front of me. What would Nanette be wearing? Crowds of people waited expectantly, children hanging off the rails. To my left, as I pushed the trolley in front of me, I saw her through the crowd. She was dressed in a royal blue pinafore and her hair was cropped, highlighting her beautiful eyes. She looked fantastic. I walked in her direction. My parents were obviously expecting me to come to them first, but I felt an overwhelming desire to hold my Netty. It took all my strength to tear myself away from her softness and the smell of her Opium perfume.

My parents gave me the traditional kiss on each cheek and there was much laughter. It was good to be back on Australian soil among people who loved me. This was my home and I was going to stay here.

On the way back to Macleod I was assailed by questions which were all made bearable by the fact that I could feel Netty's thigh against mine. She kept looking at me all the time as if to reassure herself I was here in the flesh.

In the corridor at my parents' place, I brushed past her, feeling momentarily the softness of her breasts, that softness I had missed for so long. She pressed against me and I bent to kiss her.

'I told you your Mum would want to keep you here when you got back,' she whispered fiercely in my ear.

'My son, I've brewed some real coffee for you,' my mother called from the kitchen, almost as if on cue.

'See, she just wants to feed her boy and doesn't want me around.' Finally we managed to leave.

Back at the Amityville Horror House, she pulled the shirt over my head, her mouth seeking my nipples. I moaned. She knew exactly where to arouse me. The pleasure was greater than any of my fantasies, but it was the softness of her skin and her gentleness that moved me most. With Vivaldi's *Four Seasons* playing on the cassette player in the bedroom, I abandoned myself to her.

FOUR

To Have and to Hold

The constable is standing at the front door of our house in Nubeena. I know why he's here. I'm expecting him. Inside the house he hands me a plastic bag. Netty, here are all your rings, your earrings, your chain and your gold bracelet – the ones you were wearing when you died. I'm going to wear one of your sapphire studs in my left ear and it will always be there. I sit on the couch and stare at your engagement ring. The ruby, when I hold it up to the window, still sparkles. You looked after it so well, Netty, soaking it in ether soap so it would keep the same sparkle it had when I first saw it.

The coloured stones sparkled boldly under the fluorescent lighting in the jewellery shop window. I stood transfixed. Necklaces and watches competed with rubies, sapphires and emeralds. Everything shone and sparkled. This was the eighth day in a row that I had passed this jewellery store in Puckle Street, but it was only in the past two days I had stopped to look. I was working as a relief pharmacist further up the street – my first job since returning from Europe eight weeks ago.

Puckle Street was the main shopping centre in Moonee Ponds, an older northern suburb of Melbourne and the well-known territory of the comedian Barry Humphries' alter ego, housewife Dame Edna Everage. Moonee Ponds was a real melting pot of cultures. Smells of souvlakis cooking from the nearby take-away and hot loaves of bread baking in the bakery across the road filled my senses as I walked by each day.

In the pharmacy I grappled with the spelling of the numerous surnames – Italian, Greek, Macedonian and Maltese. Some lunch-times I ventured to the Moonee Ponds market just behind Puckle Street. It was sheer entertainment ambling through there with its coffee aromas and vast display cabinets of cheeses, pickled peppers and continental sausages. I often purchased a pasta dura roll which I packed with Swiss Jarlsberg cheese and prosciutto. Stallholders would spruik their specials with booming voices, creating an atmos-phere I had grown to love while travelling in Europe.

As I furiously dispensed prescriptions and counselled customers on the correct way to use their medication, my thoughts would drift to Nanette. Since I had been back, I had actually spoken the words out loud that I had written so often in my letters: 'I love you'.

On the first occasion, Nanette wasn't quite sure how to react. She just smiled coyly and scrunched up her face in embarrassment. Next time, she was more prepared. 'Prove it then.' Very quickly this became the standard response to even simple greetings or compli-mentary remarks. It started to niggle at me in a similar way to the 'Where are my flowers?' question just over twelve months ago.

I was also finding living back with my family frustrating. Where was I going? What was I doing? Their questions were relentless, so I would often stay at Nanette's. However, this meant waking up at 6 a.m. to get home in time to keep up appearances and not get abused.

Nanette was ecstatic to have me back and pranced about with a renewed vitality which even surpassed her antics on Ward 5. She spoke with great enthusiasm about the other staff in the X-ray department. Her descriptions of the procedures were well beyond my physiology knowledge, but she rattled off terminology like a specialist in the field.

While I was in Europe, Nanette had also learned how to tap dance. With drawing pins embedded front and back of her nursing shoes she would do routines to Glenn Miller's 'In the Mood' or 'Chattanooga Choo Choo'. I was happy with the way our relationship was evolving – Nanette was so easy to love. I felt relaxed and content.

After Christmas, I joined my family for our ritual holiday at our beach house at Rye on the picturesque Mornington Peninsula, about 100 kilometres south-east of Melbourne. Nanette had only been able to come down on the weekends because she was working, but during these visits I began to notice that the subversive jousting between her and my mother was becoming a regular event. We spent a lot of time in the house playing cards and games, so the atmosphere was less than relaxed. I found myself on sentry duty ready to defuse any possible explosion between them. Perhaps I should have told my mother to ease off, but I was a little immature and, looking back, I didn't really know how to handle it. Gradually, I began to spend less time at the beach house to avoid the tension.

On the Thursday before the upcoming Australia Day long weekend the weather reports predicted a scorcher. Maybe this weekend we should make the effort, I thought. That night Nanette and I went off to see *Raiders of the Lost Ark* at the Northlands cinema in Preston, the closest big shopping centre to Ivanhoe.

After the movie, we were cuddling in the carpark when I decided to broach the subject:

'How about we go down the beach house this weekend?'

Nanette pulled out of my arms and stormed off. I had become used to these fiery displays of anger which I knew wouldn't last long. She was a typical Aries. After lots of careful coaxing on my behalf, we reached a compromise.

'It'll be hot. My brothers'll be down there. Everyone will be there and we'll have a good time,' I began pleading.

Silence.

Then, I thought of a solution.

'How about I take you away on a romantic weekend the following week to make up for it?'

'Mmm,' she said, non-committally, but at least it wasn't 'No'.

Back at the Amityville Horror House we stopped on the verandah. 'I really love you, Nanette,' was my honest and sincere whisper to which she gave her usual flippant reply: 'Well, prove it then.'

I felt a wave of irritation, but remembered my victory for the long weekend, so I didn't say anything. There was, of course, one alternative. Ask Nanette to marry me. That would silence her. That night we slept together, but the thought of the alternative plagued my dreams. I tossed and turned under Nanette's doona until she finally woke up.

'What's the matter? How come you're not snoring?'

I pretended to go back to sleep. How was I going to do it? Where would I do it? Was it the right thing to do? What would my parents say? I'm only twenty-two. Am I ready for this commitment? Do I know what I'm really letting myself in for? But this girl was everything I always wanted. And more. I remembered telling my parents only a year before: 'I'm never going to get married.' My mind was a swirling tornado of questions undermined by doubts.

Morning arrived. We parted with a quick peck on the cheek as Nanette buzzed back and forth. I knew today was going to be my day of reckoning. Arriving for work at the Puckle Street pharmacy, my mind was still sorting out the order in which I was going to propose. It had to be romantic.

After work that day, I made my way to the jewellers up the street. I knew exactly how many minutes it would take to reach the window. There it was. A blood-red ruby on a white-gold band glistening on the black velvet cushion with opulent light adorning its high setting. Twelve small, outer diamonds and eight inner diamonds sparkled around it. I already knew what she would like after past shopping experiences when Nanette would gaze wistfully at rings in jewellers' windows. The question of a wedding hovered in the air, but it had never been broached.

'Yes, that's excellent,' I told the shop assistant. 'The setting is magnificent. I'll have it,' I said, watching the light refracting through the scarlet depths of the stone.

I began pulling a wad of $50 notes from the pay packet inside my pocket. The counting ended at $900 – almost a fortnight's pay. She gradually gathered up the money. 'This must be for someone really sensational,' she smiled, relaxed now she had made a sale.

'Yes, it sure is. It's for the lovely girl who's going to be my wife.'

On the way down to the beach house, we took our time, as Nanette was in no rush to get there. We stopped at our favourite plant nursery, a chance for me to marvel at the wonderful collection of plants and bonsai. I loved gardening and bonsai had become a recent passion. We sat on the lush green lawn at the front of the nursery and ate ice cream.

Back in the car, I fell back into the familiar reverie, contemplating how I was actually going to propose. What would she say? She could refuse. How was I going to tell my parents? I imagined they would be happy for me so I hadn't given them prior warning.

And to a more pressing question. Where to ask *that* question? It had to be really visually spectacular. The surf beach at the end of Canterbury Jetty Road in Sorrento appeared to be the best choice. Memories, from only a few years before, of jumping off a huge twenty-metre naturally formed sandstone pillar. This had given my brothers and me many an adrenalin rush whilst often resulting in having our bathers gathered halfway up our bottoms.

The opportunity came on Sunday night. When I suggested a drive down to the back beach, Nanette's eyes lit up. Here's a chance to 'suck face' – her favourite expression for kissing – I could see her thinking. While at the beach house, with Mum hovering in the background, we kept touching to a minimum.

That evening Nanette was wearing a beige and pink floral jumpsuit with no bra. She was proud of her cleavage and happy not to cover it up. A resin fruit necklace which I had bought for her the previous day hung around her neck and the customary scarf was in her hair. I was wearing loose jeans so she wouldn't notice the box in my pocket.

When we arrived at the cliffs, I took her in my arms. Time seemed suspended. The weathered sandstone cliffs covered in coastal heath and banksias fell away beneath us. Occasionally, a swallow flitted past as if to boast its ability to fly, swooping over the ocean and up again in the draught of wind. Nanette's curls swirled with the sea air.

'Do you sometimes wonder why we're here?' she asked, staring out to sea after we'd kissed.

'Yeah, but why worry about it?'

'I always have the feeling I'm here for another purpose,' she answered slowly.

The breathtaking view held us motionless for what seemed like hours. With no-one else around, it was as if we were the only ones on earth.

'Let's go for a walk round to the other side where that pillar is,' I suggested.

'It's a bit far. Let's just sit down here.'

Her response wasn't what I'd expected. Now more forcefully, trying to infect her with my enthusiasm, I said: 'Do you realise that you can actually climb up that incredible rock outcrop over there? That one at the end of the cliffs. I used to jump off there as a kid.'

'We're not kids now. You wouldn't get me up there for quids.'

'Wait till you see it when we get closer. It's not that bad,' I pulled her hand, suddenly seized with panic at the thought my plan might not eventuate.

She agreed, reluctantly, and we walked along the cliff edge for ten minutes.

As we approached the pillar, I smiled invitingly: 'Come on, let's climb up there.'

'No. No way. No.' She seemed adamant.

The waves crashed mercilessly onto the sandstone cliffs, drowning out any other sound. Instinctively, I reached into my pocket and held its contents in my outstretched hand.

'Well, I suppose you don't want this either?'

She grabbed it, chuckling. 'What is this? Are you playing a joke? It's not funny, you know.'

'Well, open it and see.

As the box sprang open under her probing fingers, Nanette's eyes widened in amazement. For one of the few times in her life, she was silent, unable to speak. She placed it on her finger and turned away from me, transfixed by the ruby and diamonds. I was watching her amused, but still anxious.

'Well then, will you marry me?' I blurted out. I had to know.

'Yes ... yes, yes,' she was walking around in circles as if in disbelief.

We walked to the phone box at the end of the street to ring Keith and Grace.

'Can I have your permission to take Nanette's hand in marriage?' I asked Keith.

In Keith's dry fashion he replied, 'Which bus are you leaving on then?' Grace was delighted.

As we approached my family's beach house, I became more pensive. It was just on dusk.

I strolled into the lounge-room where I could hear the television was on. My brothers and my parents were engrossed in the set. John looked up.

'How was the drive?'

We stood there for what seemed like a minute or two. Then I said, 'Nanette and I have decided to get engaged,' and Nanette extended her ring-clad left hand. At first I thought I wasn't going to get any response. Finally my mum spoke, barely taking her eyes off the screen: 'So does this mean it's serious then?'

Ashamed and embarrassed by their response, I wrapped my arms around Nanette. The elation of just half an hour before had vanished. Nanette's eyes told the story. It was as if they were saying to me,

'Should I really have accepted your offer if this is going to be how I'll be treated?'

Not preparing my parents for this was obviously a monumental mistake on my behalf. I felt terrible about what I had done. I had acted solely on my emotions and now I'd inadvertently hurt Nanette. But I knew my decision was the right one.

Nanette disappeared quietly into her bedroom without speaking to me. I knew this wasn't going to be easy, but if it meant holding on to Nanette, I was prepared to take up the challenge.

'This isn't right,' I say to Bronwyn, Nanette's sister. 'Nanette and Maddie would never have gone out without nail polish. And look at Netty's lips. They're not bright red.'

I am in the funeral parlour and my three girls are lying in their coloured caskets on stands. Before I saw them, I felt scared. More scared even than seeing them lying on the road. Would they look the same? Would they look the way I remembered them? But the girls look so peaceful, as if they are asleep. I kiss them and feel their skin and play with Maddie's hair. It's still soft and fluffy. Alannah's rounded cheeks look as they always did. She looks like she is going to open her eyes and come back to me. But Netty's lips are not right and she can't be buried without nail polish.

Bronwyn immediately understands. 'I'll go and get some,' she offers. 'I'll leave you alone with them for a while.'

I am looking at you, Netty, in your beautiful ivory wedding dress with the fine-patterned lace on the sleeves and on the bodice. You nearly had ulcers over this dress, didn't you? And you were going to lend it out to be used in our theatre production 'Dimboola' down on the peninsula. It seemed like the right choice to be buried in. I found it in the video recorder box on top of the wardrobe. Now you are leaving, Netty, I want you to wear it. But, my greatest wish is that I should be lying here with you all. Life doesn't have any meaning when I'm not with you. Will it ever have any meaning again? To have and to hold ... till death do us part.

The weather on 8 December 1985, our wedding day, was full of portent, the sky an ominous black with the torrential rain streaming down unforgivingly.

The windscreen wipers cleared away the heavy stream of rain that poured steadily down the windscreen of the white Toyota Celica as we moved slowly down Bell Street in Heidelberg. My bow tie and starched white collar felt formal and strange. I looked down at the polished black shoes and was pleased to see that so far, by jumping the puddles, I had managed to keep them mud-free. When I closed my eyes, I could smell the scent of gardenia, encircled by baby's breath, pinned to the left lapel of my black hired suit.

As we drove along 'Walk of Life' from Dire Straits played on the radio. I felt tears well up in my eyes as I sang along at the top of my voice. My eyes were drawn across the charcoal darkness of the cold front that moved steadily towards us across the cityscape of northern Melbourne. There, in the distance, where St Theresa's Catholic Church stood, a shaft of sunlight pierced the blackness. If I believed in miracles ...

When we arrived at the church, I walked nervously towards its high bluestone front and through the open heavy steel doors at the entrance. Majestic stained glass windows and a vast interior greeted me as I went down the aisle. A handful of people had gathered behind the pews.

At the end of the aisle, we went into the sacristy to confer with the priest. I could feel a distinct dampness under my arms, even though I knew it wasn't hot. Chris McCann, an old friend from school, was my best man and my brother Steve, the groomsman.

'Chris, are you sure you've got the ring?' I asked tersely.

'Of course,' Chris reassured me.

I began to circle the room.

It felt not unlike the warm-up before a game of Australian Rules football, the main difference being the black double-breasted jacket I was wearing, which felt constricting.

As 2.30 p.m. approached, Father Colin Bourke and the three of us made our way to the altar. Familiar faces now sat on both sides of the aisle and I felt overwhelmed that they were looking at us. We waited for what seemed like an eternity – probably more like fifteen minutes – until the majority of the heads swung 180 degrees back up the aisle. Nanette, Bronwyn and Glenice had arrived, silhouetted in the door. As Netty came into sight, her beauty mesmerised me. Her full-length ivory dress had lace all over the bodice and arms. The purity of it gave her features an angelic glow. In her hands she carried the wedding bouquet, which was made up of white roses and gardenias with a few faint splashes of green. The sweet scent of it filled the air around her as she neared – gardenias were Nanette's favourite flower. As I watched her approach, I thought how lucky I was to be marrying her.

The photographer ducked in and there was another flash. Behind the veil in the flashlight, I could see she was fighting to camouflage a bundle of nerves and butterflies.

Nanette's morning hadn't been without drama. The photographer was late turning up at Bronwyn's house in Moonee Ponds, which had made them late for the church.

But the sun was shining and here was Nanette in front of me at the altar. With the ceremony well in progress, sweat was running from my forehead as the most important moment of my life to date approached.

After the readings, psalms and hymns the point of realisation arrived. For our vows we had chosen to face each other. The priest stood on the step above me: 'Do you take this woman Nanette, to have, to hold, to honour and cherish, in sickness and in health, till death do you part?'

The lump slipped from my throat and the solid, proud words came from my lips. 'I do.'

Having repeated this question to Nanette, I can still remember today the loving, endearing way in which she answered.

Chris reached into his jacket pocket for the ring. To my disbelief, he kept grappling inside his pocket. I think I stopped breathing. Then, he reached into the shirt pocket and there it was.

There was a ripple of amusement from the congregation.

Up to this point in my life, there had been only three other times when I had cried. On this day the tears flowed freely.

'Don't make me cry, bub. My mascara'll run and I'll look like a ferret,' she whispered as she nibbled my ear after we embraced passionately.

Walking back down the aisle, we both felt an immense sense of relief. Outside, kisses and hugs were followed by more of the same. The Croatian contingent insisted on the traditional kiss on both cheeks which meant getting around to everyone took some time. Cameras clicked incessantly as all combinations of poses with family and friends were covered. Eventually we were shunted off to our waiting cars – vintage white Bentleys. As I sank back into the burgundy leather, I felt like royalty. The wedding photos were to have been taken in the gardens in Essendon. But, after the rain earlier in the day and the prospect of traipsing through mud, it was decided to retire to the beautiful reception venue, Edenhope, in Ascot Vale, slightly closer to the city. It was a majestic old Victorian building, built in 1875. Inside, opulent chandeliers hung from the ceiling and tasteful antiques were scattered around the room. The walls of the reception room were plush red velvet.

The magnificent landscaped grounds lent the wedding photos a wonderful olde world charm.

It wasn't until we adjourned to the change rooms that I realised just how worked up Netty had been.

'Would you like a champagne now, my darling?' I asked smiling.

'I think so, but I'm not sure how the two dozen ulcers in my stomach will handle it.'

'You're serious? You actually don't want a champagne?'

'I'm just so tired and stressed out.'

'What time did you get up?'

'Oh, about 5.30 and I hardly slept all night.'

'How did the bridal breakfast go?'

'Oh, Bronwyn had the whole thing organised as usual. After that we had our hair done and the make-up was so over the top, we had to fix it ourselves. I was so strung out I was telling the joke about the head.'

'Which one?'

'You know the one where it's the head's birthday party. When he goes to open the presents, he says, "Oh no, not more hats".'

After a couple of mouthfuls of champagne Netty relaxed enough to squeeze up to me and say, 'I really love you, Walter. You're my boy.'

I smiled and thought, 'That sounds more like my Netty.'

In the reception room, drinks flowed freely as guests settled in for an entertaining evening. When the girls had freshened up their make-up we were ready.

'Ladies and gentlemen, please stand to welcome Mr and Mrs Mikac,' was the welcome on the public address system. Clapping, cheering and loud whistling abounded as we walked arm in arm to the bridal table. The intense feeling of pleasure and happiness was what I remember most.

The two wedding cakes on a separate small table, covered with a white cloth near the dance hall, were to become a major talking point at the reception. This had been one area where we could not compromise. One was a traditional Australian fruit cake in two layers. The second was continental-style (Crokenbocce) and consisted of a huge mountain of profiteroles filled with rich custard. Over the top of this had been drizzled a thick toffee-like treacle. It looked sensational and ensured that even the ever-hungry Croatian crowd were filled to the brink. The proceedings were going very smoothly with people dancing and enjoying themselves. Years of ballroom dancing lessons made the bridal waltz a breeze for me, as I led Nanette around the dance floor.

Later, the final goodbyes heralded more kisses, hugs and a bounty of tears.

The hordes were left to mop up the last of the drinks on the tables as Nanette and I departed for our new life together.

We approached the two towers of the Regent Hotel in Collins Street and I pulled into the grand entrance of the hotel and got out onto the red carpet. Having booked the honeymoon suite, I still had enough energy to feel quietly excited. Nanette was wearing mauve chiffon loose-fitting pants and a matching long-sleeved jacket her mother had made for her. The enormity of the day was showing on her drawn face. She looked like she had finished a triathlon rather than having got married.

'You looked absolutely beautiful today, Net. I'm very proud of you.' To which she could only manage a faint smile.

Our suite was on the 43rd floor with magnificent views southwards over the Yarra River. Like a little boy I excitedly ran over to the wall of windows.

'Wow. Look at this, Net.'

I checked out all the familiar landmarks from a totally different perspective. What impressed me most was the flashing neon 'Allens' sign on the far bank of the river and the changing positions of the sign which mimicked a lolly being unwrapped.

By the time I got back from the bathroom Nanette was already in bed. Her eyes were closed.

'Netty,' I said cuddling up behind her. 'Are you still awake? You do realise what night this is, don't you?'

'Mmm,' she said, sleepily. 'Aw, yes, it was a beautiful day, wasn't it?' Then she added in a resigned tone, 'Okay, let's get it over with.'

The following day, we were off on our honeymoon. The lady at the check-in counter in Tullamarine Airport looked up as we approached. 'Mr and Mrs Mikac, would either of you like a window seat?'

We smiled at each other. We were husband and wife. Those months of meticulous planning were now over and we were about to depart for ten blissful days together.

After a stop-off in Singapore our destination was the Maldive Islands, an atoll of some 1200 tiny islands in the Indian Ocean. The island of Bandos was to be our own little paradise for seven days. With its archetypal waving palms and coral reef which extended about fifty metres from the beach it proved to be beyond our wildest expectations.

On a hammock suspended in the palm trees by the water's edge Nanette would spend hours reading and sunbaking with her feet dangling into the warm water. This tranquillity allowed me to spend each day snorkelling and being bewildered by the array of marine life inhabiting the reef. When I was able to convince Netty to join me, the fish would nibble at the red nail polish on her toes. This entertained her no end. As the fish congregated for the biting and it increased in frequency, she'd shriek and jump out laughing.

We arrived back in Melbourne one week before Christmas. The harmonious beginning to our lives together was all but forgotten as we were thrown into the hustle and bustle of the huge shopping centres and feverish pre-Christmas spenders. After our relaxing honeymoon, it all came as a culture shock.

Our home for the next year was at Locksley Road, Ivanhoe, in the flat that Nanette had moved into after we had got engaged. Netty had bought me a tropical fish tank as my Christmas present, which I took great pride in setting up. We would lie in bed and hold each other in the dark watching the delicate and smooth movements of the angel fish floating through the water.

With the honeymoon over, much as though we could have spent weeks like this, we had to go back to work. I was managing a small but busy pharmacy in the Preston Market in the northern suburbs. Netty went back to the Radiology department.

Married life was going well, but there were some major stumbling blocks – housework, cooking and co-operation. All things I had to learn. Although I was quite adept at vacuuming, ironing and washing, doing it on a regular basis was another story. On Saturday afternoons, I'd trundle off to cricket while Netty stood in the lounge-room with the vacuum nozzle in her hands. It took a while to realise how selfish I was being. After all, we were both working demanding full-time jobs, so why not share the house duties equally? A compromise scenario saw us work in tandem early on a Saturday morning. I would dust and vacuum as Netty did the washing and the kitchen.

Netty enjoyed cooking immensely which is probably why she was so good at it. Although on one occasion she cooked some rice for dinner. Having never had to cook for myself, I had the impression that the end result was always a success. This particular night, the rice was overcooked and very gluggy. Tired after a day at work, I said, 'I'm not eating this shit.'

Netty proceeded to empty the plate on my lap. It was a story we laughed at often in the years to follow. After the retribution I learned my lesson – any future comments were only constructive or complimentary.

Netty would experiment with Thai, Indian, Greek or any other cuisine that we'd been lucky enough to have been out to sample. The resulting dishes were always greatly appreciated by friends who would come over for dinner parties. Meanwhile my chemistry skills ignited a quest to learn about the art of winemaking. This resulted in generous quantities of good wine accompanying dinner. As for me, being a well-fed Croatian lad, I simply loved to eat and the fact that Netty loved to cook made us a perfect combination.

When we had been married for just over a year we bought a house in Montmorency, a green corridor in Melbourne's north-eastern suburbs near Eltham. It had a deck at the back with views looking north-west towards Mount Macedon.

My parents' reaction to the purchase was lukewarm.

'It'll do for a while, I suppose.'

I found myself longing for their approval even though I knew we would always perceive things differently.

'You can knock it down and build units if you want,' my father said.

Keith and Grace would often come to stay overnight, which made Netty feel very special. Grace's skill in decorating came to the fore as she directed where to position prints and furniture. Grace claimed one armchair as hers and it soon became her throne. From this position I would serve up cup after cup of weak, black tea. During her upbringing in the orphanage she had missed out on many things that others consider normal, so she loved being pampered. Some evenings Nanette would give her a full facial, while I'd whip up some cocktails. Brandy Alexander was her favourite, with its creamy, frothy texture, and she was always appreciative of the quality of the Chinese food from the take-away down the road. I would also give her pedicures. 'I feel like the Queen of Sheba,' she'd say.

Those early years were full of love and fun.

Life was about living each day with purpose and making the most of it. We had lots of dinner parties, wine-tasting nights and How-to-Host-a-Murder nights. Something as innocent as a barbeque would often spill over into a couple of ports and singing around the pianola.

We were proud of our first home.

After completing a landscaping course, I had constructed a Japanese garden out the front with a cascading waterfall which was a popular talking point.

Like most newlyweds, we took for granted the certainty of our future together.

FIVE

And Then We Were Four

L *ani, I can feel you dancing around me. I am proud of you, my*
darling girl. In fact, I can sense you all. Please show yourselves
to me. I know the three of you can see me. Why can't I see you? It's
not fair. Nothing about life is fair at the moment. What on earth am
I doing here on this volcanic island, Rangitoto, in the middle of
Auckland Harbour? I should be dispensing prescriptions in my phar-
macy in Tasmania. Nothing about my life is normal and may never
be again.

Netty, are you there? I've come to New Zealand to visit Jo Winter
who lost her husband, Jason, that day at Port Arthur. I met this
extraordinary person after the memorial service at St David's Cathe-
dral in Hobart. We were sitting in a large group when this very
attractive lady with a red scarf draped over one shoulder came up
to us. 'I'm not sure what your circumstance is but I've lost my
husband which I want to share with you.' These words somehow

*showed me a glimmer of light when all around me was dark. My
family and I talked with Jo, and Jason's parents for ages. I am a
positive person but these people amazed me.*

*A bond was formed and now, in June 1996, I am visiting them in
New Zealand. Am I doing the right thing? I thought I might feel
uncomfortable as I don't really know anyone here. But as it turns
out, it's giving me a chance to collect my thoughts and regain some
harmony. Spending time with Jo, her father, Mick, and her baby son,
Mitchell, who were all in the Broad Arrow Cafe and have survived.
In the cafe that day, Jo sang lullabies to Mitchell to keep him quiet
as the gunman walked around selecting his victims.*

*The days passed differently in New Zealand. I was far away from
the memories back home and had time to reflect. Being in a family
environment, having a roast and crunchy potatoes for dinner,
brought back a bit of normality to my life. In the evenings, Jo and I
talked over a few glasses of wine about how we were coping. At her
father's house I slept in the same bed she used as a child. All these
tiny things helped me to cope.*

*So today, I've come sightseeing and am on this volcanic island by
myself. Here in the glade there is moss and greenery everywhere.
The canopy of trees, eerie silence and huge seat-like boulders makes
it feel like fairies should abound here. I am sure the breathing on
my neck is Netty's. I'm sure I can smell my beloved. Netty, are you
enjoying it here? I know you're around me. Lani and Maddie are
skipping incessantly. The brush of Maddie's golden locks glances my
thigh. I swivel to try and follow her direction. She must be smiling;
she's having fun with her sister and Mum. Lani, your hair must look
gorgeous, flowing and flying as you pirouette. Glistening around
your soft lips. I can still think of the moment you entered our world.
My tentative hands placed you in the loving arms of Netty. Our body
and our blood.*

It was 8 o'clock on Monday morning, 28 August 1989, and I was
battling with peak-hour city traffic. All things being equal, we would

be cuddling our new addition to the world sometime today. St Vincent's Private Hospital, where Nanette had checked in the previous day, was on the fringe of the CBD of Melbourne. The presence of speed cameras down this route did little to deter my foot impatiently coercing the accelerator pedal.

I entered the ward, running late and feeling more than a little stressed. Nanette, sitting up in bed surrounded by pillows, looked a little apprehensive, her characteristic joviality missing. She was over a week overdue and wanted to get childbirth over and done with. I knew how desperately she wanted to hold that baby after nine months of it being in her womb.

We already had surrogate children. After settling in to Montmorency, we bought an Australian terrier/Jack Russell cross called Molly and a fat beagle pup called Becky to keep her company. They were spoiled with play toys, bones and all kinds of treats. They even had their own presents of dog chewies wrapped under the Christmas tree.

Our decision to start a real family had been made one night in late 1988, at the Patee Thai in Brunswick Street, Fitzroy. We had just finished the entree when Nanette announced she wanted to have a child. The idea hadn't come out of the blue. We had our own house, I had a steady job at the Preston Market Pharmacy, a tiny shop the size of a matchbox where all the local ethnic shopkeepers used to drop in to say hello each morning. During one trip in January 1988 to Ballarat, as a joke I had even written a postcard to our two imaginary children, Thomas and Alannah.

Our first child's conception went ahead, as planned, at the end of that year and now the long awaited date had arrived.

At 10 a.m., Dr Peter Maher, the obstetrician and gynaecologist, arrived. He was an imposing figure at over six foot, with a solid build, well-groomed hair and a full ginger beard. He was dressed in his customary suit and sported one of his endless supply of bow ties. His humour matched Nanette's.

'You're looking good today. Probably too good to have a baby. Are you sure you're ready?' was his opening comment.

Nanette tried to respond, but I could sense, for once, she was over-awed by the magnitude of the task ahead.

As the nurse followed Dr Maher's instructions, the oxytocin drip, a synthetic version of a drug that the body normally produces to begin labour, began to run into Nanette's arm. Being a nurse herself, Nanette knew there was no turning back now. With the IV flowing steadily we were able to sit back and wait. I read the paper, a novelty I rarely enjoyed, while we shared a plate of sandwiches.

'I just hope it's healthy,' Netty said. 'I can't wait to see those ten fingers and toes.'

She had climbed the steps to motherhood fairly easily, despite the obligatory nausea and morning sickness. At first, she continued working in the X-ray department, but wearing the heavy protective lead coats wore her out by the end of the day so the CAT Scan room became her domain instead. At the initial ultrasound session we saw our baby move for the first time. The living being in Netty's womb was only about eight centimetres long and you could see the minute contractions of the heart. To say this was a humbling moment would be a gross understatement.

The baby would often do 'flip flops', as Nanette called them, her belly moving with gymnast-like fervour. We would watch, laugh and wonder. Sometimes Netty would get out her stethoscope and we'd listen to the heartbeat.

Just before 3 p.m., the nursing shift changed over, but Nanette had still not dilated much. A very efficient-looking nurse called Pauline scuttled in to check Nanette.

'You've dilated up to eight centimetres. We'd better call Dr Maher. It's not very far off.'

A device called a halter monitor was placed around Nanette's tummy to keep tabs on the baby's heart rate. It was about this time, for me, that the prospect of becoming a father started to become a reality.

Would I do a good job? Would my child accept me and love me? At the same time, I felt a glowing, warm feeling in my chest at the thought of having my own family to care for.

'Everything's looking fine,' Dr Maher assured us when he arrived.

Giving Nanette's curls a ruffle to lessen her apprehension, he turned to me with a wry smile. The eagerness on my face must have been standing out like a beacon.

'Would you like to gown up then, Walter?'

I was taken aback that he expected me to join in, but I made my way to the basin to scrub up.

Gowned up and ready to go, I nervously shuffled to Dr Maher's side. Ducking around to Nanette, I kissed her forehead whilst telling how much I loved her and how proud I was. She managed a very faint grin, but looked uncomfortable. After receiving a couple of large inhalations of nitrous oxide gas, she relaxed a little. Soon she began to grimace and in my nervous state I became convinced things may be going wrong. The baby's heart rate was dropping. I could hear it on the bips from the monitor and see it on the screen. I felt a sinking feeling deep in my stomach.

'Nanette, what would you like me to do?' I asked seizing her hand.

'Get bloody lost,' she replied.

I was aghast. Here I was trying to be supportive and caring. She rarely ever swore and certainly not like that. I felt confused and didn't know what to do, not realising this all meant transition had begun. I later learned that the slowing of the heart rate and Nanette's indifference to me were merely part of the occasion of childbirth.

When I could see the baby's hair emerging, I became quite excited. With every call of 'push' from Pauline I could see our child coming closer and closer. Peter Maher performed his job with the ease of a consummate professional which certainly had a relaxing, calming effect. Gently positioning my hand under the minute neck as instructed, I watched in awe as Nanette gave one last burst of panting, clearly wanting to get the job over and done with. One final call of 'push' and our daughter Alannah Louise Mikac entered the world. Having checked the cord wasn't around the baby's neck, Peter handed her over to me. 'It's a girl!' I called out to Nanette whose smile was truly ecstatic. Her cheeks were quite red, hair only slightly ruffled and make-up firmly intact. She smiled as I placed Alannah at

6lb 14oz on her chest. At 4.15 p.m. Nanette held her tightly to her chest and proclaimed: 'Welcome, my beautiful little daughter.'

You were such a joy to us, Alannah. As first-time parents we blundered our way through the steps of parenthood for which we were totally unprepared. I would rock you to sleep. Sometimes it took 300 rocks, you know, before your eyes would close and your breathing would slow and we would tiptoe out of the room. I remember, even before you came home from hospital, hanging up the mobiles we'd got as presents, blowing on them and watching them spin around. Making space in the laundry for the big nappy bucket. When I gave you your first bath, I held your little arms so carefully. I was frightened I would pull too hard. I put your jumpsuit on back to front and couldn't work out why it didn't do up properly. Mummy laughed so much, she said: 'I sound like an out-of-work chook. I'm glad that wasn't the nappy you were putting on.'

Netty, those early days of parenting were particularly tough for you.

We argued often over petty, domestic issues. Looking back, that was the biggest strain on our relationship. Where once we'd sit down with a beer or wine before dinner, after Lani arrived, we were clearing the backlog of nappies or sterilising bottles to prevent colic. Our lives were irrevocably changed.

You developed a breast abscess and had to go into hospital, leaving your beloved daughter at home in my care. Luckily, Grace was there to teach me how to give our little Lani a bottle. I tried hard to be a good dad. Sometimes, I know I could have done better. Like the day I went to run a marathon when you were sick with the abscess. You were so ill and begged me to stay at home. But I was obsessed with running my first marathon. Completing the gruelling 42 kilometres was all-encompassing and it was a pinnacle of endurance that I wanted to experience. I failed to understand that you were battling with your own test of endurance. You even told me the abscess was worse than the pain of childbirth, but I was caught up in my goal and my own selfishness. On the day of the marathon, because I wasn't there, you had to ring Chris McCann as you were running such a temperature. I know selfishness is one of my worst traits. I am always aware of it.

Life was also tough on the job front for me and things were made worse by the fact that we had less money because you weren't working. Remember that job I had at the place in West Heidelberg where the customers were so sick. The boss, Leigh Sampson, was a guiding light, caring for those who came into the pharmacy as if he was the neighbourhood Messiah. It was a rough place full of housing commission estates. I was so naive thinking they simply needed counselling and more education. Some of these people had asthma and emphysema, were on every inhalation medicine available, and yet they still smoked.

I was naive in my role as a father, too. Remember how I used to come home exhausted and full of despair and tell you I needed half an hour to myself. You used to get so mad, as you'd been looking after Alannah all day by yourself. I shouldn't have been so thoughtless. I didn't understand for a long time, Netty, how hard you were finding it in your new role without the stimulation of work. You enjoyed the company of intelligent people and most of all you needed an arena in which to perform. From your jokes to your tap dancing; from the need to help sick people to the need to feel useful and worthwhile. I remember you saying: 'I can make people laugh, Walter. I want to make people laugh. That is my gift!' And the funny thing is, Netty, that's what I loved so much about you. You made each day another adventure, another experience to have and moment to be savoured.

I found a letter I wrote you back then:

To my dearest Netty,
I thought I'd write you this letter to tell you I love you more than ever. Perhaps, in recent times we have taken each other for granted. Now that Alannah is becoming easier to look after, I think it's essential that we still have time for each other. I realize I can be

extremely stubborn and frustrating at times, which I have to resolve. I want you to know I respect and love you more now than ever before. Your braveness and strength during your pregnancy and birth were fantastic. I envy the courage you showed during your trauma with your breast abscess. I love you with all my heart and want to grow with you as we watch our beautiful Lani grow up and develop.

These are my deep and sincere feelings to you.

Love Walter

The fine cracks, that could have developed back then into gaping holes, Netty, were rendered over by our beautiful Lani. I am watching the video where you caught me out in my birthday suit in the bath with Alannah, hiding myself under the bubbles while she crawls around wondering what her Daddy is up to. Things improved as Lani grew up. We changed our routine, curling up in front of the fire with a bottle of wine, no longer going on our regular Saturday night out. Those were healing times, times which we spent talking to each other.

Alannah was the first grandchild on my side of the family and Keith and Grace's eighth. When Alannah was six months old, Keith and Grace went on a two-year trip around Australia. Nanette said goodbye with tears in her eyes. She desperately wanted Grace's help and support in these early months of motherhood. But it was alone that we ventured into the unknown territory of parenthood. Despite our fears, it was also a glorious process of discovery. That joyous smile and such unconditional love is something only a parent can know.

Netty went back to work when Alannah was eight months old. At first, she felt guilty, but we both saw that Alannah benefited from being with other children. And Netty won back her independence. With the extra money she earned, we would go on what she called 'our little adventures' which took us all over the state. From places like the gold-mining towns of Bendigo and Ballarat, to areas of

natural beauty like the Grampians in Victoria's west or short overnight stays to Healesville or Warburton just outside of Melbourne.
Dinner would traditionally be at the local pub with a bottle of wine
or champagne to take back to our room.

When Alannah was two years old we decided to have our second
child. We thought that while we were still in the habit of washing
nappies and getting up in the middle of the night, we might as well
have another one. Plus they would only be three years apart.

It was during one of those trips – to Daylesford, an area famous
for its natural mineral springs – in early November 1991 that Maddie
was conceived. The motel where we stayed had big lawns in front
where Alannah ran wild. After discovering she could catch one of
the young chickens she continued chasing it and trying to pick it up.

When Nani and Pa returned from their trip to find another grandchild was on the way, they had a surprise for us too. On their cir-
cumnavigation of Tasmania they had chosen a quiet seafront home
for their retirement. It was at White Beach on the Tasman Peninsula,
some 100 kilometres south-east of Hobart, only about ten minutes'
drive from the historic penal settlement of Port Arthur.

*What ifs, Netty. What ifs. 'What ifs' plague my life. What if they had
never moved to White Beach? To that strip of peninsula that was to
harbour so much heartache for all of us. Grace died there, you died
there, our two girls died there. We all knew nothing of our fate back
then.*

*I am reading a letter from your mother to you dated 5 July 1994.
She only got to live in the White Beach house for two years. In her
letter to you Grace writes: 'I guess if I knew my condition was terminal before we moved here then we may have considered otherwise,
but I guess it is far too late for regrets.'*

*I find it hard not to live without regrets, Netty, not yet, perhaps
never. What if Grace and Keith had chosen somewhere else to settle
down? We could be living in Queensland now or Western Australia.
What if Grace had never thought of the idea of opening a pharmacy*

at Nubeena? What if it didn't matter to you so much that your mother had moved away from Melbourne? What if?

In May 1992, Keith and Grace moved to Tasmania. Netty was six months pregnant with Maddie and could not hide her disappointment. No more spontaneous weekend trips to Romsey for donkey rides and home-grown vegetables. Netty's worst fear had always been that Keith and Grace weren't going to be involved in our children growing up. Now that fear had become a reality. I tried to reason that we'd be able to visit them and that if it helped she could take the children down more often. Deep down, I knew it didn't stop her hurting. It was as if this scenario had rekindled some kind of painful childhood memory. It was as if she was being abandoned again as she felt she had been as a child during Grace's many absences.

Even the second pregnancy didn't take her mind off things. Our second child was even more active in the womb than Alannah and her entry into the world was also different.

On Saturday, 15 August 1992, I stirred at around 8.15 a.m. knowing that Netty had been up for more than an hour. Her contractions had begun. About forty minutes later, Bronwyn arrived to pick up Alannah and we were in the car heading for the Freemasons Private Hospital in Wellington Parade, Fitzroy.

The contractions were just under ten minutes apart. While trying to remain calm, I was obviously tense.

'Hold on, Net. We'll be there in no time.'

'I hope so or else I'll be delivering on the Eastern Freeway.'

Ten minutes later, she was calling out as each contraction started. 'How long in between those ones?' she asked, wincing.

I knew in this situation that I had to stay calm. They were about four minutes apart. I casually said, 'It's still okay. Around six minutes. You'll be fine.'

About fifteen minutes later, with handbrake coming into play, I pulled up to a screeching halt outside the hospital. Netty beckoned to me to run around and open her door. Grabbing her hand to lever her out of the car, I nursed her through the entrance and into the elevator. As we stepped out of the elevator the desk of the delivery suite was in sight. The nurse was obviously aware of the situation and dashed over to assist. With Netty in the middle we burst into the suite like a steam train.

'How's it going then?' asked the midwife.

'You're not going to believe this, but I have to push,' said Netty in a matter-of-fact kind of way.

Disbelieving what she was being told, the midwife stretched on her examination glove and performed the tried and true test. The astonished expression on her face told the story.

'Quick, let's get your clothes off and get a gown on you.'

'Can I scrub up and help out?' I asked naively, unable to see the head crowning as Netty lay on the delivery bed.

'Shut up, Walter,' shouted Net.

'Let's try to slow this down a bit, otherwise you'll tear badly. Try and pant just like in the classes,' ordered the midwife.

The doctor was not going to make it. Even pain relief fell by the wayside. The baby's head was nearly through the opening as I watched, dumbfounded. Snapping back to the event, I rushed to Netty's side to lend support. The agony on her face told the story. As I clutched her tightly in my arms she broke the skin on my forearm with the force of her nails. With one final recoil of her body Nanette signalled the job was completed. My arms relaxed marginally as the fingers extracted themselves from my forearm. There was a smile of relief on Netty's face as the midwife held up our new addition.

'Congratulations, Mr and Mrs Mikac, on a beautiful, healthy daughter.'

Beaming, Netty turned to me and said, 'Madeline Grace Mikac,' as the nurse placed Madeline on her chest. My contribution to Maddie's arrival was cutting the cord.

The lightning speed of the birth meant that Madeline looked like she had spent fifteen rounds in the ring with Muhammad Ali.

'I think she looks a lot like Tony Mundine,' Netty said ruefully.

We were assured that Madeline's rate of entry into the world was the cause of her squashed face. Netty appreciated the narcotics given to alleviate her sudden pain. With Madeline having a sleep, we could enjoy morning tea followed by a sumptuous lunch with a celebratory bottle of wine and joked that the hospital should have been called the Freemasons Hilton.

The early weeks of having Madeline home weren't anywhere near as traumatic as with Alannah. 'Maddie', as she quickly became called, was more relaxed. Unlike Alannah, she refused a dummy, preferring the fingers in the mouth. Always the index and ring fingers of the right hand. She fed, slept and seemed contented.

Christmas 1992 was our first as a family of four. Maddie was four months old, propped up with cushions on our club lounge. Alannah and I knelt in front of the Christmas tree to give out the presents. Nanette sat in striped pyjamas cross-legged on the couch, eating cereal. Alannah ripped her first present open. A battery-operated guitar with sing-a-long microphone.

'Wow, Lani!' Nanette said, getting more enjoyment from the occasion than Alannah. 'Imagine how much money you'll be able to make now that you can busk professionally.'

The guitar was Alannah's first musical instrument. She began busking with her cassette player at the Eltham Craft Market. She'd take her hard-earned money and beetle off to the next stall to buy doll's clothes with the proceeds.

Maddie's first Christmas present was a replica Madeline doll from the television series of the same name, which was bigger than Maddie herself. We laughed at her antics as she clawed at the wrapping paper. We had arranged to have a banquet at our house that day, with wine and copious quantities of seafood. My family were all there. Bronwyn came, too, with Daniel and Hannah, and Nanette's brother Rodney with his wife Jenny and their kids. Nanette soldiered on, occasionally breastfeeding, cooking and washing, and we ended up in the evening around the pianola. Only Keith and Grace were absent having decided to spend their first Christmas in Tasmania.

In February 1993 we travelled down to see them for two weeks. I played with the girls on the beach every day and we both felt happy that Keith and Grace had found somewhere so peaceful to live.

It wasn't our first trip to Tasmania. In 1986, we'd done a ten-day holiday on our own. We even went to Port Arthur, which you loved at first sight, Netty. So did I. We looked at Tasmanian house prices back then, but we didn't really believe that we'd end up living there. And then, in 1993, we were back, drawn unwittingly like a magnet to this island that was to play such a large part in our future.

We have a video of that first holiday to White Beach, the first time we'd travelled together as a family of four. As I watch the video again, I am watching your legs, Netty, as you walk across the tarmac after we say goodbye to Keith and Grace, your long, beautiful legs under a short blue skirt, Maddie on your hip. Your legs are femininely firm and taper perfectly to lovely thin ankles. Okay, you had two children by then. You were never slender, but after more than seven years of marriage, Netty, I still found you gorgeous and was excited by you.

After we returned from Tasmania, Netty was offered a half-nightshift nursing position in the Accident and Emergency department of the Austin Hospital, which meant shifts from 9 p.m. to 2 a.m. a few times a week.

Having decided to renovate, and knowing the extra money would be useful, we began a life of tag team, slapping hands as I came home from my managing position at Ivan Grauer Pharmacy in Watsonia, seven kilometres from where we lived, and Netty walked out the door. Our life continued at a frenetic pace.

By June 1993, we had a new bathroom with a large corner spa, a new bedroom for Alannah and a huge living room for the kids.

As each room was completed I started painting in earnest. With Netty off to work in the evenings and Maddie in bed, I would begin.

Alannah, armed with brush, would progressively paint stick figures around the room while I would follow behind her with the roller filling in the spaces. This gave her great delight as she would describe each figure before she painted it. Netty would often arrive from work after 2 a.m., to see me with paint roller in hand.

'I can't believe you're still up. Are you coming to bed now?' she'd say in an annoyed tone.

'Yeah, I'll just be ten minutes. I want to finish this ceiling.'

When I'd finally sneak into bed, I would still be wide awake. Usually a cuddle led to a little more. Making love was often the best panacea for sleep.

We found a reliable babysitter called Emily Gioules which meant we could get out more. There was only one thing wrong as far as I was concerned. I still yearned for my own business. I'd scour the papers for positions as far away as Queensland if they mentioned a partnership. I wanted to be able to provide my family with all the things they wanted, as well as having a lifestyle where we could spend as much time as possible together.

In late 1993, I took up the suggestion of my boss, Ivan Grauer, to attend a motivational seminar. Ivan and I had been discussing a partnership and he had attended many such seminars.

Sitting in the fourth row of the vast expanse of Dallas Brookes Hall, I joined the thunderous applause after Dr Wayne Dyer talked about being what you wanted to be and Dr Deepak Chopra spoke about the body's ability to heal and rejuvenate itself through the power of the mind. The principles they outlined struck a note with me and I arrived home in a blaze of enthusiasm to a tired Netty who was breastfeeding Maddie and would rather have gone to sleep than listen to my rantings.

Maybe I didn't need to be more motivated, Netty. Why wasn't I happy with my lot? We had a beautiful house that we'd renovated to suit us. Alannah was happy living at Montmorency and going to kinder. Lani, at your first dance school Christmas concert you wore your hair tied back into a bun and with full make-up, I hardly recognised you as my little baby. You were such a performer. Even after you slipped during your tap routine, you were back up on your feet like a consummate professional. And the grand finale, Alannah – you were the Christmas tree surrounded by all your little four-year-old friends with flashing bud lights which pierced the darkness. Remember your Uncle John and I racing up to the stage with posies of flowers? If a smile ever said, 'I believe in myself and know that I'm good' then this smile was it. The diva holding two bunches of flowers – in her element. Performing and loving it.

By February 1994, we learnt of Grace's illness, a rare respiratory disease in which the lungs gradually lose their capacity to function. So little was known of this condition, except that inevitably it was terminal. Nanette decided to take the girls and visit Tasmania. At the last minute I thought I would go, too.

It was while we were sitting on Keith and Grace's verandah watching the white cappers beating on the beach outside that Grace uttered the words that were to change our lives forever.

'Walter, you should think about starting a pharmacy down here. We really need one and the doctors have been crying out for a pharmacist for ages. A recent survey showed a pharmacy as being the most demanded service on the peninsula.'

The comment came out of the blue. I was a born-and-bred city boy, so the idea of living in a quiet rural township had never held any attraction. Then Grace said the magical words that set me in motion: 'Imagine setting up your own business. You'd be so well respected here.'

'Maybe you should go and talk to the doctors. You've got nothing to lose,' Netty added.

I momentarily pictured myself standing behind the counter of my own pharmacy. A very alluring scene.

'Oh well,' I said slowly, 'What about I go and see the doctors tomorrow?'

The local gazette had all the information I required and Grace would surely be able to fill in any gaps. I met Steve and Pam Ireland, who were the local general practitioners servicing the entire peninsula and who also operated a limited pharmacy service. Kerrie Shoobridge, the receptionist at the surgery, informed me that Pam was on today.

Meeting Pam, I felt somewhat intimidated by her presence. A solidly built lady with a pleasant face and straight, dark brown hair she gave the impression of not interacting with people well. Her manner, without being unpleasant, was blunt and matter of fact.

'We've been screaming to the health department for years to get a proper pharmacy here. You'd have to buy all our stock and computer, too, if you were to take the pharmacy over.'

Hang on, hang on, I thought. I've just come here to ask a few questions and this lady's got me buying everything. I then explained I'd have to apply to the Federal Government for a licence as it wasn't as simple as just starting a pharmacy. There were strict guidelines in place. Pam agreed to give me their figures which would help me calculate if it would be financially viable. Armed with all the relevant information, we headed back to Melbourne.

Having looked at the figures and prepared a professional submission and been recommended by the Irelands, I had an inner confidence that it would work out. After posting my submission, we sat back to await the verdict. In the meantime, all kinds of questions popped up in our heads. Why would we want to leave the house we'd spent so much time and effort on? How difficult would it be to uproot and move across Bass Strait? What if the business didn't work out or if we hated it? What if Grace died before we moved there?

The whole prospect was frightening, yet exciting. The lifestyle we could only have imagined was close to becoming reality. The sixty-hour weeks I was currently working at Watsonia would be replaced by a more leisurely workplace with only some forty hours at the coal face. A huge hunk of time that I could spend taking my girls to the beach, gardening or simply being around to watch them thrive and grow up.

The night in April that the letter arrived that was to determine our fate, I arrived home totally bushed.

'Walter, there's a few letters here for you that look important,' Nanette called from the kitchen as I walked through the front door.

Flopping back onto the bed, I didn't have the energy to respond. 'How are you, bub? How are my little darlings?'

Alannah ran into our bedroom and catapulted herself full length onto my stomach. 'Daddy, daddy, I wuv you. You're the best daddy in all the world.'

This demonstration of love and energy swept away my tiredness and I hugged Lani. A waddling Maddie wasn't far behind. I reached over to pick her up and unceremoniously dumped her on top of Alannah. Hysterical laughter followed with each new wave of bouncing on the bed. They both loved it. The rougher and noisier it got, the better. As it wound down in intensity, Netty strolled in and laid next to us. A big group cuddle made me forget the day entirely. I was home and this was where I wanted to be.

'Darling, here's those letters I was telling you about.'

'Right, actually this one is from the Health Insurance Commission. This could be some news about the pharmacy.' I scanned down the letter to the line that read 'Your application for a new pharmacy in Nubeena has been approved'. I thrust the letter at Netty and yelled, 'We've got it, honey. We've got it. Our very own pharmacy. Can you believe it?'

Net shrieked as she grabbed my arm tightly and kissed me on the lips. 'I'm so proud of you, bub. This is going to be fantastic. Girls, you're going to be able to see Nani every day if you want.'

'Will we have a beautiful house with lots of animals?' asked Alannah enthusiastically.

'Yes, lots of ducks, chickens and maybe a sheep or a pony for you.'

'Wow. That'll be fun. Maddie and I can feed the baby chickens. Can we go tomorrow?'

For Netty, having time with her mother was extremely important. So, despite having a comfortable home, a $50,000 per annum job and nearly all our friends and relatives nearby, we decided to leave Melbourne. Leaving the security of our house was the biggest obstacle. My parents were not ecstatic about the decision, but I explained that this was an opportunity to be grasped. If we didn't take it now, in years to come we might regret it.

Little did I know how much I would regret it. If onlys. If only the Health Insurance Commission had rejected my application. That would have been the end of it. It would have been a good idea, but that's what it would have remained. It would not have become a reality. It seemed like the right thing to do, to move to a place that was a safe and peaceful environment for our children, where they could grow up in a beautiful place and we could escape the frantic pace of a city and its ever-increasing crime. Yes, I pictured myself standing behind the counter of my own pharmacy, my own boss with my family living close by. Was I so wrong to want this?

SIX

The Spirit of Tasmania

I *am sitting on the deck of the* Spirit of Tasmania, *reading a book. Everywhere around me, people are crowding the decks to have their first glimpse of this innocent island. Tourists, like we once were, arriving blissfully unaware of what this island means to me. I don't even bother to look over the rails as we approach Devonport. Everything on this trip reminds me of when we moved here, Netty. I even think back to the trip we made alone in 1986 with ten days of bed and breakfasts and no responsibilities. But, it's the trip with the family I remember most. We were venturing into a wonderful new life. Or so we thought.*

Lost in memories, I sink back into the deckchair avoiding the general tone of excitement on deck. Other people with their own dreams and their own children planning for their future together without a thought that the future may not happen the way they expect it to. When we sailed to Tasmania in 1994, Netty, you were sailing to your fate along with our beautiful daughters. And now, in February 1997, I am returning to this place which has given me so much misery, returning with a conviction that I will write about our life together. It is the one thing that holds me together. I will write a book about what a wonderful family I had and the incredible waste of life brought about by the actions of a pathetic creature who had access to an arsenal of firearms, weapons designed to kill.

I owe this book to you, Netty, and Lani and Maddie.

I now have a tattoo, Netty. You know I always hated tattoos. But it was the one way I could have a physical reminder. Three angels, each with the same colour hair as each of you, entwined in a vine, linked together forever. Your names indelibly engraved on my body.

I wish, as I sit on the deck of this ferry, that I was like these people, that I wasn't returning to this island alone.

We left Melbourne on 1 August 1994 on the *Spirit of Tasmania*. On the boat Netty and I managed to snatch a drink at the bar while Lani and Maddie were the centre of attention as they whirled around on the dancefloor. I bedded down the girls, and then we had an early night in our cabin. We had our two cars, the faithful old blue Mitsubishi Sigma, fully laden with bonsai plants, packing boxes and suitcases. Nanette drove the classy, sporty red Fiat, the back seat decked out with baby seats and just enough room to fit the dogs.

'I think we'll buy a Pajero so we can do the deliveries for the pharmacy,' I said.

'Good idea, then we can go on trips at weekends,' Netty answered. 'A 4WD's a great idea.'

'Hey,' I said, taking another sip of beer, 'Imagine the sign on the door: "Tasman Pharmacy – Proprietor Walter Mikac".'

Netty jumped up and down in her seat. 'And Gracie, the old bag, she'll be round the corner and Lani and Maddie can visit every day. Yippeedooda.'

After docking at Devonport we began the four and a half hour trip to the Tasman Peninsula. It was a circus, with children and animals jumping around.

'They're driving me nuts, Wal,' Nanette said when we stopped our convoy en route for a cup of coffee. 'The dogs keep whimpering and the girls just want to be unbuckled and run around.'

There was no turning back now. Before we left, we'd been through two months of frantic activity. Organising people to rent our house, getting removalists to clear away a massive accumulation of belongings, finishing jobs and the obligatory farewell functions. We had garage sales, sitting under umbrellas at the top of the drive where we had to get rid of hundreds of bonsais and other plants. One of my best bonsais that was too large to take to Tasmania fetched us $100 and we scored a pair of Blundstone boots each.

At Station Pier, I had the difficult task of saying goodbye to my family. The hugs were firmer with a much stronger sensation of leaving the nest than ever before.

Our arrival in the small village of Nubeena was a culture shock. There was no-one in sight and nothing was open. Even the take-away was closed. It was like a ghost town. After the busy suburb of Montmorency it was like a town in hibernation.

After spending the first night with Keith and Grace, we found a house to rent in Koonya, ten kilometres out of Nubeena. It was a picture-postcard log cabin with stained glass windows and high gables on ten acres which ran down to the sea at Norfolk Bay. Old roses rambled over the house and in the garden dry stone walls segregated the huge lawn area where the children played.

The bedrooms had no heating and, with the cool Tasmanian nights, we ended up in one room. Netty and the girls slept in our queen-size bed, while I occupied a single bed mattress on the floor lying at the foot of their bed. Mornings would mean my two little munchkins jumping on me or squeezing me with those soft, cherub-like arms. We spent fair amounts of time in there. Netty and I drinking morning cups of tea while the girls watched television or played with their multitude of Barbie dolls. Madeline was still being breastfed and would sporadically jump in for a quick suckle. She was two years old, but clearly found the 'boozi', as Netty called it, a comfort. Maddie would often twiddle with the other nipple while she drank. It was our special time together.

We enrolled Alannah in kindergarten at the Tasman District School. At the tender age of four, she set off by bus each morning to her new world of friends and learning.

I had first seen the old Church of Christ building that was to become my pharmacy on the day we arrived in Tasmania. The property, on the main corner of the township, was in a decrepit state. But it was in the ideal location – 100 metres up the road from the local doctors' surgery and nursing home, while its prominent corner position maximised passing traffic. So I took the plunge and decided to lease it.

There was much work to be done. It was hardly visible from the street due to a canopy of overgrown wattles and shrubs, and the full extent of the peeling paint and rotting faciaboards hadn't been evident on my first visit. The once transparent roof sheeting on the front verandah was now opaque with large holes allowing in sunshine. Opening the front door revealed a further chapter of decay. Veneer wood panelling, dipping floors and gaudy decor meant everything would have to ripped out. And this was after I had spent so long trying to convince the owners to lease it to me as commercial premises and terminate the lease of the current tenant. Not for the first time in my life, as I stood in the street outside looking at my future, I thought I'd bitten off more than I could chew.

My first Saturday in Nubeena involved clearing plants and trees from the front yard of the pharmacy site. The next ten days were devoted to repairing and painting the exterior. Long days up and down ladders finally resulted in an amazing transformation. The heritage colours reconstituted the old character of the building and passing locals would stop and ogle in surprise. Internally four major walls were removed, counters were constructed, sloping floors were corrected with the help of a shop-fitter from Burnie in north-west Tasmania. Netty would drop in at lunchtime bringing soup and scrumptious sandwiches. This made her feel part of the effort and allowed her to drive 'into town' as she called it. She was extremely proud of what had been done in such a short time. When the enormous sign was erected in the carpark, saying 'Tasman Pharmacy', I realised our dream had come to life.

We opened for trade on 1 September, exactly one month, short one day, after we'd arrived in town. Our friend and pharmacy supplier, Julia McCance, helped me stock the shelves. I'd done my pharmacy training with Julia's partner, Brad, in Melbourne. Brad managed a pharmacy in Hobart and he and Julia lived nearby in a double-storeyed renovated Victorian mansion.

Julia stayed with me until the early hours of the morning when all the pharmacy shelves were stocked.

Just before we opened the doors for business that morning, Netty hugged me.

'Walter, I'm so proud of you. We've finally achieved what we wanted.'

'I can't really believe the day has come,' I admitted. 'Darling, thanks for all your love and support. I've probably been a pain to live with over the last few months. I'm sorry.'

'You certainly haven't been there very much. I miss you. I want to spend time with you. Let's go for a weekend away as soon as possible.'

The pharmacy was to bring more purpose into Netty's life. Initially she had found it difficult living in such an isolated spot, as she was used to company and visiting shopping centres. Here, she knew no-one except Keith and Grace.

After the pharmacy opened, Netty sometimes helped behind the counter. She cracked jokes with the customers and enjoyed spreading her own brand of humour which sometimes confused the locals. The response to the new premises was varied.

'This is like a real pharmacy. Like the ones in town [Hobart],' one woman said.

Many of them just came in for a look. But reaction, on the whole, was positive.

All of this helped take Nanette's mind off her mother's illness.

Grace, who still lived at home, was now spending more time in bed and occasionally needed oxygen. Netty visited her with the girls as often as she could. Although she knew Grace was dying, it was different confronting it face to face.

The week after we arrived in Tasmania, Nanette received a letter Grace had drafted to all of her children. It had a profound effect on Netty.

For the last few months, I have had the privilege and advantage of reflecting on my life and the purpose of it ... On reading some wise sayings recently, one that stuck in my mind was written by the Scottish poet Robert Burns: 'The purpose of life is a life of purpose.' My darlings, I beg of you to love and support each other whenever possible, for my sake, as well as your own. Love and be careful of your partners and your beloved children. For, finally we are as we love, it is love that measures our stature, so if you want to be loved, be lovable. Love is above all the gift of oneself ...

With all my love from your everloving Mother

Shortly after we arrived in Nubeena we went to watch the local football grand final. Port Arthur was playing Eaglehawk Neck, the place where the Tasman and Forestier Peninsulas joined. In convict days it was crossed by a dog line to deter escapees. Netty and the girls went to the game separately, while I went directly from work. I looked after the children at the game which was a well-earned break for Netty, as she had had so much time with them recently.

'Why don't you go along for a few drinks, honey, at the Port Arthur Motor Inn? You've been working pretty hard. Go and meet some of the locals,' Netty said at the end of the match.

'Oh, I'm tired, but I suppose I should get out to get known around the district. It'll be good PR.'

'Just don't be home too late.'

With these parting words, I walked up the hill to the Motor Inn at the top of the Port Arthur Historic Site.

'G'day, mate. How you going? Aren't you the new chemist

man?' said the bloke sitting at the bar. His two front teeth were missing.

'Yeah, my name's Walter. Pretty good win today by the lads.'

'Bloody oath, Wal. They really put in. A great effort,' said another older man. 'Tell you what, putting in a chemist down here is something we've waited years for. Good on ya.'

The celebrations continued and suddenly, before I realised it, it was 9 p.m. It occurred to me that this was the first time I'd relaxed since leaving Melbourne.

In the back bar, the cover went onto the pool table and people began dancing on the top. I hadn't eaten anything all evening and the last I remember of the evening was slumping back into the corner and drifting off to sleep. I awoke, startled, as an ice bucket full of cold water was tipped on my head. As I struggled to my feet and walked to the carpark, a man approached me asking for a lift home.

He looked like something out of a horror movie. Thick glasses, a massive mop of brown hair and teeth that hadn't seen a toothbrush for months. But, after such an evening, I was feeling benevolent.

'You can sleep on the couch at our place.'

I would live to regret my offer. As we pulled up outside our house, Netty was at the front door in her pink silk pyjamas.

'Where on earth have you been? I've been worried sick. Do you know what time it is, you selfish mongrel?'

I realised it was 2 a.m.

'I'm sorry, honey. I should have rung, but I got caught up.'

'I've heard that one before. So it's the old line you lost track of time? Are you all right?'

'Yes, I'm fine.'

As we spoke, Netty was peering into the car.

'You bastard, who's this woman you've brought back here?'

'It's okay, darling. He's going to sleep on the couch.'

'What? I can't believe you, Walter. Get inside before I leave you out in the car to sleep.'

It took till the end of the next day, a long time for Netty who was prone to 'fire up' and cool down in a relatively short period, until I finally won a passionate kiss.

Our life was happy enough at Koonya although we struggled through winter. One morning in September in our log cabin, Alannah opened the curtains: 'Mummy, Daddy, someone's painted everything white outside.'

'What do you mean, Lani?'

We looked to see two or three inches of snow lying in the yard.

'Wow, Dad, does this mean we can use your skis in the yard?' asked Lani.

We went outside and threw snowballs until the bitter cold sent us indoors again.

Lani, whenever I drive past the pharmacy now I can see you walking across the road from school, your bag on your back, looking hot and flustered. I remember I used to cross the road and grab you by the hand. When we got to the pharmacy, you'd show me what you'd done that day.

'Daddy, if I'm good can I have a present from the shop?' you'd ask, requesting a toy ring or stationery set.

'I expect you to be good all the time. You don't need a present for that,' I'd tell you. But you usually won. Before the day was out, you'd be drawing on your new pad or book.

I've found the Pocahontas diary that you loved writing in. You'd written about the time Mummy and I went to Hobart with the Haltons and the Irelands.

14/4/96. 'My Mum and Dad are going away today. I will miss them. I love them with all of my hart [sic]. I will love them forever.'

After a few weeks, we started to get to know more people in the community. We hosted a murder mystery night. Our guests were the local policeman, Chris Iles, and his wife Carmen, Steve and Pam

Ireland, and Richard and Kerrie Shoobridge. The night got out of control when a soda siphon taken from the bar was used to play commandoes and spray each other. From that night on the locals knew we'd be an acquisition to the social set.

The locals were also coming in increasing numbers to the pharmacy. During the day, Netty and our shopgirl, Louise Broughton, unpacked new orders. Everything was tested.

'You have to know about the products you're selling, don't you,' was Net's standard reply, as she applied lipstick and dispensed nail polish.

On the days that Julia McCance was visiting, the two would excitedly try any new cosmetic products. They had become firm friends since our move to the Tasman Peninsula.

Maddie, who spent a lot of time in the pharmacy, would kidnap the pricing gun and eat Furry Friends chocolate bars, two or three of which were always stashed under the counter.

By early November 1994 we felt settled enough to buy a house. It seemed a sound decision given that we had already committed to the pharmacy. 'A Renovator's Delight' would be the term used by a slick city agent for the large family home we found on one and a half acres with stables and a dam. The best part was that it was only 600 metres from the pharmacy.

'It's a bit of a mess, but there's not many houses of this size down here,' the real estate agent told us, making no excuses for it.

It was a psychedelic trip from the sixties, rented for many years with dreadful consequences. Pot plants inside had rotted through the carpet in places. Games of darts against one of the walls had left hundreds of puncture marks around the silhouette of the board. The decor was swirls and paisley with nothing matching. Somehow we could see beyond the surface. Clearing the forest in the front yard would reveal a magnificent view of the bay, while a new kitchen and fittings could totally transform the inside. But it would mean more work for me.

Netty was excited. 'Honey, we'll be in town. It'll be a walk to school for the girls. I can bring you down your lunch.'

Steve and Pam Ireland visited the house shortly after we bought it and introduced a tone of realism.

'What have you got yourself in for?' said Steve. 'Just another little project?'

'I know that when we finish this I'm never going to want to paint again,' I replied.

Our new life, once we got used to it, meant I could play golf on Wednesday afternoons, we had fish and chips on the beach some evenings and whenever it was warm, we plunged into the sea. This was the lifestyle we had been looking for. There was no traffic. We could walk to the beach. Life was simple.

We never locked our car in Nubeena. Sometimes, we wouldn't lock the house at night. It was a safe place compared to Melbourne, we thought.

Netty enlisted for parents' help in Alannah's class. The kids absolutely loved her and Maddie became their mascot. Tuesday was her canteen day at the school. Maddie would position herself on the serving bench, waving an icy pole as the kids were systematically served. She'd help Netty pack the orders and, of course, Alannah was so proud to have her mum there. The dogs, Molly and Becky, both now seven years old, loved our new life, especially the walks along the beach.

When Molly died that November I cried for three hours. I held her at the road where she lay, killed instantly by a passing car, then I carried her up to the house. She had been there from the start, when I was bathing Alannah as a baby, at the kids' parties sniffing for treats and in the backyard barking at the lawnmower.

Netty was devastated too.

'Why didn't you put her on the lead, Walter?' she accused me between tears, her arms around Molly's body.

Then, some time later, after a cup of tea, Netty said, 'If we feel this bad about our dog dying, imagine how you'd feel if you lost one of your children. I just don't think I'd be able to cope.'

'At least we can go out and get another dog, but you can't go out and get another child,' I said.

To have and to hold. 8 December 1985. The day we began our lives together.

Nanette as a baby in 1960 with siblings (left to right) Rodney, the twins Bronwyn and Peter, and Graeme. Her mother Grace had five children under the age of four.

All dressed up and ready for my first foray onto the dance floor.

The cheeky smile in this school photo was wiped off my eight-year-old face when a 'D' appeared on my report card next to behaviour

At Shepparton in 1963/64. Young 'Netty Petty' Moulton (left) as Nanette called herself with curls at the fore. Her sister, Bronwyn, is far right with a family friend in the middle. Every time I look at this photo I can see how alike she and Maddie were.

September school holidays 1976. Netty in front of an Aussie dunny displaying her 'sense of the ridiculous'.

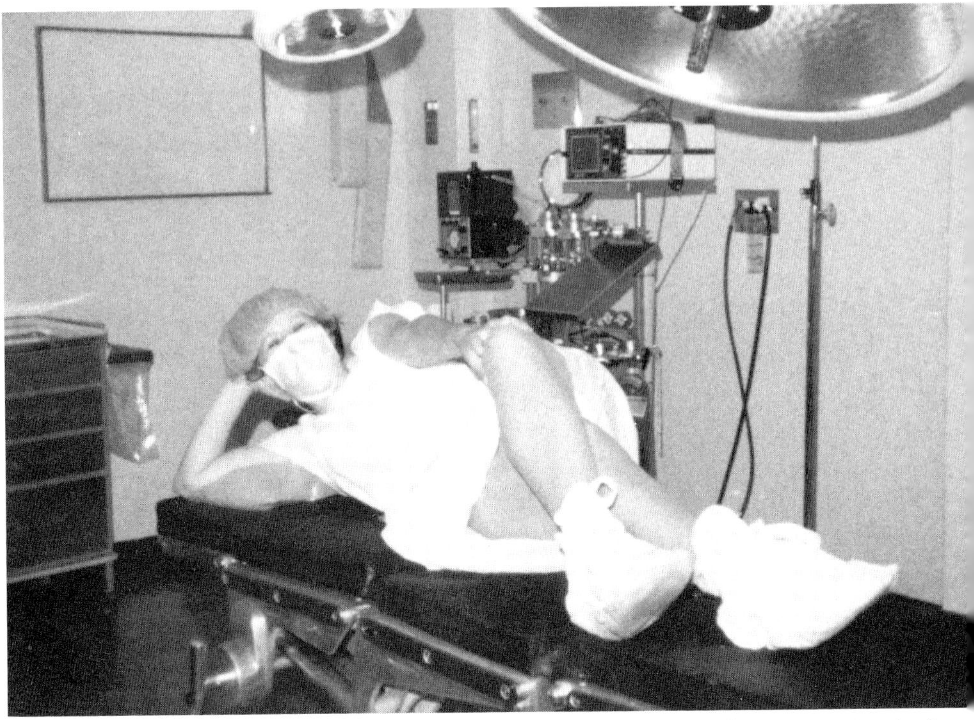

Nanette 'setting up' for theatre during her nursing training at the Austin Hospital, Heidelberg. She used to tap dance on her rounds in the neuro-surgery ward to amuse the patients.

Nanette in an uncharacteristically demure mood at the Heidelberg Festival in 1984 when we were courting. Her unusally shaped, attractive blue eyes are captured perfectly in this photo.

Netty and Glenice at their nursing graduation ceremony in 1981. Nanette did a 'Two Ronnies' routine which brought the house down.

My parents, Danny and Milka Mikac, with proud smiles in the kitchen of our family home before the tragedy struck — that same carefree spirit has vanished.

Nanette's parents, Keith and Grace Moulton, and Dougall the dog, looking relaxed at Tawonga in Victoria, where Netty was born.

Our engagement party at Bronwyn's house in Moonee Ponds.
When I told Nanette I loved her she kept saying, 'Prove it'. So I did.

Chris McCann
and my brother
Steven having
fun getting Netty's
garter off on our
wedding day. I
look on unamused.

With Netty in 1985 at London Bridge near Port Campbell on Victoria's south-west coast. The middle section has since collapsed.

On holiday in Tasmania with Netty in November 1986. This was our first visit to the Port Arthur Historic Site. Little did we know we would be living nearby eight years later and it would be where our life together would end.

The proud smile of a mum. Netty with Alannah at six months visiting Glenice in hospital after the birth of her son, Rick.

Netty outside our first home in Montmorency on 27 August 1989, the day before she gave birth to our first daughter, Alannah.

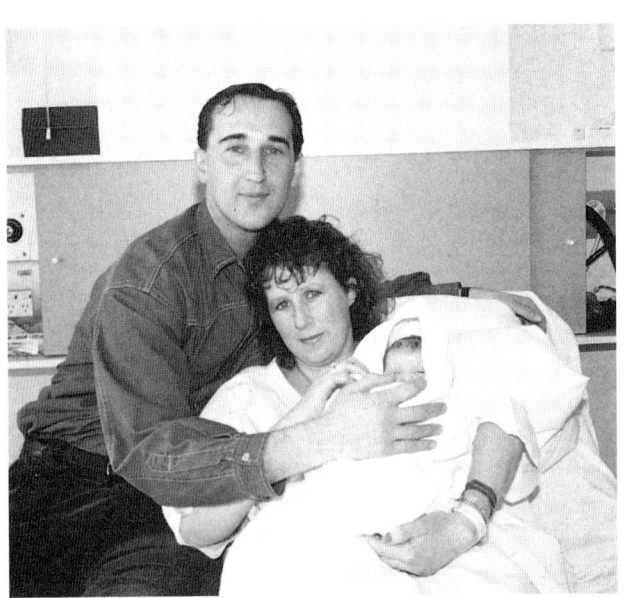

This photo was on the wall at our house in Nubeena along with all our baby photos. The stunning blue eyes and golden curls of Maddie at six months.

Proud parents at the arrival of Madeline Grace on 15 August 1992. A ten-minute labour ensured Netty's make-up didn't need to be touched up. Maddie looked like boxer Tony Mundine, her arrival into the world was so fast.

We cried together, arms round each other that night.

The next day Netty went out and bought a black and white cocker spaniel. Our new puppy was called Beethoven, after the dog in the movie of the same name. We also acquired a kitten called Wilbur about the same time.

'He's my own responsible pet,' Alannah used to say about Wilbur, who slept in the bedroom either on Netty or Alannah's chest.

I am alone with death now and I haven't just lost a child. I've lost all of you. All of those times together, Lani, Maddie and you, Netty. And then Beethoven. Beethoven died the week after he arrived in Melbourne last November. It was the final straw, one that I could hardly bear. Wilbur and Becky are all I have left.

I do not have any of you to share in my grief. No-one else can console me. I don't want consoling. You were right, Netty – sometimes I don't know if I can cope or whether you would have been able to.

SEVEN

After Life

The headstone's been up at Melbourne's Warringal Cemetery for two weeks and I haven't been able to see it because I've been in Tasmania writing the book. I'm nervous about seeing it for the first time. Those three names, all with the same date of death. Will it be too much for me? Will it send me over the edge? I don't know. Will it do their memory justice? The names of the girls who represented everything to me in life: 'Died tragically at Port Arthur on April 28th, 1996. Beloved wife and adored daughters of Walter. My love for you will never die.' Grace's name is also on the headstone. Netty's mum and then her mother. Four generations within one plot. Just after you died, I had to decide where you should be buried. I thought of Port Arthur. It was your favourite spot and the place where you all died. But what would happen if I left Tasmania? Then Keith told me there was a space next to Grace at this cemetery in Melbourne, my home city. You would be with your mother, Netty, and the girls would be with theirs.

As Christmas 1994 approached, Grace was steadily losing her independence. We knew it could be our last Christmas together. On Christmas Day we arrived at Keith and Grace's house with two crays. Netty dressed the girls to the hilt and all of them wore Christmas earrings.

'Nani, you should have seen us in my Sunday School play,' Alannah said, lying in bed with Grace. 'I was the shepherd and Maddie was one of the angels. She kept sucking her two fingers all the way through. Next year I want to be Mary, though. She's the real star.'

Grace laughed heartily. Alannah's way of describing things usually had a way of uplifting people. Grace was no exception.

'Lani, you've certainly got a way with words,' she said.

After Christmas, we began work on our new house, ripping everything out, renovating, sanding, painting. Three months later it was ready for us to move in.

'Is this going to be my room?' yelled Alannah, running through the house.

'And mine,' called Maddie, following not far behind her big sister.

'This room is big enough for me to set up the whole Barbie house, Mum,' shouted Alannah.

Netty, I could see, was in seventh heaven.

'This view is great, bub. Look at the salmon farm over there and that yacht sailing into the bay. This is going to be fun.'

'It looks just great, doesn't it?' was all I could say, exhausted at the end of two projects and the prospect of landscaping the garden still ahead of me.

But, this was where we would call 'home'.

I tackled the landscaping with vigour, often working at night under the floodlight from the deck. I built a pond, and after the hollows were filled with plastic liner and water, the girls dangled their legs over the side. They spent many hours fishing out the goldfish with a net, then throwing it back in again. We acquired a lamb which the girls called Lily. She used to love being bottlefed and eating the new growth off my roses.

In six months, the house had been transformed. One day, I sat on the verandah and picked up a magazine.

'What's wrong, bub?' Nanette said, lounging in the deckchair next to me. 'Why aren't you working in the garden?'

'Because everything's got to grow now. I've finished.'

This was the house that nobody wanted and now it was somewhere to be proud of.

In the early months of 1995, Grace had been admitted to the Tasman District Nursing Home. Keith had made a monumental effort to keep her at home, including constructing a lift when she couldn't manage the stairs. It was a full-time job managing the home, oxygen bottles, and other household jobs. At the nursing home fellow patients quickly became the extended family, and Netty and the girls visited at every opportunity to try to 'cheer Nan up'.

After all the hard work on the house and the pharmacy and coping with Grace's illness, we decided in April to go on a trip we'd won the year before to visit Movieworld at the Gold Coast. I loved entering competitions and over the years had won several. Netty was concerned about leaving Grace, but decided that we deserved a break.

We stopped at Byron Bay first as we'd heard so much about it. We walked to the lighthouse and looked out over the vast ocean and the rich sand, gazing out to sea and looking for whales. Next came the skyscrapers and hustle and bustle of the Gold Coast, to which we were so unaccustomed after sleepy Nubeena. But the real treat for the children came with the trips to Movieworld and then Seaworld. Entering the enormous Movieworld archway, Lani squeezed my hand tightly. Breakfast with the Stars was first on the agenda.

I gripped the seat inside the Batmobile as we were tossed and thrown all over the place, careering through skyscapers and down alleys. Lani loved it.

'Mum and Dad, can we come here again? I'm having the best day of my life,' she said.

* * *

It was our last holiday together and all I have left are the memories. I am glad we took so many photos – like the one at the lighthouse in Byron Bay, with you in your straw hat, Netty, and everyone is smiling. That time is so precious to me now.

One of Nanette and the girls' favourite spots on the Tasman Peninsula was the Port Arthur Historic Site. The gardens, the oak-lined avenues, the honey-coloured ruins. In a place of such majestic beauty, it was hard to imagine the suffering of the convicts who had lived within its walls. We often called in to the Broad Arrow Cafe, fed the seagulls at the waterfront with the leftovers and wandered around the grounds. Netty was immediately drawn to the site – her love of history and the supernatural meant it held a real fascination for her. She never tired of visiting it and right from the start she had strange experiences there.

One night, she recounted what had happened during her visit to the site that day. Cell Number One at the Model Prison was the home of an insane highwayman, Denis Quigley. It would take five officers to hold him down and he exercised in a padded cell.

'You know that feeling of eyes burning in the back of your head,' she told me. 'Well, I had this sensation of someone being there. The hair on the back of my neck was really prickling and I felt uneasy. I just kept edging away, I had to get away and escape. It was like he was sneering. Really malevolent. Nasty. Evil. As soon as the guide took us away, the sensation passed.'

When she returned to the cell, the feeling that he was watching her was still there. Nanette even became agitated telling me about it.

That August, the historic site advertised for ghost tour guides. It seemed that providence had intervened. It offered Nanette a perfect opportunity to display her talents as well as a chance to explore her interest in the supernatural. Here was a job she could excel in and it would give her a focus other than the children and the pharmacy.

She was nervous in her first interview with Andrew Simmonds, the ghost tour supervisor, but she managed to convince him she had the necessary qualities. By September, equipped with her black patent leather Esprit runners and the black parka provided, Nanette began guiding her own night-time tours through the ruins.

The following month I presented a lecture on colonial medicine at the historic site. Collecting old pharmacy and medicine memorabilia had become a hobby of mine, so I packaged a collection of leech jars, old medicine bottles and medical instruments, including a Victorian douche which inspired a few jokes.

Lindsay Simpson, who was writing a historical novel about the convicts at Port Arthur, turned up to the lecture. It was the first time we'd met. By coincidence, that night we both ended up on one of Nanette's ghost tours, my first experience of seeing Netty in action. We began at the Information Centre. Two people were chosen as lantern bearers and then we walked across to the other side of the site and the Commandant's Cottage. From there, we visited the Model Prison followed by a visit to the room where the post-mortems were carried out.

'Now that you're all in, could someone please close the door,' Nanette said mischievously.

No-one was keen on doing the task.

'Oh well, maybe we can ask one of the ghosts to do it for us then.'

I watched the fearful faces, full of anticipation, around me. Then she drew the audience closer to the dissection table by lowering the volume of her voice. On the table was the skull of a sheep, a handy prop for the ghost tour guides. As they all came closer, Netty sharply scraped the skull across the dissection table. Everyone jumped back in horror. Some screamed. Netty was delighted. She then led the group to the end of the tour via the old church.

The church was another place that spooked you, Netty. You often saw lights there, like sparklers, as if someone with a camera had been taking flash photographs outside of the walls. Sometimes half of your group saw the lights too. Once the lantern bearer went around the perimeter of the church, but there was no-one there.

Lindsay was also impressed by your performance that night and decided to interview you about your job for an article on ghosts she was writing for a weekly magazine.

On the interview tape you talked of seeing these lights.

Another night while driving home on the road where you were murdered the inside lights of the car came on and you couldn't turn them off . . .

So many strange things that you could not account for, almost as if you were coming into contact with an undercurrent of messages that could not be explained. You did have a psychic side to you. You know I have always been the analytical one and perhaps I should have listened more to what you felt. Did any of these strange occurrences bear any portent of your fate? I am listening to your voice on the tape of the interview you did with Lindsay. You are talking of reincarnation:

'I love history and, as I said, I do believe there is something out there, something that I don't really know. I just sort of sense there's something out there. Often, I think there's another time phase going on and that I have lived in another time.'

It was at the end of that ghost tour that I approached Lindsay to ask if Nanette could join the writing course she was running. It was funded by the Australia Council and was being run in the Junior Medical Officer's Quarters on the site. I told her Netty could write, but didn't have enough confidence. Lindsay was very encouraging and we convinced Netty to enrol in the six-week creative writing course that ran through November and December. Maddie often came along and played under the table with Lindsay's dog, Camus.

I think of the words you wrote, Netty, when you were doing Lindsay's course. I remember typing up your story for the writing workshop. You always dreamed of having your writing published. Now your wish has come true.

THE SCHOOLGIRL'S DARE
by NANETTE MIKAC

Terrified. The young schoolgirl felt her stomach churning and her mouth was dry as she entered the shop and heard the bell ringing above the doorway. Her hands were cold in anticipation. The shop-keeper, behind the counter, was on the phone. He glanced furtively in her direction. Who was he talking to? He was laughing and seemed relaxed. She envied him.

Across the street, her friends were waiting. She knew what she was doing was wrong but she also knew that if she didn't go through with the dare, her life would be hell.

Do it now before he gets off the phone, she thought. But, he was walking towards her, his feet sounding loud on the vinyl floor. It would soon be over. She didn't care if she was caught.

The door of the shop jangled and opened. The man and the girl both turned towards the newcomer. A middle-aged lady entered.

The girl looked back at the shelves, under the cover of the distraction. A fairy globe. She picked it up and shook it. The glitter sparkled in the fluorescent light of the shop and settled on the little fairy's wings.

Suddenly, she became aware that the woman was standing behind her. She jumped, startled, then smiled, hoping she would go away.

The girl was the same age as the lady's youngest granddaughter. Immediately, the old lady's heart went out to her. She was a victim of her peers. The old lady had guessed what was going on as soon as she saw the group of giggling girls across the street.

'Pretty, isn't it?' the older lady remarked, picking up the globe the girl had put down. The girl nodded, looking suspicious. The woman walked towards the counter, carrying the globe.

She knows, the girl whispered to herself. She could feel the tears welling up in her eyes. All she wanted to do was run. This was the most awful thing that'd ever happened to her. A dare could not be worth all of this anguish.

'Excuse me,' the older woman said, turning to her across the shop.

'I know you'll think me a silly old lady, but you remind me of my granddaughter. She lives interstate and I can't carry it in my luggage. So, I was wondering whether I could buy it for you.'

The girl clutched the globe, which had been wrapped in green tissue paper by the man in the shop and placed in a plastic bag. She was gone in moments with a few splutters of thanks.

As she skipped across the street, the man in the shop watched. He turned to the older woman to ask if that was all, but she was gazing, transfixed, at the schoolgirls on the other side of the road.

'Such small things become so enormous when you're that age,' she said to no-one in particular.

Forty years ago, perhaps more, she remembered the same pain she'd seen mirrored in the girl's eyes. Some things never change. Now, she could put that memory to rest.

The shopkeeper was about to reply but was saved by the strident ringing of the telephone.

Our tenth, and last, wedding anniversary in December 1995 was spent in Hobart. Nanette and I had decided to stay the night at Wrest Point Casino and enjoyed a wonderful meal at a Thai restaurant to celebrate. In the lift on the way back up to our room, in an impulsive moment, I decided to prepare early for the night ahead by taking off my pants.

'I'll carry them,' Netty offered.

As the lift door opened, she bolted to our room and locked the door. I was left there standing in my underpants, hammering on the door.

'You were only being an exhibitionist,' she said over breakfast the next morning. 'Attention-seeking behaviour.'

'At least I waited until we left the restaurant,' I bantered.

That weekend Rebekah Whitfield, a fourteen-year-old girl from the local school, looked after the children. She was our regular babysitter and adored Lani and Maddie. They would play together for hours. The girls would always look forward to her visits.

One evening, early in the New Year, I dropped in to see Grace after work. She told me to turn on the cassette player because she couldn't manage it.

'This is the music I want played at my funeral,' she said in a matter-of-fact way.

I tucked her into bed and I knew I was saying goodbye. It wouldn't be long before she departed this world. Her face was terribly swollen due to steroids and she was in great pain.

The day she died on – 11 January 1996 – we couldn't find Alannah anywhere. We eventually found her sitting beside Grace holding her grandmother's lifeless hand. We'd discussed whether Lani and Maddie should see Grace after she'd died and decided that death needed to be confronted, even at such an early age. But Lani had taken it into her own hands.

'I hope you'll be comfortable in Heaven, Nani,' Lani told her, her small hand still clasping her grandmother's.

Three months later you were all dead. How I hope this for all of you – that you find comfort wherever you are.

EIGHT

Swept Along with the Current

I am sitting in Hobart's Salamanca Place. The leaves on the plane trees in the park are turning to gold. The changing hue of the leaves, so like Europe, is beautiful, but it also brings back painful memories I wish I could obliterate. Autumn signals the inevitable change towards another winter. Another season I wish was not arriving. It is April, almost a year to the date when I last spent time with my family. It's as if it were yesterday.

I didn't want to come back here and face all the memories. But it wasn't through choice. I needed to be here to write the book with Lindsay. She has three children and couldn't come to me in Melbourne.

I try to look at this town objectively. In this hub of Hobart cafe life, near the wharf, people are sitting outside under umbrellas sipping cafe lattes. The pace of life is so laid back. People have time to smile at you, chat to you, be nice to you. Friends drop in, rather than make a formal arrangement. All in all, it's a pretty good place to live.

This time last year, I was just an ordinary person in an ordinary situation. I suppose I never thought I was 'ordinary'. Nobody does. But, my life was like so many other people's – a father and husband striving for a quiet and successful life.

All of that has now gone. Instead, I have an overwhelming sense of being alone. I am no longer answerable to anyone. No responsibilities, no commitment required. A strange concept after caring for others for such a long time. My brain still finds it hard to reprogramme. I can go out any time of day or night without leaving a message or making a phone call. No-one cares where I am. Sometimes, I need to know someone cares or is thinking about me. I've even rung friends at 5 a.m. They usually know it's me because no-one else rings at that time. And they're understanding, but it's not the same as having a partner who cares.

Life is nomadic. A few weeks here, a night there, another flight or a different bed. The predictable life I once had is what I yearn for. Lying on the couch watching 'Blue Heelers' or 'ER', two of our favourite programmes. Lying in front of the fire cuddling Nanette. Having a little time to myself, reading the paper after the three of them were safely tucked up in bed. Those times were so simple and so good.

I can be in a crowded room now and feel so isolated. No-one in the room knows how I feel.

Sometimes I get asked, 'Are you really able to enjoy yourself? Do you have a good time?' There have to be good times. If I spent my whole time in the deepest cellars of grief how would I find the light to re-enter my life? The darkness would simply consume me. I need to give myself a chance to survive. I will not give in. I have compassion for the world. A compassion for what is good on this planet. There burns in me an innate desire to make this world a better place, a desire that has been nurtured since living surrounded by the beauty of Tasmania.

I first saw the rapids of the mighty Franklin River in Tasmania's south-west in March 1996 while I was standing on top of Frenchman's Cap gazing across the South-West National Park. In front of me was the largest tract of temperate rainforest left in the world. I felt insignificant against such pristine beauty, overawed that the world still had such places to offer.

Rafting the river, the reason for the trip, was my next experience. Halfway down the river we approached the Cauldron. I was feeling apprehensive. These were the big rapids with drops of two metres. It was day four of the trip.

The pact to raft the Franklin arose after a few beers on Australia Day with Steve Ireland, Eddie Halton and Richard Shoobridge. We'd decided to pierce our ears in the kitchen late that night. The victims stood over the sink and I approached them one by one, wielding the piercing gun from the pharmacy.

'Why don't we all go parachuting?' Eddie ventured, wearing his new gold stud.

'What about rafting down the Franklin?' Steve said. 'I've always wanted to do that. That'd be awesome.'

'Yeah, I've always wanted to do something like that – a huge adventure,' I said.

'We could do a "Deliverance",' said Richard. 'In the backwoods of Tasmania.'

And that was how it started. Now, in March, we were facing the consequences. For three hours that day we'd carried the two rafts, the toilet, cooking gear and our wet packs between us across enormous boulders down the river.

Gigantic ancient Huon pines grew almost down to water level. On the second day we'd passed through the Irenabyss Gorge, where the water ran twenty metres deep. Black cormorants flew overhead. Smooth copper-coloured quartzite rocks glistened above us.

By the fourth day of the trip, I was missing Netty and the girls terribly. In ten years I'd never spent more than one or two nights away from them. I just wanted to be back home in my own bed. But the grandeur of the wilderness forced me to confront this solitary experience though, in spite of the companionship of the others, I sometimes still felt alone.

On the seventh day, we scaled a 500-metre cliff, holding onto ropes and carrying thirty-kilogram backpacks. At the top we examined our welts, marvelled at our resilience and then jumped into a 4WD and headed for Queenstown on Tasmania's west coast.

When I got back, it was as if I was the missing hero, smothered in kisses and cuddles. They'd been to the Bream Creek Show and they had a showbag for me. I lay in front of the woodheater in the lounge-room and basked in their affection.

They were there when I got back, when I needed them. But they're not here now. They're not there on a busy Easter Saturday morning at my local supermarket in Melbourne's Heidelberg. I'm just starting to do some of the chores most people consider normal. Approaching the laundry section, I become aware that I need to buy everything to start a new household. Where do I start? Sure, I'm handy around the house, but now I had to think of everything. I'd never had to do that before. As my trolley swells to near capacity, people stare at the contents. Was there something wrong with my selections or were they wondering how many people I was buying for? Oh well, who cares? I just didn't feel comfortable and I wanted to get out of there.

As I approached the checkout, a mountainous pile of Easter eggs stood in front of me. I gaze, transfixed, waiting for the question. 'Dad, can I have one of those? I've been real good.' But the question never came. The children were not with me. I wouldn't need to buy Easter eggs this year.

Waiting at the checkout, I think back to Easter Sunday almost a year ago, to the service in the quaint, cedar-lined church in Koonya, some ten minutes from our home. Lani and Maddie sitting on the floor by my feet. They had behaved gorgeously during the service despite the continual counting out of their basket of tiny Easter eggs. That vision embodies everything I have lost.

At the gravesite, I place a little basket of Easter eggs on the marble tablet near the headstone. All colours. Also a scented pink rose plant. Accompanying these offerings is a note to them which reads, 'Dear Netty, Lani, and Maddie, You should be here to enjoy these with me. I love you all very much and always will.' I lie down on the grey marble top. I need to be as close to them as possible. A weird sensation overtakes me. I can feel the beating of my heart, but feel it is in unison with another heartbeat. I am sure that it is Alannah's.

* * *

I find I am becoming obsessed with everything that happened in those last few weeks. Ironically, Netty and I were separated twice during this time. My trip down the Franklin and the last weekend before they were killed when Netty went away. I suddenly needed to find out everything about that weekend she had with Julia McCance on Maria Island. I ask Julia what they talked about that weekend. What was on Netty's mind? Where was her life at when it was so cruelly taken from her?

Julia gets upset when she remembers their conversations. But I have to know. I have to know everything about my Netty. So Julia begins to piece the painful memories together for me. I am surprised by how much she remembers of their conversations.

Netty was philosophical that weekend as she and Julia sat on the fossil cliffs at Maria Island, gazing out at Schouten Island and sharing a pack of peanuts. It was the last week of Nanette's life, something she could never have known as she took in the beauty of the sight before her.

Maria Island, off Tasmania's east coast, has an old penitentiary once used for convicts. Today it is used as accommodation for bushwalkers and campers who visit the island to see the native wildlife.

Nanette watched the waves beneath crash onto the rocks. It was a rare weekend away from the family and, having initially felt peculiar about the lack of responsibility, she was beginning to unwind.

'I really feel needed for the first time in my life, you know, Julia,' Nanette said. 'There's my job, and Walter and the girls, of course, but for so long I've been the pharmacist's wife. Now I've got my independence. I love my job and I'm finally being paid to entertain. It couldn't be better. It's turned out so well moving to Tasmania.'

Julia agreed. 'If someone'd said to us when you and I met five years ago that we'd both be living in Tasmania, I'd never have believed it,' she said.

'That's true. I know Grace is no longer here, but I feel this was the right step to make. The best thing we ever did was move away and set up life here for ourselves.'

'Yeah, that helped your independence,' Julia said.

'And the kids love it here,' Nanette said. 'Alannah walks to school across the paddock. Maddie collects the mail from the post office. It's so safe here compared to Melbourne. And I'm making some good friends. People who care about *me* – Nanette – and don't judge me by what I do.'

Back on the mainland at the East Coaster Resort, at the pub near the wharf, Julia and Nanette continued to reminisce over glasses of champagne.

'We don't need to drive anywhere,' Nanette said. 'It's so nice to get away. No responsibilities.'

'Yeah, let's get stuck into it,' Julia said.

Back at the hotel room, they drank a bottle of red wine and the topic changed to old boyfriends.

'I was a real wild thing,' Julia said. 'I did some things that amaze me when I look back at them. When I met you, I'd only just started going out with Brad – remember some of the things he and Walter got up to when they were doing pharmacy together?'

'They were the same kind of guys. Brad's got Walter's sense of humour,' Nanette said. 'I don't have any regrets about my early days. But, I never thought I'd meet someone like Walter. Even after ten years, I still enjoy having sex. I bought a sexy new bra last week and Walter loved it.'

'There's something about being in a relationship for a long time,'

Julia warmed to the topic. 'It makes you feel secure. I trust Brad implicitly. I have no doubts about his loyalty even after four years.'

'Yep, but you'd think things'd go stale after a few years, wouldn't you? I mean, don't other people's lives get like that? Yours and Brad's don't, nor does mine and Walter's. Being with Walter is never boring. You don't know what to expect next. Having Alannah and Madeline is the best thing I've ever done. They are a product of the two of us. But the best thing is the cuddling. Being held by someone who cares for you and loves you. Feeling wanted.' Nanette took another gulp of wine. 'I'm going to ring them, Julia. Just one phone call to see how they are.'

Julia had been ringing our house all afternoon on the day of the massacre. But there was no reply. At first, she wasn't concerned. Nanette was probably helping at the site. After all, she was a trained nurse. No doubt they'd be using her skills. But at 10.30 p.m. someone did answer the phone. Julia thought it was the babysitter. 'Thank goodness, there's someone there. I was starting to get worried,' she said. 'It's Julia. Who's this?'

I picked up the phone from the neighbour who'd answered it.

'Is everything all right?' Julia asked. 'Are Nanette and the girls okay?'

'No, they're not,' I said, my voice wooden. 'They've gone to heaven.' Julia's scream pierced down the phone line, searing my heart. I could hear her leave the phone and run across the room. Her anguish reminded me these words I had to get used to speaking were real. I, too, dropped the phone and it was left dangling – like my life.

While Netty was away that weekend, I spent the time with the girls. We had a magical two days together – helping dress the Barbie dolls, sprawled on the lounge-room floor watching videos and playing

Memory. On the Sunday, as a treat, we drove to Hobart to see a movie.

'JUMANJI – ARE YOU GAME?' was boldly printed on the billboard at the cinema. I can still hear Alannah saying those words over and over. She was so excited. This was an adventure for Lani, Maddie and myself. Drinks and the biggest bucket of popcorn. When the movie got scary, Maddie held up the bucket in front of her eyes.

As we walked up the aisle after the movie I said, 'Let's go and see Mummy. She'll be back soon.'

We all wanted to see her smiling face, so we drove across the Derwent River to Brad and Julia's. The first thing Nanette said was: 'Did you miss me?' as the girls jumped around and we hugged her. She didn't need an answer.

In that last week, it was almost as though we were preparing for the dreadful thing that was going to happen. I played Nintendo with Lani for the first time the night before. Netty told me to go to the pub after the football that afternoon. 'No,' I answered 'I'd rather be with you.' There was also a special mid-week lunch with Netty, an unexpected treat.

On the Wednesday afternoon, Maddie was in childcare and Lani was at school. The pharmacy shut at midday because the doctors' surgery had finished up early. We sometimes went to the take-away across the street, but today I thought of something better. When Netty came to pick me up, I said: 'I hope you're happy with how you're dressed, 'cause I'm taking you out to lunch.'

The cafe at Eaglehawk Neck was one of our favourite places on the peninsula. Netty sat opposite me as we looked out over the azure blue water of the bay. The large open wood fire was burning. Red velvet curtains, baltic pine boards on the walls and ceilings and splendid memorabilia gave this place a great ambience.

It was 24 April and Grace's birthday. She'd been dead for only three months, but gradually Netty was coming to terms with it.

We ordered some soup and a glass of red wine.

'You know, Wal, I'm really glad we decided to move down here,' she said.

'It's certainly been a growing experience,' I agreed. 'But, if the opportunity to buy another pharmacy in Hobart comes up, I wouldn't mind moving. We could always keep a shack down here, but as far as the kids' education goes, it's going to be better in town.'

'I'm just glad that I can be here for Dad. Keith was so devoted to Mum, even when she was so demanding at times. I absolutely love him. We had a very precious bond as I was growing up.'

'He seems to be travelling all right but it must be difficult being on your own. I'll try and take him out golfing if I can.'

I remember the sun's rays coming through the window as we shared the warm salad of lamb, the last meal we ate on our own. We both agreed it was yummy. We'd often share each other's meals, Netty. Trying new tastes together was one of our little rituals. We fed each other from our single fork that lunchtime, the way we often did. Did I tell you I loved you? I search my memory and I hope I did. I know I told you I didn't want to take you for granted.

I still regret the silly argument we had the following day. I suggested we get a cleaning lady. I was just trying to help. You had your job as a ghost tour guide and I thought it was all getting too much for you. But you thought I was criticising your housekeeping abilities. It was only minor, but I can't help wishing it hadn't happened. If I'd only known it was one of the last days of our life together . . .

* * *

I am arranging our furniture in my new house in Melbourne. I put the girls' beds in the garage. I don't want to get rid of them. And then there are all sorts of bits and pieces from our past life together and I'm not sure where to put them. I rifle through your bedside drawer, Netty, Bankcard slips with your signature, a cheque that was signed for some books for the kids at school, your nursing scissors and watch. Then I come across the blue badge with 'Almost Famous' on it. I remember you wearing it when you worked as a nurse. You poor darling, now you really are famous, but not for the reason you would have imagined. I can't let you be forgotten. You touched so many people, you were an extraordinary woman. How can I enshrine your memory, girls? Netty, you always wanted to be a writer. With that no longer possible, should I do the next best thing? I'm going to share your uniqueness with the world. A book in your honour will give you a place in history. Long after I pass on, your names will remain in perpetuity. This will give me a great sense of achievement.

We lived the life of an ordinary family. We had the same ups and downs, but we managed to maintain our direction in life. I've talked to so many people since all of this happened who are unhappy in their lives. I seem to see things with greater clarity. Their work, health and relationships are far from satisfactory. Yet they stay in that situation. Why? Life is so short. The events of 28 April 1996 have at least taught me this. Why waste time? My perspective on life has changed irrevocably. We had what the world aspired to: Contentment. Happiness. Normality. Love.

Can I write a book? So many people tell me it's not something they could do. Where do I start? I'm a pharmacist, not a wordsmith. But as the words start appearing, I know I can write a book, especially with the help I am getting along the way. Our memories give me the strength to do anything I set my mind to. I can write a great book – I hope – encouraging people to live life to the utmost, to filter out things that are superfluous. Restore focus to their life.

You could have written a great book, Nanette. I am seeking help from the same person that guided you in that writing course only five months before you died. Together, Lindsay and I are unravelling some of my thoughts. Each day more words appear as I grapple with my emotions and my desire to be honest in my account.

Writing is a whole new way of life for me. It gives me a focus. I find myself confiding in my laptop, writing about the rollercoaster of emotions I am experiencing. Sometimes I feel I have no control, that there is an outpouring from deep within my soul.

Awake again. I scribble a couple of thoughts on the pad that lies next to my bed. My aim is to try and remember every emotion possible. It needs to be documented or with time it will fade. I talked to Sue Burgess, whose seventeen-year-old daughter, Nicole, was killed at Port Arthur. We marvelled at how we thought all of those little details would always be with us. But, already, I can't exactly remember how I felt all those months ago. I write it down so I can recall everything if I desire. And what shall I call the book? What will be a fitting tribute? Titles are starting to fill the pages of my diary. So many possibilities. It needs to be a title that is strong, yet simple. Short, yet positive. A statement of my time with them. 'Holes in my heart ... Ode to my Family ... Till Death do us Part.' No. Not quite the right image.

I go for a run, where I once ran as an under-11 footballer, through an avenue of trees at the old golf course near my parents' place. Yes! My breath is short but the words are there, they are spoken. 'To have and to hold.'

To hold them all just one last time.

NINE

Our Last Morning

*D*on't speak so loudly. Don't swear. It hurts. So much violence.
I'm in a bubble and I want to float away across a gentle sea.
I don't want anyone or anything to pierce the fragility of my existence. Images of civil war in Somalia or Bosnia flash up on the
television. Violence. I don't want anyone to get hurt. As for me – I
can't be hurt any more. Death can't hurt me, but I can't tolerate
aggression. My mother is speaking too loudly.

'This is the way I always speak,' she answers.

'Well, could you just speak quietly for the moment?' I implore.

Let me float away for a while, let me be. Left to my own thoughts.
Left to my own dreams. But sleep is not always kind to me. Time
passes more quickly when I'm awake. I feel safer because I can
control what I'm thinking.

In the dream I had last night, Nanette finally answers me after
almost a year of silence. In most other dreams, she is there but has
no voice. The girls, too. They don't talk to me. In one dream, Lani
is skipping up the path next to my parents' house, skipping towards
me. She is coming so close, I reach out for her and she skirts past

almost as if she's flowing through my outstretched arms. I am so excited at seeing her that I fall out of bed.

When Nanette spoke to me in my dream, we were in a crowd. I was searching, as always, for her face and this time she was there. She was looking at me, dressed in a white or cream robe as if she was indifferent, simply waiting for me to do something, to say something. 'I wish I'd been with you. I should have been there,' I said.

'There's nothing you could have done,' she replied.

I wake up and can't get back to sleep. I don't want to close my eyes. I can see them again lying on the roadside. I must stay awake. I must go out. I must be with people. I must do something.

The nightmares defy explanation. Gruesome images of what it may have been like in the Broad Arrow Cafe. Accounts from people who were in there, like John and Gaye Fidler and Jo Winter, echo in my head. The images are often graphic, but with time, immunity sets in. Clearly a self-protection mechanism. Thank goodness for this ability.

People keep writing to me saying that I still have my memories and no-one can take them away from me. True. Wonderful memories that make me smile and feel warm inside. But can they sustain me when I don't have touch, smell, taste, hearing or sensation of my girls? What I really need to know is whether there is an afterlife. Can I bank on seeing them again one day? Will they be as they were or have aged like myself? I wish I knew.

Will they be reincarnated and enter my life sometime in the future? As the new house cleaner or the university lecturer? The librarian or the nurse or the tour guide? After all, this is something you had strong thoughts on, Netty. Will you be able to influence my life in the future? My greatest wish is that you will. Help me be a better person.

I'm so sorry that I wasn't there.

Breakfast on Sunday 28 April was croissants from the Parson's Bay Bakery, our favourite Sunday fare. It was about 8.30 a.m. when I carried them into the kitchen with the obligatory weekend paper under my arm.

'Now, sit down and read the paper and I'll make your breakfast,' Netty said briskly. 'And then you'd better get yourself organised because Eddie'll be here right on nine o'clock. He's always on time, unlike someone else we know.'

Netty was right. Eddie was always punctual. I sat on the floral club lounge and put my feet up on the coffee table and began to read the paper.

The bay below shimmered as the sun rose from behind the hills. It was going to be a perfect day. It was such a shame I was playing golf, I thought, momentarily putting the paper down and looking out of the window.

Lani and Maddie were lying sprawled on the floor watching *The Lion King* for the umpteenth time. I used to recite 'Akuna Matata' when we were walking the dogs, working in the garden or even in the bath.

I feel like unpacking The Lion King *video and watching it with you again. So often we'd sing 'Akuna Matata' together and prance around stupidly. I miss that, girls. And I'm sorry. I can't stop the tears from rolling down my face. I want your soft, little bodies near me. Touching me. The song 'Circle of Life' from* The Lion King *always made me so proud of you both. Thank you for making me such a happy dad. The thought of you not being able to have children really upsets me. I know they would have been so beautiful. Unfortunately that will never be, my darlings. I wanted to give you away on your wedding day, a dream I think every father cherishes. The circle of life has been cut drastically short, especially considering the violence of your deaths.*

Please help me, could you, girls. I know that life does continue, albeit insignificantly. Days drift along. Months seem like years. Babies are being born and other people are certainly dying.

'Here's your coffee, darling,' Net said, coming out from the kitchen.

'Are you still going to Port Arthur today?' I asked.

'Yeah, I think so. I was thinking of stopping at the Koonya markets on the way.'

'Why don't you take the girls on the boat to the Isle of the Dead tour? They'd enjoy that. They haven't been since Steven was over from Melbourne in November last year.'

'Yeah, that was a while ago. That's a good idea and it's a nice day. You won't be back until late in the afternoon, will you?'

'No, I won't. I was just thinking I wish I wasn't going today. But I'm sponsoring the tournament – the Tasman Pharmacy Eclectic – I'll have to be there.'

It was back in January that Clive Wells, the secretary of the Tasman Golf Club, had come into the pharmacy.

'There's only one possibility to play the tournament two weeks in a row. And that means 28 April. And then the following week, 5 May.'

My first reaction was that I couldn't do it. It coincided with the weekend of my birthday on the 29th. I should have said 'No'.

Why didn't I say 'No'?

I rarely played golf on a Sunday. It seemed like the waste of a day with the family.

One of the Dunblane mothers, whose six-year-old boy was killed in the massacre, said in an ITV documentary: 'If I'd known what was going to happen that day, I wouldn't have sent him to school.'

I know exactly what she means.

All of the things I could have done to change what happened I should have done in these last short minutes we had together. But how could anyone ever know that such a horrific thing was possible? Even in their worst nightmares. What was coming to me that day, as I sat reading the newspaper in the comfort of my own home with the people I loved most in all the world, I could never ever have contemplated.

Netty brought out the croissants she'd filled with ham and cheese, and there was another cup of coffee.

'Here you are, Lani,' Netty said. 'Come and get your croissants.'

'Me, too, my potatoes,' Maddie said.

'Not potatoes, darling, croissants,' Nanette said. 'They're called croissants.'

'You know what Lani said to me last night after she convinced me to play Nintendo?' I said as I reached for a croissant. 'I wanted to watch the football, but I felt I should play with her.'

'What did she say?' Netty asked, taking a drink of her 'nectar of the gods' tea.

'She said: "Well done, Dad. At least you tried. I'm really proud of you".'

Net almost choked on her tea laughing.

'And you should've seen the look on her face. It was like I was the child and she was the parent. And then I read to her – you know, that book Grace gave her for her birthday last year.'

'Oh yes, *My Underwater Adventure*, where Grace had the kids' names printed as the characters in the story,' Netty said.

'That's it. Well, while I was reading to her, so unlike Lani, she actually said: "I want to go to sleep now." And not long after that, you arrived home. How was your night?'

'They were a really good group. They really got into it.'

'How did the dissection room go.'

'Oh, really well. I scared the living daylights out of them. "Now, are you all comfortable, had something to eat and drink, been to the toilet? Then follow me".' Nanette mimicked holding up the lantern ready to begin the tour.

'And what was their favourite story last night?'

'We got to the Commandant's House and they *loved* the story about the rocking chair. I told them how Nanny used to sit there and how people had taken photos of it and a mysterious presence appeared on the photos afterwards. They all wanted to see the photos on the board back at the Information Office – you know those ones with the weird flashlight.'

'And did you tell them about the woman who felt the pulse when she sat on the rocking chair?'

A pillow flew through the air and I put up my arms to fend it off.

'Oh yes, they loved that. But we didn't see the lights at the church last night, you know, those lights like sparklers ... Oh, hon, it was so nice to come home to the hot water bottle in my bed around my pyjamas. It was a lovely surprise ...'

I got a letter, Netty, from a lady called Brooke who was on your last ghost tour. She said you made it 'a fascinating, exciting, amazing experience' and that you had such enthusiasm and passion, such a friendly, open spirit and such a love of your work that she was swept away. When the tour finished, you stood out in the rain to speak to her. You even spoke to her about me and our children and how wonderful our life was in Tasmania. Unbelievably, she saw you, Lani and Maddie again the next day, only an hour before your deaths, boarding the ferry to go to the Isle of the Dead.

She writes: 'Your daughters were exactly as Nanette described them. Madeline was "let's go, go, go ... now, now, now" and was halfway up the jetty before you could blink. Alannah had the prettiest freckles across her nose, such a lovely smile and beautiful, soft hair. They were so full of life and spoke to me with such excitement about going on the cruise, especially Alannah because she "just really likes it".'

You even told her I was playing golf and that the girls always chose Port Arthur as a place to spend the day.

You told her Port Arthur was one of your favourite places.

The letter finishes: 'I will always remember their wonderful smiles. They were very special people. I wanted you to know how much your beautiful family touched my life, how much they loved you and how full of joy they were.'

The pillow hit me on the head. The fight was now on in earnest.

'Hey, watch the time,' Netty said, looking at her watch.

Lani and I were wrestling on the floor and pretty soon Maddie joined in. It was time for the Sandwich game. I ruefully looked at the clock on the mantelpiece.

'Girls, I should get ready –'

'Aw, dad, peese?' Maddie begged, bouncing on my chest.

I gave up, getting up on my hands and knees. Lani was circling around behind me, pillow in her hand ready to pounce. I turned around smiling, ready to grab her.

I can still hear her laughter, now, ringing in my ears, the clarity undiminished even after all these months.

Maddie was on the attack now from behind, charging like a miniature bull and hurling herself through the air on top of my back.

'Ouch . . .' But then the pillow hit me full on the face. I stood no chance. As I managed to grasp Maddie, Lani continued belting me with the pillow mercilessly.

'Walter? Are you getting ready?' Nanette called from the kitchen. 'You're so frustrating sometimes . . . You're not even dressed. Where's your clubs? I suppose they're still in the shed . . .' She came into the lounge-room, pulling Maddie off as she got ready for another assault. 'You're just like a big kid. Eddie'll be here in six minutes.'

'That's okay. I've got ten minutes to get ready.'

Eddie arrived at a quarter past nine. He knew I wouldn't be ready at nine.

Finally, I was dressed in dark slacks, a royal blue polo-top and my lucky golf socks, a birthday present from Nanette. I picked up my red golf bag from the carport after giving Netty and the girls kisses and hugs and headed towards Eddie's white Pajero.

The girls and Netty came out to the carport. In spite of the sunshine I'd seen earlier, it was nippy outside, typical autumn weather. Lani was wearing my Blundstone boots and her white nightie with tiny blue spots. Maddie was in her pink pyjamas.

'See you, Chubby. Be good for Mum,' I called. 'Buy me a present from the market, Lani.'

Nanette was still in her red tartan pyjamas, her hair a mop of curls without her customary bow. She was wearing my steel-capped boots.

'Have a good day. See you when you get back,' she called.

As Eddie reversed back down the driveway onto George Street, I could see them waving in unison.

I can see them again now. That final goodbye. Is it a dream or is it real? That image is with me – they are still alive and warm as I saw them last. The way I saw them that morning. I want to remember them that way, and not how I remember that other recurring image of them lying dead on the road. Can I programme my dreams like inserting a videotape? If I knew I could, I would play and replay those good times, those cuddles, those games, those kisses.

If I can't physically be with them, then why can't they stay inside my head? Some nights when I'm writing I get a premonition that I'm going to dream about them that night. It's like the warning signs of a migraine approaching. Some nights their presence fills my dreams completely. But how can I talk to them in my dreams? How could that be possible? This is the right-hand side of my brain talking. The analytical part. Walter the pharmacist. I was a university graduate, a pharmacist with a good analytical mind. I should be able to work out which neurotransmitters in my brain are causing these disturbances. Is it serotonin or acetylcholine?

It doesn't matter, but I need to somehow stop it. I ring up Allan Anderson, the pastor I've been speaking to since all of this happened. He's an expert in dealing with death and bereavement. He was at Port Arthur the day after the tragedy to help the local community and has become the only person I could talk to openly about anything, whether it's feelings, fears in my life today, other relationships. Allan is not judgemental. He listens and then gives a range of responses.

In the months after I lost the girls, I visited a leading psychiatrist, Dr Ian Sale, in Hobart, but I found that less beneficial. Doctor Sale is very good, but what I really need is reassurance. I need to know my behaviour is normal in these very abnormal circumstances. People judge you as if you are in normal circumstances. Nothing could be further from the truth. Doctor Sale listens to all I have to say and documents it. But he doesn't respond when I disclose some of my worst fears. My fear of being in large open spaces. I feel unsafe and vulnerable in places like airports. Wherever there are lots of people in a public place. Crowded cafes or sporting events. I have this sense of foreboding that a person is going to start firing a gun at all these innocent people. It is still with me today. Then there's the horror of closing my eyes. I know what I will see first – the sight of them lying near the roadside, and the other bodies that I saw in body bags.

Often when I close my eyes I see that same scene. It is sharp and in focus. The details are recounted with such precision. Hopefully this will continue to be the case. It is like the default screen that pops up on a computer after a few minutes of non-use.

The Tasman Golf Course is on the same peninsula as Point Puer, the penal settlement across the water from Port Arthur, where the young male convicts lived such miserable lives 150 years ago. It's a beautiful little course with views down the ninth fairway towards Mt Brown and across Maingon Bay to Cape Raoul. The coastline here is rugged and isolated with huge swells pounding the dolerite cliffs, some of the highest sea cliffs in Australia. Near Mt Brown is Crescent Beach with sand dunes thirty metres high.

Hitting off the first tee across Carnarvon Bay, I thought of the girls and how close they were. They might even be at the Isle of the Dead, within shouting distance from the seventh hole. What would they be up to, I wondered. They'd be enjoying the ride on the boat and they'd probably had 'chippies' at the cafe.

We were at the thirteenth hole and had just finished putting out on the par three when we heard the sound. A succession of loud, hollow noises.

'What's that? I think it's coming from the site, across the bay,' Eddie asked.

'It sounds like a post-hole digger because it just keeps going,' I said.

'Maybe it's a re-enactment,' Eddie said. 'Like Beating Retreat or something.'

If I'd known what those noises were, what could I have done? It was a quiet Sunday afternoon on a golf course. The noises echoed across the silence of the bay and still echo in my ears now. Could I have got there in time? It stopped and re-started. Which noise was it that killed them? It took six months for me to find out. When they played the video during the court case, it was obvious then which shots they were.

'It couldn't happen to me.' People are so sure and smug that it won't. It always happens to someone else, someone you have read about in the news or see on television. 'Isn't it terrible?' people say. 'How awful for that poor man or that poor family.' But it hasn't happened to them; they can give their platitudes and be shocked and still be comforted by the thought that it hasn't happened to them. Why did it happen to me? Have I done something that deserves the worst punishment anyone could ever have been expected to endure? Why?

In many ways, the impact of 28 April has had repercussions from which none of us will recover. That we have a society that has created someone who could carry out such deeds. We have lost our innocence. Violence on this scale no longer belongs in war zones.

'Mummy, can this happen again here?' a young child asks after the massacre. The parent is unable to reassure the child. They cannot tell a lie. In their heart they know they're not telling the truth. The repercussions of this tragedy have rippled far beyond the people whose lives are bound up on this little peninsula. Like the other

tragedy on the other side of the planet at Dunblane in Scotland, the ripples are gaining in strength until they become gigantic waves threatening to submerge us all. When two waves meet, they merge into a big tidal wave. It's inevitable that some people will drown. Will I be one of them or can I keep my head above water?

After Eddie and I finished the last five holes we headed for the clubhouse at the top of the hill.

A car drove towards the clubhouse and parked round the back. The family, tourists who'd been on their way to the Port Arthur Historic Site, got out.

'There's been a shooting at Port Arthur,' they told us and a group of golfers who'd just finished the course. 'We were diverted up here.'

'Maybe they didn't like the service at the shop,' one of the golfers joked.

We chuckled. The possibility was ludicrous.

Entering the clubhouse, we handed our score cards over.

'A beer?' Eddie asked.

'Yep, it's been hard work out there,' I answered. 'I'll have a quick one and stay for the presentation, and then I'll head home.'

It was ten past two. The tourist's words stayed with me as I sipped on my can of beer. What if it was true? It couldn't be, but I'd ring Nanette. I looked at my watch. She'd be home by now. The girls would be bored, they'd have had lunch and it would be time to go home.

I asked the barman for the key to the phone and rang our number. There was no answer. I let the phone keep ringing. Maybe they'd just arrived or they were outside.

They should be home. Where were they? A growing discomfort had started in the pit of my stomach. Something wasn't right. But there could be another explanation. Perhaps they'd gone to visit Keith at White Beach. But Nanette hadn't said anything about it this morning. I rang Keith.

'Have you seen Nanette and the girls?' I asked.

'No, they haven't been here,' he answered. 'Why?'

'Well, they went to the site today and they're not home yet and I'm a little bit worried because someone here said there'd been some shooting or something.'

I rang Kerrie Shoobridge, but got the answering machine.

I rang the Port Arthur Historic Site Information Office. I knew the number off by heart. It was Nanette's work number.

The woman who answered was non-committal.

'Have you seen Nanette and the girls today?'

'Yes, they've definitely been here. I saw them, but I don't know where they are now. I have to go.'

I wanted to ask her what had happened, but she obviously didn't have time to talk.

'Are you all right?' Eddie asked when I came back to the bar. 'Were they home?'

'No, they're not, but I'm not sure where they are,' I answered slowly. 'They should be home. We'd better get going. I want to get back to the house.'

On the way home, as we approached the historic site, we saw a group of people congregated in a house on the corner. I recognised one of the locals, a man called Dale Wellard.

We pulled over and I wound down the window.

'What's going on at the site?' Eddie asked. 'What's happened?'

'There's been shootings,' Dale said. 'Someone's on the loose with a gun and there's been people killed. One of them is Lizzie Howard.'

'Are you sure?' I asked in disbelief. 'Lizzie Howard?'

Lizzie Howard was a young girl who had recently got married and had just started work at the souvenir shop in the Broad Arrow Cafe.

'Yes. I'm pretty sure, mate. It's mayhem down there,' Dale said.

'I wonder if we'll still be doing play rehearsals tonight?' Eddie said as we drove off.

'It depends on what's happened, I suppose,' I said. 'Steve and Pam'll probably get called out.'

Back at the house there was silence – no-one home. Everything was tidy. The dishes were done, beds made, there were no toys on the floor. I left a note on the bench.

'Dear Netty, I'm going to the site to look for you. I'll see you when I get back, Love "Your Boy".'

As I put the note down on the bench, I noticed one of Netty's signed ghost tour certificates: 'I've completed a ghost tour at Port Arthur ...' Strange, I thought. What was this doing on the kitchen bench?

'I want to go back to the site,' I said as soon as I saw Eddie. 'Can I borrow one of your cars?'

At Eddie's supermarket, speculation was rife.

'Who is it?'

'He was driving a Volvo, you know,' one man said.

'And he had a surfboard on the top of the car.'

'Is it someone we know?' a woman asked.

'There's a few weirdos around. It's not that bloke with the beard ... I've always thought he was a bit strange.'

Behind the wheel of Eddie's Lancer, I drove by myself towards Port Arthur. All kinds of thoughts flitted through my mind. How could a shooting happen there? I hope the children are okay. I hope they haven't been hurt. No, there's no way possible anything could happen to them. They'll be all right. At the access road into the site, before the toll booth, people were standing across the road forming a barricade and I recognised some of them. I wound down the window.

'I need to go in. I think Nanette and the girls are still there,' I said.

'You can't come in this way,' I was told. 'You'll have to use the entrance round by the Motor Inn.'

I did a U-turn and as I was turning, I saw four white mounds underneath sheets not far from the toll booth. I know now they were bodies. Did I know then? I must have, but it didn't register. Had I looked past the toll booth, only ten metres further, I would have known right away what happened. Their bodies would still have been warm. I wish that had been the case. The next few hours of anguish may have been eased. The not knowing, the searching, clinging to hope until it was brutally extinguished.

It was 4 p.m. when I parked in the carpark of the Motor Inn and walked down the asphalt road across the historic site.

What did I see when I was walking? The penitentiary, where I'd photographed Lani and Maddie so many times, was still the same. There were the ruins of the old church, built in 1836, on the hill. Port Arthur. It had come to mean so much in our lives. In the ten years since we first saw these ruins, it seemed unchanged. That vast acreage of lawns, the English oaks between Champ Street, the main street of the settlement, and the Information Office. In the distance, the Commandant's Cottage behind the military barracks. We walked through these ruins hand in hand, climbing up the steps of the penitentiary, reading the history of the convicts, the suffering and the pain of those wretched souls transported across the seas.

At the turn of the century, after the convicts had left, people wanted to tear everything down. But instead of that, they simply changed its name to Carnarvon and turned it into a tourist town with a hotel complete with murals. But the ghosts of the convicts remained.

Netty, I should have listened when you told me about your spiritual encounters. As I walked across the lawn, alone, towards the Broad Arrow Cafe, I was taking those steps that were to bring me closer to the reality I wish I never had to face. I can't recall the helicopters or the commotion, no matter how hard I try. I had tunnel vision. I had to find you and the girls.

Even though there were lots of people at the Port Arthur Historic Site, it was deathly quiet. Ambulances stood outside the cafe. Nobody knew what to do. There was no crying, I remember that much, just stark disbelief. But my memory plays tricks with me. I remember speaking with someone outside the cafe.

'Have you seen Nanette and the girls?' It was the question I kept repeating all afternoon.

'Yes,' the person replied. 'They headed towards the old church after the shooting started.'

There was a glimmer of hope. I had to find them – this thought superseded everything else. I was no longer taking anything in. I talked to people I knew, but I can't remember what I said, or what they said in reply. I just wanted to see Netty and the girls and hold them in my arms.

I ran back to the Motor Inn, scouring the faces. Yet every face looking towards me seemed vacant, uncomprehending. The restaurant and the foyer were packed with people, waiting. A police officer was taking down people's names. Tables stood in the middle of the room laden with sweets and biscuits.

Vicki McLaughlin, one of the guides at the site, approached me.

'The girls should be all right, Walter,' she said. 'They were walking with me towards the old church, but they didn't stay with me. I don't know why. There was so much chaos.'

'Thank goodness,' I said out loud.

They had to be hiding somewhere, or perhaps they were injured in some way.

'You don't have any idea where they could have gone?' I asked.

'No, have you looked around here?'

'Yes, I've been searching for quite a while now.'

'Well, there are some people in other buildings around the site, the Junior Medical Officer's Quarters and the overseer's cottage near the Model Prison,' she said.

I visited both places, asking again. Nobody seemed to respond. It was as if they couldn't understand what I was saying, as if I was in a dream where I was all alone and speaking in another language. Where were they? Didn't anybody care? Nobody offered to come and help me look. I was becoming increasingly desperate.

I ran back to the Visitors' Information Office near the cafe. There were fewer people standing around now. I approached the cafe, walking towards the concrete steps leading up to the verandah. Pam Ireland was coming out of the door of the cafe.

'Walter, what are you up to, mate? What are you doing?'

'I can't find Nanette and the girls, but I know that they were here.'

I started walking towards the cafe. I must have known the cafe was littered with dead bodies, but somehow it was of no concern. I had to search every bit of that place to find them. Pam grabbed me by the arm, holding me back.

'You can't go in there. They're not in there.'

'Are you sure?'

'No. They're definitely not in there.'

I looked at her in bewilderment. Where were they then?

Thank goodness I hadn't gone in. Some people who lost loved ones ventured into that place. What they saw in there defies description. John Burgess found the body of his seventeen-year-old daughter Nicole, cousin of Lizzie Howard, who was killed behind the counter of the souvenir shop adjoining the cafe. He had to return some time later just to confirm what he had seen. It could not have happened. He was in a state of disbelief.

I had lunch with Eddie Halton and Steve Ireland recently, just before the first anniversary. I showed them some of the book. So much didn't need to be said. There is an unspoken bond between us. I am sure it will last all our lives.

At lunch Eddie and I talked of the sounds of the gunfire we heard on the golf course. How what struck both of us was its methodical regularity. It was the gunman choosing his victims. He took time to decide who was going to die next, inflicting maximum terror on those left behind.

I completed the same circuit again. I started at the Motor Inn. There was a news flash on the television up on the wall. It talked of the gunman, but I wasn't interested. By then, people seemed more relaxed. They were sitting in front of the fire, on the ground. A long queue of people was still formed waiting to register their names with police.

'There's been a mass shooting at Tasmania's Port Arthur Historic Site today with the number of victims as yet unknown. It is suspected that at least twenty people have been shot dead ...'

Is it possible? Could the worst have happened. No, immediately I pushed the thought to the back of my mind.

On my third visit, I began looking for our vehicle. I had to confirm whether they were here or not. I found our dark blue 'Tasman Pharmacy' Pajero near the wharf where the ferry left for the Isle of the Dead tours. I checked inside. There were some toys in the back and the baby seat, but no clues to their whereabouts. They had to be here somewhere. They were still here. The evidence was irrefutable.

I headed back towards the Information Office past the Broad Arrow Cafe. Pam Ireland approached me from behind. She held my arm. I was probably shaking all over, like I was going to sink into a hole in the ground. It was getting dark. I had been searching for nearly two hours.

'Pam, I know they've got to be here somewhere,' I said. 'The car's there. I've been right around the site twice now and there's no sign of them. It's getting dark and cold and Nanette wouldn't have the girls out. She'd try and bring them inside somewhere.'

'Okay, mate, have they been reported missing?'

'Actually, that's just where I was going – to talk to the policeman at the Information Office.'

The police officer picked up a blank piece of paper from his folder. I watched as he wrote down the three names, checking the spelling as he wrote.

After I finished, Paul Cooper, another guide who worked at the site, took me by the arm, acting on Pam's instructions, and led me across to 'Clougha', one of the historic houses up towards the old church. Inside the hallway, people were standing around, some heads were down, others huddled in groups of twos and threes. As I stood in the hall next to Paul, I saw a solitary figure across the room, leaning against a table. It was Steve Howard and the look on his face is still with me today. Such a look of disbelief, like a zombie. He'd lost Lizzie, I remembered, as I looked at him. Poor thing, losing his wife.

It still hadn't registered with me that I could be in the same boat, or worse. I wonder now if anyone knew of my family's fate in those early hours. And if so, why didn't they tell me? I remember how shocked I was to learn that I knew one of the victims. Lizzie Howard was someone I knew well. A beautiful-looking girl who came into the pharmacy regularly to get Ventolin for her asthma. How could that happen to someone who had such a love of life? I felt sorry for him, compassion, the sort of compassion people now feel for me. I wonder what I looked like when I found out. Eddie told me that when he found me much later that night in the Youth Hostel covered by an old grey blanket with holes in it, I was shaking uncontrollably. He said it crossed his mind that this might be what he looked like when he was having one of his epileptic fits.

I can't remember how much time passed, but at some stage, while I was in Clougha, Pam Ireland came up the hallway. It must have been close to 7 p.m. She looked at me, straight into my eyes, and held me with both hands.

'Walter, the bodies that are up on the road near the toll booth. It's Nanette and the girls.'

'No! No. It can't be. You've made a mistake.'

'It is them, Walter. I've just been up there to identify them.'

I gave out a primal scream from the inner depths of my body.

'No, no, no . . . it can't be. Not all of them. Not my babies. Not my Netty. No . . .'

Life had no meaning in those moments. I didn't care whether I existed or not. If they were gone, I wanted to be gone, too.

What happened then? Who said what to whom? I can't remember, just numbness as if I was under an anaesthetic, but I could still comprehend . . . just.

Someone had a two-way radio. Unbelievably, as we huddled together in the historic house, news came that shots were being fired somewhere near the site.

'Cannot confirm the suspect confined to Seascape Guesthouse. Possibly still at large on historic site. Treat as siege situation . . .'

The words didn't register with me. I still had no idea who was responsible for the shooting, nor had I even bothered to ask, so obsessed was I about finding my family.

But the words had a charged effect on the people inside Clougha. The crowd were mainly women and some began to panic.

'Where are we going to hide?'

'He's coming back.'

'We're all going to die.'

Hysteria started building, some women screamed. Nobody knew what to do.

Kaye Fox, a volunteer ambulance officer who taught Alannah how to swim, and Ruth Noye, who was also a volunteer, materialised by my side. Kaye had been up to the road with Pam when they'd identified the girls' bodies. Kaye and Ruth held me tightly as I sat on a chair.

I didn't care if I died. In fact, I wanted to. I could run out through the front door into his line of fire. That would be how it would end. Let's get it over and done with. Then we can all be at peace together.

The lights were turned off so we would not be so conspicuous and silence fell. But I didn't want to be quiet. Many of the people lay on the floor anticipating something nobody could imagine unless they were having a nightmare.

Whoever had the radio called for help. 'We need a police escort. You need to get us out of here. It's not safe. We're like sitting ducks.'

Everyone was numb. No-one spoke. Eventually the police escort arrived, two uniformed police, I think, but I can't recall. We were moved to the Motor Inn and by 8 p.m. we were sent to the youth hostel. My legs moved one in front of the other. In the youth hostel, I was put in a room alone with Pam and Steve Ireland.

'Do you want to ring Keith and let him know?' Pam asked.

I had been wondering what to do. What would he say? What would I say? How could I tell him? I couldn't. He'd already lost Grace, his greatest treasure.

'I don't know, Pam. I don't know what to do.'

I was sitting on an old couch in the sunroom of the hostel. It was freezing, all windows facing the cold and no heater. I was shivering uncontrollably. All I could think of was the girls lying there exposed in this damp, dark air. They deserved some comfort, some warmth. I couldn't leave them there.

'I have to go and see them,' I said to Pam and Steve. 'Netty and my babies,' in between sobs.

Pam got up and went outside. She was back shortly afterwards.

'It's not possible, Walter. The siege area hasn't been contained, the police said. He's still at large and nobody's allowed to walk around the site.'

'I don't care about my safety. I couldn't care less. I *have* to be with them. You don't understand. I want to hold them. They'll get cold. They need me.'

'Walter, mate, you just can't go,' Steve said, whispering in my ear and holding me tightly. 'Pam will organise it for the morning. It's the only way it can happen.'

Pam sat on the other side of me with her arm around my neck.

It was 9 p.m. by the time we got back to the house. My note to Netty, written in such a carefree way just hours before, was still on the bench, untouched. The house was dark, cold, empty and silent. Reminders they weren't home. Not only were they not home, but they weren't coming back. I sobbed uncontrollably. Keith and Eddie had returned to the house with me. Keith had been told about the girls at one of the roadblocks near the historic site earlier in the evening.

I walked into the girls' rooms. On Alannah's dressing table was a blue velvet headband. I wound it three times around my wrist. In Maddie's room, I picked up a pink headband with 'Ankle Biters' written on it and put it on my other wrist.

Eddie rang his wife, Pam, at home. He was in a state of shock and did not prepare her for the news.

'Nanette and the girls have been shot and killed,' he said. 'I'm with Walter. Come up as soon as you can.'

I sat on the couch, holding Nanette's tartan pyjamas, which still held her scent. My face was wet with tears.

'I just don't know what to say to you,' Eddie said, holding me.

'This must be a bad dream. It's a bad dream, isn't it? They'll be back in the morning,' I said. 'But how could they all die? Surely he could have left me one.'

Suddenly I brightened.

'It might not be them. There's been a mistake. How do I know it is them? I haven't even seen them yet.'

Keith began lighting the woodheater. Then, as if he was on automatic, he got out the vacuum cleaner. He needed to keep himself busy.

In the surreal world I now inhabited, phone calls came and went. Eddie made coffees as I sat on the lounge immobilised, the coffee still in the cup untouched. I had not eaten since lunchtime, but existence didn't seem relevant any more.

One of the phone calls was from my mother.

'Walter, are you all right?' she said. 'Tell me it's not true and Nanette and the girls are all right?'

'It is true.'

She screamed a heart-rending sound. I couldn't say any more.

Then my father was on the phone.

'Chris is organising for us to leave in the morning. We'll be there as soon as we can,' he said.

Eddie offered to stay.

'It's okay, I'll stay with Walter,' Keith said.

At some time in the early hours of the morning, I lay in our bed. I don't know how I got there. I took the girls' pyjamas from under the pillows on our bed. I lay in a foetal position on Netty's side of the bed, cuddling all of the pyjamas, including Nanette's. I left the light on. I couldn't bear to be alone. That hollow feeling, that unbearable emptiness, was to become as familiar as putting on my pyjamas. Something I have to learn to live with.

Oblivion

I am standing inside St David's Cathedral in Hobart lighting two candles at the altar. The wooden pews date back to last century. To my left is the Chapel of Hope, the area of the church dedicated to the victims of Port Arthur. A new cross is to be built. It will be a place for reflection. It is a cold autumn morning and the sun is filtering through the stained glass window of the birth of Christ behind me. The hallowed interior makes me want to pray. But I am not sure who I am praying to and what I am praying for. My prayers cannot be answered.

The night before the state service, in May last year, I'd talked of suicide to my friend, Chris McCann. Sitting in the lounge-room at Nubeena and drinking port, Chris, a detective-sergeant, said he could comprehend where I was coming from. I had the capacity to do it quickly and painlessly with my access to drugs. I had never before contemplated such a thing. We had been so happy, but now they were gone.

In the Visitors' Book near the front door, I write: 'This is a magnificent building. However, I wish I had never had to come into it. Walter Mikac.'

Three days after the shooting, my family, close friends and I decided to go to the service at St David's Anglican Cathedral. It happened on the spur of the moment – I didn't know if I'd be up to it. Parking had been arranged for us at police headquarters. Our group walked through the streets of Hobart. As we neared the church, the crowd was so tightly packed we had to push to get through. I felt repelled by such close contact. I clutched three Dutch Irises in my hands and Alannah's two diaries. Her blue velvet headband was on one wrist and Maddie's hot pink scrunchie on the other. This was the closest I could be to them now. They had worn them in their hair only days before.

The hour-long service passed in a blur. I focused on a canvas bag which sat on the floor in front of us. It might be a bomb, I thought, staring at it throughout the prayers, fixating now on violence, that no longer could I guarantee that the world was a safe place.

Standing on the steps of the church after the service, my head bowed, I kept my eyes on the bluestone steps. People were everywhere outside in a grandstand on the other side of the street. As I walked down the steps, I heard the bells tolling. I felt the strange sensation that I had been here before, walking through a similar entrance and looking down at similar aged steps. It was our wedding day. But this time Netty was not by my side. She would never be by my side again. How could I live without her?

As I walked down the footpath, an avalanche of tears flooded my vision. My brother John, clutching my right arm, cried too, unashamedly. Chris held me on the other side. I didn't want to be somewhere so public. I could hear the motor drives of the media contingent clicking incessantly. They had got their prey. But I couldn't hold back. I cried for the life that had been taken from me. I cried for what I could never get back – a life of fulfilment.

Inside nearby Hadley's Hotel, a function room had been set aside for friends and relatives of the victims. In the foyer, I caught up with Nanette's brothers Rodney and Peter and their partners, Jenny and Jo. None of us said much. We put arms around each other and cried.

As we were ushered to the function room, I had my arm around my mother, who was crying quietly. A woman took me by the other arm and led me a few steps away. She was wearing a cross and I thought she was the bishop's wife.

'If you come with me, I can help you come out of this,' she said.

I stared at her. 'Come out of what? I'm doing what I want to do.'

Inside the function room, John received similar treatment.

A woman separated John and Chris.

'Look at the floor,' she said. 'Look at the ceiling. Look at the wall. What colour is the wall?'

Chris and John looked at her, perplexed.

'What's the point? What the hell are you talking about.'

These 'counsellors' had presumably been organised by someone, but, to this day, I cannot work out what they were doing or what they were trying to achieve.

In the days after the shooting, back in Nubeena, someone walked into my life who did make a difference. At that point, my mind was closed to the whole idea of needing to talk to anyone. The man had greying neatly trimmed hair, glasses and wore a shirt with a small cross near the collar. He looked like he was in his late forties. His name was Allan Anderson and he was a pastor based at the Church of Christ in Nowra, NSW. He spoke to all of us, my family and friends who were at my house for a session of group counselling.

'You'll experience a whole range of emotions, many you've never experienced before. You'll all react differently. There is no one response. Each person copes differently with grief.'

Here we go, I thought. More platitudes.

But, he seemed to be saying things that made sense. I *did* need somebody to talk to and someone who was objective. Someone who I felt I could trust and in whom I could confide all the strange thoughts that were circling in my mind.

Afterwards, when everyone had left, he came back and we sat on the stone seats in the garden where Lani, Maddie and Nanette and I used to have afternoon tea. We talked about everything from fear, to my feelings about God, to the idea that to make love to someone else would be an act of infidelity.

I had also talked to Chris about fidelity the Tuesday night after the massacre. I had told him that after ten years of marriage, I had never been unfaithful and that, considering the way Nanette and I had parted without proper goodbyes, I felt proud to be able to say that.

'You mean to say that you've never even been tempted?' asked Chris.

'Sure I've been tempted. In fact, the opportunities have been there, but I'd ask myself: "Is a few moments of possible pleasure worth jeopardising all that I have? Netty loves me with all her heart and I could never live with the thought of being separated from my daughters".'

At that first meeting in the garden at Nubeena, Pastor Allan Anderson tackled this issue without any fuss.

'While it may seem a long way away at the moment, there will come a time when you can put your memories with them in their place in history. It's like having the best book you could ever read – you can have it on the shelf, you can have it around, you can go back to look at it, but it doesn't mean you can't go back and pick up a different book off the shelf. That doesn't mean the first book is still not the best book you've ever read. Your marriage vows state: "Till death do us part." Unfortunately, even though you would never have contemplated what has happened, you have to re-align your thinking that you are now a single person. That will take a long time to accept.'

His words brought relief. Here was someone who could give me advice, whose simple analogies made sense and who did not judge what I said. Who wasn't speaking to me as someone who knew me, but was giving me answers to questions that I found difficult to ask.

In those first few months I really clung to Allan. We chatted on the phone often. He was someone who could understand me in the face of so many people who didn't – like the woman who rang suggesting I get a supply of tranquillisers. And that to a pharmacist. Or the customer who declared a few days after my wife and daughters were killed that she loved me while I held her small baby in our garden. I had no idea how to respond, so I said: 'Thanks ... that's really nice.'

I also had to tackle the strange experience of being a celebrity – for which I had no training and no time to prepare. The media wanted a piece of the action now. I was newsworthy and deadlines could not wait.

From the day after the massacre the television cameras and newspaper journalists set up camp at the bottom of George Street in Nubeena. Occasionally my brothers, John or Steve, would go down the hill to talk to them. No, there weren't any photos. Walter didn't want to speak. That situation would not change.

But on the Tuesday after the shooting, I decided I would speak to Ray Martin on 'A Current Affair'. If the media train was approaching, I was going to meet it head on. I could dictate the terms. I would speak once and that was it. Then I got the phone call that Ray Martin was on his way to our house. What would I say? Somehow I felt assured that Netty would watch over me and, as I faced national television, I could feel her presence.

But a few weeks after the massacre, I experienced my biggest betrayal in this new world of being a media celebrity. I allowed a journalist into my house who said she was doing an article on how the community was coping with the aftermath and how we could all rebuild a future together. I still have the letter she faxed me stating this was the thrust of the story. I would just be one of several people interviewed.

'I don't want to speak to you unless it's in this context,' I said to her at the front door. 'I expressly don't want you to do a story on my family.'

She seemed unfazed and gave me assurances this was the case. She asked if she could bring a photographer inside the house. Naively, I agreed. While she spoke to me, the photographer clicked away as Chris McCann and I leant on the kitchen wall drinking a cup of coffee. She took notes, writing down descriptions of what was on the fridge. Weeks later, in Melbourne, she confronted Nanette's sister, Bronwyn, telling her she'd been inside my house and had been talking to me, implying I'd agreed to be interviewed for a profile piece. By using similar tactics of subterfuge, she managed to get hold of some personal family photographs. The resulting article was splashed across several pages of *Who Weekly* magazine with the headline 'WALTER MIKAC FACES LIFE AFTER LOSING HIS FAMILY IN THE PORT ARTHUR MASSACRE'. It was a sobering lesson to me of how ruthless the media machine was.

I am looking at my diary, a now-battered, grey hardcovered book with a red spine. I started it as a contact book between me and the outside world in those days following the shooting when I was immersed in a world where no-one could reach me. A world of shock where my brain simply closed down and refused to accept reality. People resorted to writing things down in this little book, trying to get through to me what was happening in the real world. The upcoming funeral was approaching. Decisions had to be made.

All kinds of messages were left in the book. I had to choose the order of the speakers at the funeral. Tina Arena may not be able to come, but would John Farnham do? The Pharmacy Benevolent Fund had rung. Scores of wellwishers passed on their condolences.

I have kept this diary with me since that day. It has become a jumbled record of the confusion of my recent life. Notes I have made for the book, feelings I have had at different times about various issues. Descriptions scribbled down before I forget them. Phone numbers of all these people who have crossed my path since I began this strange new existence. Jo Winter's phone number, Sue and John Burgess, the number of a good masseuse, Roland Browne, the Co-ordinator for the Coalition for Gun Control.

On Friday 3 May, I went to the funeral of Nicole Burgess and Lizzie Howard at the little white weatherboard church in Koonya where I used to take Lani and Maddie. People from all parts of the peninsula were there, residents still numb with shock paying their respects.

I also sat, with my family, at the private service at the Port Arthur Historic Site, inside the walls of the old convict church looking up at the sky where the roof had been. Large arched windows, their stained glass long gone, were all around us. Last time I'd been to a gathering here, it was Carols by Candlelight a week before Christmas. Lani, and even Maddie, had sung 'Away in a Manger'.

I remembered Netty saying, 'It's such a beautiful setting. You couldn't beat this atmosphere anywhere else in the world.'

I thought of Netty standing in the centre of this church, during a ghost tour, regaling her audience with tales of the murders that happened while the church was being built and the stories of how she had seen the inexplicable lights bouncing off the old sandstone walls.

Bronwyn's children, Daniel and Hannah, walked up with me to place the first of thirty-five red roses on the makeshift altar on the largest arched window. As the minister read the service, my mother's voice drowned out some of his words: 'Lani, Lani ... My little Maddie,' she sobbed.

As I steered a path through this jungle of pitfalls and adjusted to losing my anonymity, I grappled with my grief, sometimes becoming anxious, other times becoming oblivious to the world around me. That first week after the shooting, apart from coping with the media, I only had one focus and that was the funeral. I had decided already to call it 'a celebration'. It was to be 'a celebration of their lives'. As I have always been goal-oriented, it gave me something to centre on. I only had one chance to get it right for Nanette and the girls. This was my parting gift to them.

ELEVEN

My Parting Gift

I am picturing myself in a confession box.
   'Bless me, Father, for I have sinned. It has been quite a while since my last confession.'

The priest answers: 'Go ahead, my son.'

I tell him what has happened in my life. I say: 'I know that I've sinned. I've done things that I wish I hadn't done. But, by the same token, what sins could possibly justify the punishment I've had?'

There's silenc.e There is no answer from the priest.

What could I have done that day to have prevented what happened? Why did it happen to me?

I'd like to think there is a God or a higher power who is in control of what happens, who is the guiding force. But if that's the case why did the events of 28 April occur? When you see what happened to people that day at Port Arthur, it's hard to ever come to terms with why people need to die in that way. If they'd died in a car accident, or a boating accident . . . it might have been easier to accept. Maybe.

What was Alannah thinking in those last few moments of her life? This question gave me unbearable, inconsolable grief in those first few weeks, grief that has never been resolved. What did she know? She saw, obviously, what happened to Maddie and Nanette. And I suppose knew what was going to happen to her. For any person to have to consider such a fate, especially a child, makes it extremely difficult for me to hold on to my faith. It makes it very, very difficult. The fact that I wasn't there. As a parent you want to protect your children and to do anything to prevent them from suffering in any way. Nanette did exactly that in trying to save them. She told him: 'Please don't hurt my babies.' She gladly sacrificed herself for her children.

If there is a God, He didn't answer her prayers. And He has never answered mine.

I'm sitting on the fence at the moment. People like to assume that I've got incredible faith. Often I think it's just for their own sakes, for their own coping mechanism. They think that my strength is drawn from my faith. I don't honestly know where I've got the strength to continue. Where has the ability come from to talk in public? To be able to do television interviews, to cry every day and still wake up the next? Should I perhaps keep faith as an option like an insurance policy against the future? If I give it away, what will happen if things get even worse?

When our puppy, Beethoven, died the week after he arrived in Melbourne in November 1996, I thought I had already cried as much as I could cry, and was numb with the iniquity of it all. I had grieved, I thought, to the point of no return. But could it get worse? Could my mother or father die of a heart attack? Why was I being punished in this way? What had I done? Would fate follow me when I drove the car? Will I meet with an accident? Or will I come across a scene of carnage? I know now it is possible. I have experienced that it can happen. Something which the average person never considers. Will I consider it for the rest of my life? Will I be able to enter public places without the nagging fear that the worst can happen?

Deep inside me, there's a core. I don't know where it comes from. But it says 'hang in there'. They'll never be back, but you can continue on. You can survive. Something inside me says I do have faith in the human spirit. Looking back at the memories of my children and my wife gives me hope – the naturalness and beauty of them.

I was brought up to believe in God. As a child, I went to a Catholic school. During my trip to Europe I was overawed by the ornate Renaissance paintings, the hallowed interiors and the incredible age of the buildings. I came from a country where European structures were only 200 years old. My local church at Macleod, which I visited every Sunday with my parents, was a modern octagonal building with none of that regal bearing.

Inside these European churches, if organ music was playing, I left feeling calm and spiritual. Whenever I felt melancholy, I would seek the church.

Back then, at the age of twenty-two, religion was not deeply significant in my life, but I did believe in God or a higher power. In some of the churches, I knelt in prayer at the pew, taking comfort from this womb-like sanctuary cut off from the outside world. Then, I was praying for a safe return to Australia and for my future with Nanette, who was so far away at the other side of the world.

The faith that my parents have is very important to them and I respect that. I have respect for other people's faith. That's one of the basic freedoms people should be allowed, as long as that freedom doesn't impinge on others.

But I cannot agree with the hypocrisy and some of the things that are done in the name of religion, the wars that have been fought. The war in Ireland that has been going for decades and even further back in history, to the Crusades.

I remember, when I was very little, being carried on my dad's shoulders during an outdoor service. Religion has always been there when I've been growing up: my baptism, my first communion and my confirmation. Both Lani and Maddie were baptised and Netty had been, too, although she rarely accompanied us to church. After a religious upbringing, she chose to live without it but she never objected to me taking the girls to church.

Lani, I remember how you cried through your baptism and years later how much you wanted to make your first communion. When you came to me that Easter Sunday, weeks before you died, and asked me, I said: 'No, wait for a little while, maybe next year.' Perhaps I should have let you go. That's how I live my life now. Don't wait for tomorrow. You were old enough to understand the significance of this act. It would have been an important memory and now something you will never get to do.

As your coffin was being lowered into the ground, the white dove which was waiting to be released into the air slipped away from its white ribbon. It walked across to me. Lani, were you trying to tell me something? There was still so much you had to do. Why did you have to leave so soon?

My hands were trembling as I dressed on the morning of the girls' funeral. I pinned a gardenia to the lapel of my dark blue suit just as I'd done on our wedding day. It was imperative that I be perfectly groomed.

It was 9 May, the week before Mother's Day. This was to be our final farewell. I knew they looked great. Netty in her beautiful wedding dress with nail polish and lipstick in place, and the girls in their favourite dresses – Madeline with her Mama doll and Lani with the teddy she was given when she was born.

At 1 p.m. the white Ford LTDs arrived at my parents' house to collect us. When I arrived at the chapel at Zeltner Hall at the Austin Hospital, I couldn't believe all the people. So many. There must have been 2000, spilling out on the entrance road up to the chapel. Along the road, flowers carpeted the rockeries and lined the road. I could see that people wanted to pay their respects and show they cared. Over the public address system, Tina Arena's 'Heaven Help My Heart' was playing, the lyrics so appropriate.

Two smiling faces, that's how it used to be.
What once was forever, now a faded memory,
A perfect illusion, for a while I guess it was.
Without explanation the bloom fell off the rose.
Heaven help my heart . . .

I knew Netty would have been proud that her final farewell was such a big affair. As I walked up the driveway and into the church, it was as if my life flashed before my eyes. Friends, neighbours and customers, sporting clubs that Netty or I had been involved in, faces that had crossed our paths over our time together and even before. A small contingent from the Port Arthur Historic Site and nurses and other staff from the hospital, some still in uniform. They either knew Nanette or knew of her reputation. It was as though the hospital had stopped for the occasion. A marquee, set up in the hospital grounds, was overflowing. The Australian flag flew at half-mast. Then there was the media and members of the police force. Faces which looked down in despair, some with tears, some without, but everyone crying inside. They were all, I am sure, grappling with the question of how this could happen, needing to be reassured there was some reason behind such a senseless waste of life.

I walked slowly down the aisle with Keith and Bronwyn by my side. Mourners spilled out from each door into the sunshine outside. Inside, the sun shone through the stained glass windows high in the chapel, giving the whole room a feel of light, air and space. Flowers were everywhere, piled on a bench: gerberas in reds and yellows, apricot carnations, pink roses and chrysanthemums. I had the feeling none of this was real. As I approached the front row, where I was to sit, the sight before me increased my sense of surrealism. One normal-sized coffin edged in deep blood-red with gilt handles and two smaller coffins edged in hot pink, each of them covered in garlands of flowers.

On a pedestal next to the coffins was a framed photo of each of my beloved family. Nanette, looking towards the camera, beautifully made up, her lips cherry-red against the black velour dress with a wistful expression in her eyes; Alannah, grinning, photographed on holiday at Seaworld in Queensland with her two front teeth missing; and Maddie, in a yellow polka-dot dress in the back garden at Nubeena, the Mama doll under her arm. On a pinboard behind the coffins were Lani's and Maddie's drawings.

There had been so many decisions to be made. Bronwyn and I had conferred each day leading up to the celebration. I was left with the final decisions, including deciding to bury them in Melbourne. I must have known then I might leave Tasmania. I didn't have the heart to tackle the question of how I could possibly stay on without them and I couldn't talk to anyone about it. Everything in my life was in chaos. What could sustain me if I did stay? All of the reasons we had moved to this part of the world had disappeared.

I had to consider the service. The chapel at the Austin Hospital was the logical choice. It was the place where we had met, where we had performed together in all the hospital revues and where, now, we would say goodbye. It was also non-denominational – an important factor in these confusing times – and it was intimate, surrounded by beautiful gardens. The ideal setting for a special celebration – I had decided to call it 'a celebration'. I was mourning a tragic loss, but it had to be different. Netty would have wanted it that way. Someone had to be responsible that everything went smoothly. This was something I couldn't run away from. It would be an event. A happy event that exemplified what they were like. Something that captured the dancing, singing, laughing. Having fun. After all, this was the last thing I could do for them. It had to be good. Lani needed to be able to stand on the balcony at the wake and watch and say to me: 'Dad, can I come along to this, too? Those flowers and the music are so cool.'

I spent some time considering the music for the occasion. The ABBA songs 'Mama Mia' for Maddie, 'Dancing Queen' for Alannah, and Tina Arena's 'Sorrento Moon' for Netty to celebrate my proposal of marriage were much better than mournful tunes.

'Where's the programme?' one woman had asked. Well, it really was a programme. Just what Netty would have wanted. A classy production with Lani's and Maddie's drawings in it. A photo of us together on the front, all done in a high-quality gloss finish.

And now I was standing in front of their coffins listening to Pastor Allan Anderson, looking dapper in a navy blue suit, his dark brown hair manicured. He handled the service expertly with Father Colin

Bourke, who had married Nanette and me. Father Bourke read from the Epistle to the Corinthians – the same reading he had done at our wedding.

'Love is patient, love is kind. It does not envy, it does not boast, it is not proud ... love never fails.'

Allan then addressed the crowd, referring to the impending occasion of Mother's Day:

'Nanette truly portrayed motherhood as she died protecting her children against all odds. As a nation we have had the ability to give our mothers the safest society for their children.'

He spoke of the necessity for changing the gun laws.

'I will read to you words that Walter wrote after what happened. "Time seems to have ground to a halt, minutes feel like days and days feel like years. As we assemble here, we are reminded of questions we often have which are more to do with eternity than they are to do with time. It is here that the question 'Why?' demands our attention and we discover satisfactory answers cannot be found ... It is here our hearts turn to search for the unchanging so we can find security and comfort when all around seems to have changed".'

As I sat listening to his words my body was shaking violently, my leg bouncing up and down uncontrollably. I felt everyone would notice. Making this celebration extraordinary had held my focus in the eleven days that had passed since they had died. Sleeping, eating, nothing had any relevance. I should have taken a Valium. Then I wouldn't be such a mess, but I didn't want anything to dampen my perceptions on that day. It had to stay with me just as I experienced it.

As I listened to the words people spoke about my beloved family, Bronwyn gripped my wrist tightly on one side and Chris McCann clenched my arm on the other. I had been up till late the night before with Allan Anderson. He helped me piece together some of the feelings that I had had to this point. It was my intention to share this with everyone, but I suddenly doubted my capacity to do it. Seven nieces and nephews from Netty's side of the family lit candles. Tears cascaded down my cheeks at the thought of my daughters playing with them all.

I looked at the order of service. Andrew Simmons, the ghost tour supervisor from Port Arthur, was the first to talk about Netty. Within a few lines I found myself smiling as he talked of how she had passed her assessment as a ghost tour guide on 5 September 1995 and how she often complained she was stuck with the 'sticks and the sceptics'.

'I thought this person was a little zany, slightly eccentric, had a good sense of humour and was bright and bubbly,' he said. 'Because she owned the pharmacy, she had access to all the latest products. Once she arrived at work with removable tattoos and her flashing Christmas tree earrings were something to behold. One of the children of another staff member asked Nanette if she'd put nail polish on her lips, they were that shiny.'

Glenice spoke next. Reading from Psalm 23, she battled to hold back her tears.

'Whatever we are to each other, we still are.'

Nanette's other friend, Kate, also spoke. Her daughter Stephanie had played with Alannah at kindergarten when we still lived in Melbourne. 'Nanette,' she said, 'didn't just live life, she exploded through it taking everyone and everything with her. If you were worried about something, Nanette'd say: "Everything works out, Kate, and if it doesn't la-de-dah." Anyone who's read *Peter Pan* will know if you want to fly, you think happy thoughts. That was Nanette's gift. She made you fly.'

Kate said that Stephanie had found it hard to understand what had happened to Lani. But, she told her mother: 'Lani always looked like an angel and now she's a real one.'

Nanette's sister-in-law, Jenny Moulton, spoke of the mud-pack facials Netty insisted on giving her which involved sticking straws up her nose. She also talked about how Nanette had introduced her to Rodney, her brother.

Jenny read the poem I included in the programme and in the professionally made video. Ironically, Nanette's brother sent it to her three weeks before she died. The author is unknown, but the words are beautiful. It's called 'We Did Not Die'. And in my heart I know it is true.

Do not stand at our grave and weep,
We are not there; we do not sleep,
We are a thousand winds that blow.
We are the diamond glints on snow.
We are the sunlight on ripened grain.
We are the gentle autumn's rain.
When you waken in the morning's hush,
We are the swift uplifting rush
Of quiet birds in circled flight.
We are the soft stars that shine at night.
Do not stand at our graves and cry.
We are not there. We did not die.

These intimate words spoken by so many people who knew you all helped soothe the pain. I found myself laughing. Laughing through the tears, momentarily accepting grief. The good and the bad. All-encompassing. This laughter had a mysterious effect on me. I stopped shaking and the tenseness in my arms relaxed. I felt good. Here was someone confirming to the world what I had known from the day I had met Netty. That she was funny, eccentric and a little crazy. Unpredictable. All those mysterious things that make each of us individual. Some of us are more individual than others. Nanette stood at the pinnacle of individuality. As each of our friends spoke of Nanette, Alannah and Madeline, I relaxed further.

Finally Allan Anderson signalled for me to come up to the stage – the same stage we had performed on during the many revues at the hospital. My speech sat folded in the palm of my hand. Allan stood close behind me in case I faltered. Looking out at the assembled crowd, I felt Netty looking over me, giving me the strength I needed.

'During the past ten days, I've had more thoughts than I could have imagined in a lifetime. The one thing I have to focus on is a letter I received from a friend of mine who hasn't yet met a person to share his life with. He said, "It is better to have loved and lost than not to have loved at all".'

'I ask you to quietly hold the hand of the person next to you even though you may not know them – everybody, including those outside, should be able to join with somebody.

'Don't take your partner for granted, don't take your children for granted. Don't take life for granted and last and most importantly – don't take tomorrow for granted.

'The memories flood in. The air I breathe, the sky I see, the soft skin to touch, the bodies to feel at night. The steps I take, the ground I feel. These are the thoughts that come back and they cannot be erased.

'The sounds and noises of every living moment. Remember that the power of love and creation will always triumph over the power of destruction and revenge. Please get on with your lives and live your lives in the spirit of love. It's this spirit that Alannah left me with in her diary. The word that appears in every page is the word "love".

'Did they know how much I really love them? My answer came as I looked through Alannah's drawings. "I love you Mum and Dad and I 'no' [sic] you love me. Love Alannah."

'My soul was instantly buoyed and I felt as though I was a dove that had been set free. Love is celebrated when it begins and mourned when it finishes, but let not the love and laughter of Nanette, Alannah and Madeline ever be forgotten. Celebrate life and let it continue.'

As the pall-bearers carried the coffins up the aisle, women carrying Alannah and Maddie and men, including my two brothers, carrying Netty, ABBA's 'Dancing Queen' trumpeted loudly from the loud-speakers set high in the chapel wall. As Netty's coffin was lowered into the hearse, the music reached a crescendo. It was a fitting final exit.

A lone piper played 'Scotland the Brave' and joined Pastor Allan Anderson, Wilma Righi from the funeral directors, and Father Bourke

The family at White Beach near Nubeena, Tasmania, in February 1993 on our first trip to visit Netty's parents.

Me and my girls outside Hastings Caves in southern Tasmania in January 1996, three months before they died. Alannah's proud hold on her dad's arm and Maddie's innocent face say it all.

Alannah and Maddie before we moved to Tasmania. Alannah's last entry in her Pocahontas diary on 16.4.96 was, 'My sister is a fantastic sister. I love her. I love her with all of my heart.'

Alannah, aged three, in the back garden of our house at Montmorency. She had watched a video of Peter Pan and wanted to describe imagination. Having painted her body, she was ready to fly.

Alannah, aged six, with Barbie top and handbag. The little 'Future Miss Australia'. She had an amazing comprehension of life and was ready to conquer all.

The look on Netty's face I treasure most — her pride in being a mother.

Maddie at Hobart airport in November 1995 after my brother Steven visited. Her transition from baby to a unique little person was just beginning. 'Me too, me too' was the oft-repeated demand.

Two excited little munchkins in bed with their nanny, Grace, on Christmas Day 1994 — our first at Nubeena. Grace died only three months before Nanette, Lani and Maddie.

Netty and I in a congratulatory hug outside the Tasman Pharmacy in September 1994.
A life-changing decision to move to Tasmania would mean a better lifestyle
and a safe place to bring up the children.

Nanette, the ghost tour guide, in full flight performing for her audience in October 1995.
'I feel that I'm really needed. I'm doing something I love and getting paid to do it.'
She always wore her shiny patent leather Esprit shoes.

A relaxed family portrait after walking to the Byron Bay lighthouse in April 1995. Netty's contented look is mirrored by Maddie picking her nose and Lani and I holding hands.

'Breakfast with the Stars' at Movieworld in April 1995, our last big holiday together. The excited faces looking forward to a great day together.

Sisterly love. Lani and Maddie in my uncle's garden at Easter 1995. The girls were always Netty's first consideration – pride in their appearance meant everything to her.

Time spent together. The girls and I getting to know 'Joey' the wallaby at Freycinet Peninsula on Tasmania's east coast in October 1995. Netty always referred to our trips away as 'our little adventures'.

The convict family on the verandah at our house in Nubeena in December 1995. Taken just before Net and girls went to Hobart for the Christmas pageant.

What I have lost…

LEFT: *Nanette, a stunningly gorgeous bridesmaid at a friend's wedding in 1992.*
BELOW: *Alannah and Maddie wearing their Christmas presents on Boxing Day 1995 in front of the penitentiary at Port Arthur. The historic site was one of Netty's favourite spots for picnics.*

In
Loving Memory
– of –
NANETTE PATRICIA MIKAC
NEE MOULTON
8. 4. 1960 – 28. 4. 1996
AGED 36 YEARS.
ALANNAH LOUISE MIKAC
28. 8. 1989 – 28. 4. 1996
AGED 6 YEARS.
MADELINE GRACE MIKAC
15. 8. 1992 – 28. 4. 1996
AGED 3 YEARS.
ALL DIED TRAGICALLY
AT PORT ARTHUR, TASMANIA
CHERISHED WIFE AND
ADORED DAUGHTERS
OF WALTER
MY LOVE FOR YOU WILL NE...
GRACE...

'My love for you will never die' – the inscription to my family on the headstone at Warringal Cemetery, Heidelberg. Lying on the granite grave gives me strength and inspiration to continue.

as they walked slowly in front of the hearses on their way to the cemetery, the last journey for my beloved family before their final resting place.

At the cemetery, the piper played 'Amazing Grace' and large crowds gathered around the cavity in the ground, the coffins resting next to them. Their faces and tears said it all.

White doves were released, representing the presence of the Holy Spirit of God. One by one, the coffins were lowered one on top of the other after being given their final earthly blessing. I kissed a perfumed red rose for each of them and dropped them into the grave. As I was doing so, I said the words that now appear on the headstone – 'My love for you will never die.' More flowers were dropped onto the coffins from Bronwyn, Daniel, Keith, my mother and brothers.

'Return to the earth from whence they came the bodies of Nanette, Alannah and Madeline,' Allan said.

When Grace knew she was going to die, she visited the cemetery with you, Netty, to see where she would be buried. I took a photo of you and Grace in the cemetery, less than two years before your deaths. Grace is holding her oxygen bottle. It is eerie looking at it now you are both no longer here and knowing that you are in that spot under the ground.

There were so many people who wanted to share the grief. After a while I became so nonplussed that I was simply pushing my arm out to shake people's hands. Things were getting hazy.

The hospital had kindly catered for afternoon tea, so many people gathered there. There was reminiscing and lots of old stories. Many of the staff from the Austin Hospital headed for the old watering hole, the Old England Hotel in Heidelberg, for a memorial drink. My body was drained of being, but I knew that our goal had been achieved and everything had been as Netty would have wanted. Now some 200 out of the 2000 who attended were heading back to my parents' place. The support shown to our family was amazing, with people bringing food, wine, drinks, flowers. It brought the entire community together. My parents' friends from the Istrian Australian Social Club catered for the occasion.

Everyone was sitting around the table quietly. Old stories were told and toasts made. We even managed some music later into the evening. Allan stayed for a few hours. Upstairs, a small group of my closest friends and family toasted each of the girls with a small glass of kruskovac, a pear liqueur from Croatia. We toasted the dogs, family and close friends. We could sense their presence quite strongly. In five minutes, most of the liqueur had gone. Then another bottle materialised.

At around 1 a.m., Chris, Steve and John carried me to the bed I had slept in as a child. They undressed me carefully and I slipped into unconsciousness.

After the funeral I received mail from everywhere celebrating my speech and a plethora of religious material – pamphlets, cassettes, books and poems.

'You have such strength and faith.' 'Your faith is incredible.'

Faith is a very mercurial concept to me at the moment. People want to misconstrue my simple message: to live each day with purpose and enjoy what you have around you.

Do I have faith? Spiritually, I feel bankrupt and alone, even though I go through the motions of attending Mass with my parents. My prayers are met with a great wall of silence. The same sort of silence I find so unnerving when I am in the car driving along without music to accompany me. When I reach out to God for explanations of what has happened, I hear nothing in return. I still seek comfort from the Serenity prayer as it makes sense to me and is a prayer I have grown up with.

'God give me serenity to accept the things that I cannot change. Courage to change the things that I can and wisdom to know the difference.'

I know I cannot change the fact that they are gone. And I suppose I still believe there is a God, or at least a guiding force. But do I have faith?

People try to comfort me with cliches about seeing my loved ones again in heaven. I remember Les Morton, one of the fathers whose child was killed at Dunblane, telling me he was an atheist. He also told me about Michael North, another father who had lost his wife to cancer and then his daughter in the Dunblane massacre. He was also an atheist.

He had engraved on his daughter Sophie's grave: 'Still smiling somewhere.'

Did it need to be in heaven?

There is an assumption that people turn to religion, particularly the Christian religion, at times of bereavement or serious illness. In doing so, religion dictates how people in these circumstances should behave. Religion offers a panacea, but only within its own rules and codes even though these may be out of touch with what's happening in the real world. Like the advice Netty and I received when we got married and Father Bourke suggested we use the rhythm method for birth control. Netty was furious. Imagine trying to tell two health professionals, or anyone for that matter, what they should do for contraception.

These codes are also open for interpretation. There are parts of the Bible which tell you that you can use any means at your disposal to make your wife obey you.

Religion is contrived, a concept that man has thought up. It's not a physical fact, like the formation of the earth's crust. Religion is a subjective belief which has various levels of commitment.

Some people believe simply by going to church each Sunday they have fulfilled their commitment.

I've often had this argument with my mother.

'Have you been to Mass?' she asks. I say: 'Mum, I do believe going to Mass is important. But what the hell does it matter if I go to Mass on Sunday if I don't leave the church and put it into practice?' I try to put into practice the adage 'Do unto others as you would have done unto you'.

No matter how committed anyone is, the greatest difficulty I think religion faces is how to deal with the reasons for evil.

Jenny Hasell, one of the mothers from Dunblane whose son, Kevin, was killed, wrote me a card. It had angels on the front:

The rain is pouring down making me look at the outside world and I start thinking where our strength to carry on lies. I think I believe in God and then I wonder about all the evil that goes on in our earth.

Worse than any of the misguided messages I received was the vitriolic and painful explanation given by a lofty source within the church and reprinted in a newspaper article.

The words came from Rev Douglas Milne, a professor of theology from South Yarra, and appeared in a pamphlet delivered to all Presbyterian churches in Victoria.

It was significant that the killings had happened on a Sunday, he said, the Sabbath 'when we should be in churches. Church attendance in Australia was at an all-time low. Is it any wonder that such things happen?'

Sunday trading, alternative lifestyles, social engineering, promiscuity, abortion and the greed of the 'Me Generation' were also sins which led to God's wrath.

'It is sin that is the root explanation of the events of that late April Sunday afternoon in Port Arthur and why these kind of events happen,' he said.

God had allowed the evil to happen at Port Arthur, according to Rev. Milne, as a warning that tragedies would get more horrific unless people changed and turned to God.

I drafted a letter of response to the church, disgusted and angry and hurt inside at such a message:

I find it profoundly offensive to suggest that the deaths of 35 innocent people, including three- and six-year old girls who both regularly attended Sunday School, would be used to justify such a claim from a so-called Christian church.

I can only say that the article obviously represents the views of a minority of Christians because we all received enormous compassion, sympathy and support from many Christians and other churches.'

And all this in the name of God.

Three days after the funeral, Nanette came to me in my dreams. We were at the wake and I saw her standing at the bottom of my parents' stairs. She was wearing a striped top I hadn't seen before and a short black skirt. She looked like she'd lost weight, like she'd been at a health farm. Her hair was cut. I walked towards her down the stairs.

'It's so good to see you back. You look great,' I said.

'What are all these people doing here?' she asked.

'They've come to welcome you back,' I answered.

TWELVE

Guns and Pyjamas

I enter the gun debate without even realising it. Two days after the massacre, I am talking about guns and how they can maim and kill with Ray Martin on 'A Current Affair'. I am sitting in the garden at Nubeena wearing Nanette's Sportsgirl blue sloppy-joe and Alannah's blue velvet headband is around my wrist. I've sprayed Nanette's perfume on the headband and every so often, I bring it up to my face to get the scent. Sometimes, I simply twist it around. I am surprised when I watch myself now on the video, how agitated I am. I am shaking uncontrollably and I hardly recognise my voice, it is so high and strained. I look up sometimes without comprehension as the questions are asked. Sometimes, I cry on camera and other times I laugh, seeking relief, seeking to escape. I am not myself, I am like a cornered rabbit.

How long was I in that state?

I must have known even then that I needed to be strong. To speak out about why this should never have been allowed to happen.

Ray Martin asked me what I would say to the man who committed this deed. I was sitting on our bed, I reached under the pillows and clutched Nanette's and the girls' pyjamas. Their socks were there, too, Netty's pink bed socks and Maddie's striped green ones and Alannah's bottle-green Tassie devil ones.

These belongings seemed to me to represent the essence of what I had lost. They weren't coming back.

'The only thing I could possibly say to him is, ''I cannot believe what has happened'' ... I'd show him the pyjamas of my wife and two daughters and ask him; ''How can I possibly live without them?'''

Guns and pyjamas such opposites – hard and soft, impersonal and intimate. Mirroring my feelings – tough and crumbling, I had to muster my strength to continue the interview.

I falter.

'I can honestly say I have never owned a gun or needed to own a gun. The main reason I'm talking to you is that I want to pass on the message to change the gun legislation to prevent such a thing ever happening again. I hope to God no person ever has to go through this again ... I just want to plead with every person. If everyone does a little bit to make sure this doesn't ever happen again – something can be done. Everyone has to lobby a politician. What I'd really love to do is to make a fund to buy every possible weapon there is in Australia and have a big meltdown ... but that's probably being too idealistic.'

In those six weeks after the shooting, time blurred. After the funeral there was no focus. I was too exhausted to do anything. I didn't need to go anywhere.

I was staying at my parents' house in Macleod, in the study where there was a spare bed. My suitcase was open on my old bedside table. Mum did my washing and I joined the family for dinner each night. My mother was pleased to have me under her wing. We shared coffees during the day and talked about the girls. But I missed my own house and my animals, the cat and two dogs. For ten years I'd lived in my own house with my own family and now I was living back with my parents. I had to work on our relationship as we were living in such close proximity. I was used to independence and now, I was being asked to justify when I would be home for dinner or if I'd be home at all. Often I couldn't give an answer. After all, I was thirty-four years old.

Thankfully, the Tasmanian Branch of the Pharmacy Guild of Australia had set up a benevolent fund which would look after the running of my pharmacy until I was able to return. Pharmacists from all over Australia showed such generosity and support, making me extremely proud of my profession.

At the back of my mind was the need to get enough courage to return to Tasmania. But when? I was confused and apprehensive about going back on my own. I was also scared at the prospect of going back to the pharmacy and the house where we lived with so many memories. What should I do? I know it's a beautiful spot, but without my family, it had no meaning. So many decisions to make and now I had to make them on my own.

In this state of bewilderment, the gun debate gathered momentum. I was in a vortex and spiralling out of control.

I had said those words on television without knowing what I felt about guns or weapons, I didn't want to be aligned to any group. In those early days, I was speaking from the heart. It seemed to me that the world was out of control. How could we live in a society that didn't care about the consequences? I had no idea you could buy weapons such as assault rifles and semi-automatics through a news-paper. When a journalist from Channel Nine, bought a semi-automatic rifle and semi-automatic shotgun from a dealer without a licence, explaining he was from interstate, I was horrified. Just as disconcerting were the people who opposed more control. I heard of a petition circulating on the Tasman Peninsula with 200 signatures saying they didn't want stricter gun laws.

Man-made technology that is designed to kill; how successfully it performed that day at Port Arthur. At the court case I shudder when the video is played to demonstrate the rapidity of the firing. It took fifteen seconds to kill twelve people, inflict grievous bodily harm upon one and wound nine. No-one stood a chance. Those people who were in the Broad Arrow Cafe that day were at the mercy of the trigger and those left behind still have the memories of watching those people die. I can see a terror in their eyes when they talk about it, it's a terror which I think will never leave them. They have looked down the barrel. They appreciate the fragility of life.

Gaye and John Fidler wrote a personal account of what happened that day which they gave to me. Gaye was once a customer of mine at Watsonia in Melbourne and I had gone to school with their children. Twice the gunman walked right up to John and miraculously, although he was injured, he was not killed. Gaye believes the gunman was aiming at John when he killed Kevin, another member of their party.

John wrote in his account; 'The whole time I was watching the gunman, he showed no emotion at all. He didn't talk, frown, yell – he just deliberately walked up to people and shot them, firing from the hip. He only had a blank look on his face, he said nothing and as I watched him walk towards our group which was about six to eight steps, there was no movement in his eyes. He was looking straight at me, and walking, not running, as if he knew we couldn't do anything to him. He just kept shooting and walking.'

How could someone, one person, cause such devastation? Surely the politicians of Tasmania and Australia are elected to protect their constituents? Even my old friend Chris McCann, after sixteen years in the police force, spoke publicly on the gun debate. He ended up leaving the force because he felt so strongly about the need for gun control.

So what could I do about it? Ironically, the girls' funeral was the day before the national gun summit.

On the plane going back to Melbourne for the funeral, I decided to write a letter to the Prime Minister, Mr John Howard. We left Hobart just over a week after the shooting. I had to wait for the police to give us clearance to release the bodies of Lani, Maddie and Nanette. That was finally done on the Friday. I was drinking a Scotch and Coke and decided to listen to the news on the headphones.

Despite the events more than a week ago at the Port Arthur Historic site where 35 people were shot dead, not all of the states will fall into line on the issue of reforming the guns laws, especially those relating to semi-automatic weapons. Police Ministers are expected to meet on May 10 to discuss the matter.

I couldn't believe the politicians could not agree to take a hard line. I owe it to you, Netty, and to Lani and Maddie to make sure this doesn't happen again.

I began to compose my letter to the Prime Minister. I had wanted to talk to him at the service at St David's three days after the massacre. I knew he was there, but I was too overcome with grief to tackle such a subject. Up until then, I had been thinking of the arrangements for the funeral, how I was affected and how I was going to cope. Now, I would have to make a stand, I would have to fight so that their lives were not lost in vain.

Jo Winter, who obviously felt the same, made an appeal to television viewers that they should become actively involved, not just sit in their lounge-rooms watching TV. They should march in the streets to prove things can be changed and that they care. No-one should ever have to go through what she and her family had suffered, she said. Going to bed every night with tears in her eyes and such unresolved pain, Jo asked whether people were going to wait until everyone was affected by such an event for the guns laws to be changed.

Dear Mr Howard,

As the person who lost his wife and two daughters at Port Arthur I am writing to you to give you the strength to ensure no person in Australia ever has to suffer such a loss. I watched the news report this morning on the plane from Hobart to Melbourne (where my family will be buried) on new legislation concerning gun laws. I applaud your resolve and every Australian will be proud of your leadership in this matter. All I can say is there must be enough of a penalty against possession of such horrific weapons. The one-off tax to buy back such weapons is a price I'm sure every Australian would gladly pay manyfold. A small price for safety. With all my heart, I implore you to restore Australia to being the best place in the world.

Walter Mikac (Pharmacist, Husband, Father)

The night before the funeral I got a late-night phone call. Someone in the family answered the phone.

'It's Mr Howard, the Prime Minister. He wants to speak to you.'

I thought at first it was a joke.

But it was his voice. 'I want you to know I am sticking to my stance on the gun legislation and I will keep my promise to make something happen.'

Those few words I had written from the heart had reached their mark. Someone was listening. I should keep fighting.

It took several weeks before I ventured out to a social occasion where there were strangers. So many dark and destructive thoughts filled my head, I didn't know how I could talk to people.

Maybe I should have stayed at home, I thought, as I entered the crowded room. I wasn't ready to go out. Someone asked me to dance, but told me she had a boyfriend. I didn't know what to say. I wasn't used to dancing with strangers. I wanted Netty. I didn't know what to do.

When my brothers saw my reaction to 'Dancing Queen', one of the first songs to be played, they came over to me immediately for support, the way they have so often done since, trying to ease my anxiety. They stood behind my chair that night, ready to bolster my sagging morale, knowing they might have to get me through many hurdles.

My brothers write me a card. On the front is a picture of the earth, dry and cracking, and some red flowers growing in the cracks. On the front of the card, it reads: 'There are defining moments in a life ... when faced with the choice of giving up or going on.'

Inside they have written:

Dear Walter,

We think you are an incredible person and we are fortunate to be your brothers. We thank you for all the times that you have helped us and for the care and concern you have shown us.

We admire the way you have become a man. A true gentleman. We believe in you. We have probably never told you how much we look up to you and think, 'There is a man who loves his family, who does everything for his wife and children, to make them happy, and is very happy doing it.' You really are a fantastic role model for your brothers and any other parent.

There will probably never be a sadder time in your life than now – for anything and everything you ever created with your love for Nanette has been taken from you to another place. This does not mean that your love for Nanette, Alannah and Madeline has gone or that theirs for you has gone either. The love you have can never be taken from you. They will still be with you in your thoughts, prayers and memories.

As we stood there last Thursday [at the funeral] we both thought how hard it would be to string a sentence together, but you got up and gave a speech that did stop a nation. For anyone who hadn't cried until this point they could do nothing but cry. We were so proud to be your brothers as we stood in awe of your strength and resolve, that day we both got a new real life hero.

At this time of immense pain we offer our hands to hold on to and to comfort you. We offer our shoulders to lean on. We want you to know that you will have our support in whatever you do now and in the future. If you need our help, we will be there.

We love you in a way only brothers can love and we cherish the bond we have between the three of us.

Love Steve and John.

Confusion over my new status as a single person followed me everywhere. The first time I went out to a pub with my brothers, I kept thinking, 'I don't belong here. I'm married. I don't feel the need to come here.' I'd been with one person for so long, it became my way of thinking.

The Depot, in the Melbourne suburb of Richmond, is a corner pub with a beer garden, live music and pool tables. It was my brothers' regular Sunday night haunt. I remember ringing from Tasmania one Sunday evening to speak to my parents and being told my brothers were out at a nightclub. I couldn't understand why. Six weeks after the shooting here I was with them. I was drinking beer after beer. At about 9 p.m. I realised I was quite drunk. I tried to crawl up on the stage. I wanted to sing, but in trying to reach the mike, I accidentally knocked over the keyboard. The bouncers asked Steve and John to take me outside. As they carried me away from the entrance to the Depot, I vomited. The next morning I only had a vague recollection of what happened. It was another world, the world inhabited by those who were single, a world I knew little about.

I wanted to get away, but I didn't know where. It had to be somewhere where there were no memories. Nanette and I had been planning on going to New Zealand at the end of the year. I had spoken on the phone a few times to Jo Winter in Auckland, after meeting her at the State memorial service in Hobart.

For her husband Jason's memorial service on 4 May I had sent a stuffed Big Bird toy in a floral basket as Jason was colourblind and yellow was the only colour he could see. I rang Jo to ask if it would be all right to come over and she said I was more than welcome.

As I booked my ticket I was filled with a sense of apprehension. I had only met Jo for half an hour under such strange circumstances and here I was boarding a plane to spend ten days in a strange country with people I hardly knew. Well, I reasoned, I could always get on the plane and come back home again.

The New Zealand trip helped my healing process. This was one of the first decisions I'd made since the funeral, and its success boosted my confidence. It gave me the courage I needed to return to Tasmania.

When I flew into Hobart from Melbourne several weeks later, my Pajero was still at the airport and I got behind the wheel and drove down to Nubeena.

* * *

I had been back in Nubeena for a few weeks when I saw Roland Browne on television speaking about getting rid of semi-automatic weapons. He was Co-ordinator for the Tasmanian Coalition for Gun Control. Since 1987 he had repeatedly been warning the community about an impending disaster. An earnest and sincere speaker, he impressed me immediately with his message. He was not emotional, but clear and composed and seemed full of common sense.

'There are still too many weapons in the community which are able to be accessed by people who are going to abuse them,' he said.

Just a month before the Port Arthur massacre, he wrote these prophetic words to the local newspaper:

> If we want to avoid Scotland's grief [the Dunblane massacre] then I suggest Tasmanian politicians note firstly that people in this state can presently get access to high-powered and semi-automatic weapons and, secondly, that the man responsible for the Dunblane shooting would, prior to the massacre, have undoubtedly been granted a gun licence in Tasmania.
>
> In the absence of prior convictions or mental health problems, a gun licence would not be refused. We should tighten up our gun laws now and not wait for the inevitable judicial inquiry if a Dunblane-type massacre occurs here. Prevention is better than cure.

Roland's words spurred me into action. Even though my personal life was in chaos, I discovered I still had some strength in reserve. I decided to ring him. Roland suggested a press conference to put pressure on Tasmania's Upper House who were sitting the following week to discuss the gun legislation. No, I don't want to do that, I said right away. Get me their names and phone numbers and I'll go and see them personally. But as the days passed, I realised it was time I made a stand.

Before the conference on 19 July at Hobart's Westside Hotel, I left Roland and my brother Steve in an upstairs room and walked out onto the balcony roof. I felt in a daze.

'Please give me the conviction to get through this one, Netty. This is really important,' I said quietly.

I realised as I walked into that hotel room to face the twenty-five members of the media the enormity of what I was doing, I felt like a lamb going to the slaughter and I was more than a little scared. People in the pro-gun lobby were so emotional they might resort to any means to defend the ownership of their weapons. I was exceedingly anxious about questions that might re-open old wounds. But Roland had the media under control. Only questions relating to the gun debate could be asked, he told them flatly.

I read from a page of notes and I gained confidence as I realised how important my message was and how persuasive I could be. I said that I would prefer to be in my pharmacy at Nubeena, but a sense of frustration had brought me out of my private hell. I called for the Federal Government to hold a referendum to give the Commonwealth powers over firearms.

'The blame would have to be apportioned both electorally and morally if something as terrible as the Port Arthur massacre should happen again,' I said.

The week after the first anniversary I had dinner with Roland Browne and his partner Kate Calwell at their house in inner-city Hobart. We ate roast lamb and potatoes as he spoke of his passion to rid the world of firearms. Kate later played her cello. We talked about the fact that the Tasmanian government could have banned semi-auto-matic rifles much earlier. He told me the Guns Bill was still before Parliament when seven people were killed in the Strathfield massacre in Sydney. As early as January 1993 the Police Minister, Dr Frank Maddill, had the power to ban these rifles and he did nothing.

We discussed some of the views of the local politicians. The West Devon MLC, Des Hiscutt, for instance, who told the Legislative Council that by burying their guns, the owners would be able to keep prohibited weapons in the family without getting fined.

'He was asked if he'd buried any guns,' Roland said. 'Do you know what? Hiscutt said he couldn't get any PVC pipe, as they were sold out, but he told everyone to use it to bury the guns on Crown land or in a remote area of their property.'

'I can't believe he said that,' I said.

Nanette's father, Keith, obviously felt the same outrage I did. He wrote a letter to the local newspaper.

'I dearly wish that a certain gun used at Port Arthur had been placed underground before we had to place my daughter and two granddaughters in that position.'

On 23 July 1996 I laid flowers on the steps of Parliament House in Hobart with gun control supporters and families and friends of victims. The previous Saturday, 3000 shooters had rallied to urge the Legislative Council to reject the tougher laws. I sat in the public gallery listening to the politicians debating the uniform national gun laws. I was astounded at how ridiculous their arguments were and the number of amendments they proposed to the legislation. But I couldn't believe the local member for the Tasman Peninsula, Steven Wilson, moving that the preamble – which stated the reasons the bill had come about was because of the massacre – be removed.

As I sat there, Netty, on that wooden bench watching the stupidity of these people who were responsible for running this State, who had been elected by the people, I knew I had to leave Tasmania. Even after all these deaths, so many of them were only protecting their own interests. Could this be the will of the people who live on this island?

I have never owned a gun and foolishly thought that was the case with most people around me. I thought that guns were the domain of people serving in the armed forces or farmers needing them on the land. How wrong I was.

At the three-month anniversary on 28 July, I laid wreaths on the steps of Melbourne's Parliament House, at a memorial service organised by the Coalition for Gun Control. They were heart-shaped wreaths of pink roses, cornflowers, jonquils and irises each with a letter to my girls.

To Nanette, I wrote: 'To my darling Nanette. My love for you will never die.'

By 11 a.m. that same day, I was in Sydney facing a Coalition for Gun Control Rally in the Domain, across the road from the Art Gallery. It was winter and it had been raining, so it was boggy under foot. The 3000 people who attended were given yellow helium-filled balloons which stood out against the grey skies and the greenery of the park. Cheryl Kernot, the leader of the Democrats, spoke, as did Keith Woollard, President of the Australian Medical Association, and a number of other people. Meeting Rebecca Peters, the Chair of the National Coalition for Gun Control, was daunting. She is an intense, slightly built person with short-cropped brown hair and steel-rimmed glasses. That first time we met, her mobile phone rang constantly. It was something, I realised when I got to know her better, that dominated her life, along with her obsession with gun control. She had spent six years as a journalist with ABC radio before completing a law degree driven by a desire to make society a better place. She told the audience that 600 people on average were killed by gunfire in Australia each year.

The issue of gun control was gripping the nation. Only a few weeks before the Prime Minister had addressed a pro-gun rally in Sale in Victoria wearing a bullet-proof vest.

I had to play my part. I was nervous when I looked out at the number of people that were there. When my turn came, I cleared my throat and pretended I was speaking at the local Rotary dinner:

I have come here to talk to you about a very simple topic. One that we may often sub-consciously not even think about or possibly consider changing. Something that is at our very core of survival ... Australians should not forget the magnitude of what happened at Port Arthur three months ago. If all the dead and injured were standing here on this stage today there would be precious little room for me ... there are thirty-five people who no longer have the ability to improve this country, but have somehow left a little candle flickering in every one of us. It becomes a case of considering how we can stand up to represent them. Reassessing priorities and not being diverted from what is important in life ... We all have the potential to change what and how things happen in this great country. I ask you in honour of those who died and those who are left behind with their memories, please make Australia a better place to live.

Letters came from far and wide to congratulate me on the stand I had taken on the gun issue. Among them were letters from a fringe element of society saying I was doing the wrong thing. One letter, from the wife of a Queensland politician, said that her husband owned a gun and that if we all gave up our weapons, they would end up in Asia where they could be used when we were invaded by the Yellow Peril. Another accused me of being a pawn in the hands of the anti-gun lobby, a mere puppet who was being manipulated. It was an unexpected sentiment that was levelled at me during the gun debate. *I* had approached Roland Browne, not the other way around, and I had clear reasons as to why I wanted these guns banned.

But perhaps the sweetest victory was when I opened the local paper, *The Heidelberger*, at my parents' house on 14 August and saw the advertisement.

> Firearm laws have changed. For all Victorians, from 2 July 1996, it is illegal to use: Semi-automatic centre fire rifles, pump-action shotguns, semi-automatic rim fire rifles and semi-automatic shotguns. Hand in these firearms and compensation will be paid on the spot.

All over Australia, mainly men, handed in their weapons. Some, said one newspaper, were even crying.

It was a step in the right direction. I'd made sure they hadn't died in vain.

THIRTEEN

Is Anyone Home?

The dogs are barking as I drive the Pajero into our driveway in Nubeena. The scene is exactly as it was when I lived here with my family, but their souls have disappeared. I want to call out 'Is anyone home?', but I know it's pointless. As I turn the handle of the front door, I have an overwhelming feeling of despair.

There are no aromas of delights cooking on the stove, no radio is playing and there are no sounds of laughter. The house is silent, the same as it was that Sunday seven weeks ago when they were killed. I wanted to be alone on my return to the house, even though my parents have come with me from Melbourne to offer support. I hoped by being alone I would get a sense of their spirit still in the house, even though I knew they wouldn't physically be there.

Our baby photos are one of the first things I see when I walk into the lounge-room. The largest photo is of Nanette in a pram surrounded by her sisters and brothers. Then there is one of me, in a white romper suit, holding a chrysanthemum in my parents' backyard. I stare at the photo of Lani. She is wearing Netty's straw hat with flowers near the brim and she has her hand under her chin. Lastly there is Maddie with her six-month-old smile, an Esprit dress and matching headband. I kiss each one of them in turn, my lips touching the cold glass inside the frame.

I walk over to the window. The view of the bay holds my gaze for a moment. But not like before. Now it seems beautiful for beauty's sake. The emptiness is excruciating. Where once it was paradise, now it is ordinary. I call out their names, waiting for an answer. I pick up the video camera, wanting to record each moment, each memory, walking from room to room talking to each of them in between tears.

What will I do about the clothes, the beds, jewellery, everything? Even your toothbrushes are still in the holder. And the toys? I can see the pink 'Future Miss Australia' sign with the gold ballet shoes hanging on Alannah's door and her Barbie playhouse still with the kitchen set up. Inside Maddie's bedroom, her plastic teapot is on her bedside table, the same pot from which we'd shared hundreds of cups of imaginary tea. How I wish I could share just one cup with you, Maddie.

Lani, how wonderful it would be to watch you play Nintendo again. Or lie on your bed and watch the football on television while you did the sums I set you. You loved learning. I'm so glad we'd instilled that in you. I pick up your school journal and pore over the last entry, dated Friday 26.4.96: 'I went to a performance and I got to go up on the stage. He spun me around. I got a balloon and it is pink. The end.'

In your school writings, I find one you wrote when you were only five. 'Wot [sic] is it like in heaven? Can you move in heaven?'

I wonder what prompted you to write this. Did you, like your mother, have some inkling as to your future?

When I see the words you wrote on your whiteboard that last morning of your life I wonder what you were thinking. I still have the board and although the words are faded they send a shudder up my spine:

Alannah Mikac
Sunday 28.4.96:
sleeping
gardening
cicling [sic]
playing

All things every child has a right to do, but your right has been taken away from you. You had a thirst for knowledge that would last all your life. There were still so many things I wanted to teach you. Algebra and science. Bonsai and golf. We were always a great team together with so much of life to experience and much laughter to share. You are my star.

Some letters from your school were waiting when I got back. They made me cry. The teacher wrote: 'Alannah stood out in a crowd with all her bright dresses and her bright personality. Let's remember Alannah as someone who was extremely happy and, in turn, made us feel the same way. She was someone we all loved.'

And Susan: 'Alannah was my friend. We played games and it was fun. She had a lamb. I liked it when Alannah's mum and Maddie worked at the canteen.'

And Richard: 'Alannah said she wanted to be a dancer when she grew up. She won't be able to be a dancer now, but she'll always be in our hearts.'

And the funny one from Grace Paton: 'Alannah was my best friend and Maddy was like a little sister. Alannah told me a rhyme. It went like this:

Pardon me for being so rude,
It was not me, it was my food.
It got so lonely down below,
It just came up to say hello.'

There were letters about you too, Maddie. Maria from Grade 5/6 wrote: 'Madeline, I feel sorry for not much life.'

Many of the children also wrote about how you helped Netty at the canteen on Tuesdays.

Every time I watch the video of the funeral, Maddie, and see your date of birth, I am pained by what little time you had on this earth. It is there on the headstone, too, an agonising reminder. For most people, 1992 is the very recent past. For you it was the year you came into the world, only to leave so soon afterwards. At least I was able to spend so much time with you. We couldn't have packed any more in.

Maddie, you were such a determined little darling. I knew whenever I headed outside, you'd be two foot behind. Your little rainbow gumboots are sitting unused by the back door in the hope that one day I'll walk outside and you'll be standing in them. I remember the afternoon teas that we'd have on the sandstone blocks. A plate of assorted, chopped up fruit and red cordial with the dogs hovering nearby. Playing games of snap and you turning six or seven cards over to get a match. Holding you on my lap while we watched 'Gladiators' and your bony little bottom wriggling incessantly. As for you, 'Netty Petty' Mikac, how do I live without the voice that has given me so much strength and love over the years? I listen to you on the video tapes I replay over and over. That laugh, that deep throaty chuckle. On one of the tapes, you are strolling through a grove of trees with Kate, who was visiting from Melbourne with her daughter Stephanie.

I say: 'Here comes a couple of walnuts,' and you are laughing with me.

I look through the bedside drawer, filming your belongings. I need to touch some of your things. The bat earrings, black with coloured stones across them, earrings with dangling globes of the world and the charm bracelet so heavy with all the charms you collected and I gave you. The wacky pens and all the cards and letters that I sent. You were the person who put up with my stubbornness, my snoring and my idiosyncrasies. Okay, sometimes I slept on the trundle bed so you could get some sleep and with Lani and Maddie in bed, too, there often wasn't enough room for me. Guide me through the darkness I'm in at the moment. I am so scared that the memories will fade and disappear.

I heard from your old friend, Louise, the other day. She sent me a letter saying how much she remembers the parties we had when we were courting. She remembers screaming around the ward at the Austin Hospital with you sitting on top of the drug trolley singing: 'We are the tarts with the carts and bring the pills for the dills.'

You brought so much joy and humour to people's lives.

Louise also wrote: 'Your words spoken at the funeral are being repeated in workplaces, in my friends' homes, at the shopping centre. I don't know where you are getting it from, but you are giving people something to hold on to, to look forward to – when it's easy just to be angry and feel like the world really is a bad place.'

I lie gently on our bed curling up like a deserted kitten. Alone and scared. What would I do with my life now?

If I pack up this house, I will never be able to come back and revisit how things were the last time I saw you. As I stand here, I look around at what our life looked like the day you all left forever. What should I do? Can I keep it like this? Some people who have lost a child keep the bedroom exactly as it was before their child died. But I have not lost one member of the family, I have lost them all. It is not just one room of the house, it is everywhere. Bath toys are still in the bathroom, Vegemite and snack packs of chips in the cupboard, *Aladdin* and *Lion King* videos are still in the cabinet next to the TV. Every door I open reminds me of you.

I am at Lindsay's house, writing this book for you. The memories of that day are still so strong. I am surrounded by boxes filled with precious things from our life together. Locks of your hair in pink and red ribbons. When I touch them, they still have the same texture I remember. I gulp in the scent of your perfume. I will never wash your pyjamas, even though they are becoming musty, they still smell of all of you. I pick up Alannah's journals and her diary and gaze at the red hearts that are scattered throughout its pages. So much love to give.

As I walk from room to room, I realise I can't live in a mausoleum. I think I knew the day after you were all killed that I couldn't continue living here. At the beginning, the decision to leave and to physically pack up my old life was too difficult. I still feel so confused. I know I have to get on with my life. But then, if I pack up this house, everything I want to preserve will vanish. People keep telling me not to make any life-changing decisions. How can I live in this house without them? How long can I remain in a state of suspended animation?

Across the dining-room window, there is a sign written by Kate and Sophie, Eddie's children. It reads: 'Welcome home Walter.' I stand for a while contemplating the words. Is this my home any more? And if this is not my home, where is it? Should I go back to Melbourne? In 1994 when we packed up and left, I didn't think I would be returning. We were leaving the city behind for a better quality of life. Now they are gone, what does this life have to offer? Perhaps I should return to the house I still own in Montmorency, our children's first home, the first home we ever owned. Should I go back to Melbourne where I had friends and family?

For the first few weeks after the funeral, I revisited the places in Melbourne that meant something to us, trying to recapture some of the spirit we shared. I was like a traveller searching for some meaning in my life, moving from place to place in an eternal quest. I went to St Theresa's church in Essendon. The sun shone as it did on our wedding day more than ten years ago. I stood on the steps and imagined the exuberant, smiling faces of our relatives and friends. You looked so beautiful that day, Netty. I was proud and wanted the whole world to see it.

I sat on the nature strip in front of the Amityville Horror House in Ivanhoe making notes and reminiscing about all the times we had made love in that front bedroom. I called in around the corner to the flat where we lived after we got married. Those quiet, intimate times with no children to distract us. Lazy Sundays when we stayed in bed till two or three in the afternoon, before getting up to go to the movies. Life had so few complications then.

I visited Lani's old friends at the childcare centre in Heidelberg. The stories of her antics ran thick and fast. The staff all remembered me playing Father Christmas. Lani was only sixteen months old, but as she sat on my knee, she recognised my watch and looked up at me with curiosity written all over her face.

At Montmorency, the woman who was renting our house was in the early stages of pregnancy. Alannah's old room was being set up as a nursery. The tenants graciously left me to spend a few hours in the house by myself. The memories were strong, but the scenery was not the same. Our belongings were no longer there. The corner spa in the bathroom conjured up the carefree laughter of Maddie and Lani as they threw piles of bubbles over me. I slump to the tiled floor, the longing to touch them was so overwhelming. How could they not be here any more? It's still so hard to accept that they're never going to come back. I sat on the carpet in the lounge-room, in the same spot where I sat with my daughters so many times before. I felt an upward surge of love flow through me. I wrote a note to the tenants as I left.

Thanks a lot for the chance to have some time here alone. I hope you enjoy living here because there is still heaps of love in this place.

* * *

Bronwyn, Daniel and Hannah arrived in Nubeena soon after I returned, in the first week of July. If left to me, packing up the belongings of Nanette, Lani and Maddie would never have been done. It was a job I had been dreading. Girls, what will I keep and what can I get rid of? I don't want to be rash and give away things you want me to keep. Each piece of clothing represents another occasion we spent together.

Everything reminds me of them and I long to see them even if it is to punish or chastise them. I dream of that moment. Anything for another word, smile or touch. You've guided me well, my babies. I've been through your wardrobes and the decisions came to me far more easily than I would have expected. Some of the clothes I have to keep even if just for a while longer. A few of the toys I'll keep forever as they are you, girls. The Madeline doll, the Humphrey doll and Mr Squiggle, the harp seal Lani got from Grace when she was born.

And I have other reminders, too. Our dogs, Becky and Beethoven, still sleep on the couch as they did before you were all taken from me. It's when I nuzzle my face close to Beethoven's fur that I feel closest to you all. Lani, your affectionate Wilbur sleeps in the bed with me sometimes, on my chest the way he did with you. He is a vital physical link to you.

After I finish packing, I survey the scene. Your lives are now in bags and boxes, labelled, but with no purpose. You all deserve so much more than this. I want your spirits to be remembered well after I depart. In doing so, part of my spirit will flow with you.

I do get strength from talking to complete strangers about how wonderful my time with you was. It's like you are now fairy dust and by talking about you I am able to sprinkle a little of your magic over others.

There are so many people who didn't have the pleasure of getting to meet the three of you. So many people want to share in my grief. I have been getting letters from total strangers, many of whom say they've never written letters like this before, that they feel moved to put pen to paper. My situation has touched a chord in the hearts of Australians everywhere as well as people living overseas.

Boxes of letters were waiting for me at the post office when I arrived back in July. One envelope was marked simply: 'To the Chemist who lost his family, Tasmania.'

My mother and father and I spent ten days replying to them all. The postage alone cost $1000. Most letters were full of love and hope, but some less helpful.

I also received books and pamphlets filled with clichés. There were religious tomes and messages about guns. And platitudes that offered no consolation.

'At least you've got your memories.' 'You'll see them again in heaven.' 'They're at peace with God now.'

Some are from friends or people we knew. Emily Gioules, who used to be our babysitter in Melbourne, writes: 'I was surprised at how you talked at the funeral and how positive you were. Hearing you say it made me feel better. I always believe everything happens for a reason, but I can't figure out one for what happened.'

After the funeral, Emily gave me a journal she had prepared about her time with the children and she told me how Netty advised her 'on guys', and how Netty told her all about our life together. Emily wrote about how she took Lani to the movies. 'I said something to her and she said: "Shh. I'm kissing my boyfriend," and she had her arm leant on the chair like she had her arm around an imaginary person. I thought she was so funny.'

Some of the letters were more confronting. One man confided he had been contemplating suicide after splitting up with his fiancée. He told me he had reconsidered this and thought if I could continue, things weren't really that bad for him. He called me his hero.

Others were from mothers who write from the heart:

'Dear Walter, I have just finished putting my two precious sons to bed, Joel, 6, and Jim, 4, prayers, cuddles, the lot. But much of the pleasure has been dampened because Michael, my husband, and I have just watched you on "A Current Affair".'

This particular letter was written by a woman whose husband attended the Broad Arrow Cafe that day as a paramedic for the Tasmanian Ambulance Service. He spent the night with the Special Operations Group at the Seascape Guesthouse where the gunman held police at bay.

'My boys are my life and I think sometimes, maybe incorrectly, that your wife, Nanette, would rather be with her children than without. It is a mother's worst nightmare,' she writes.

Another mother from Sarina in Queensland wrote: 'I myself have two children aged 4 and 1½ and like most parents have days when

I come close to breaking point with the endless chatter, questions and noise. It is at these times that the thought of you comes into my mind and I realise how lucky I am to have them and how this constant noise would be music to your ears. The memory of you and your family will be with me always.'

While I am writing this book, I am in a family environment, but it is not my family. Upstairs there is a sudden thud as one of Lindsay's children jumps on the mini-trampoline in the hallway. Someone else is screeching from the television room. Sometimes I can hear the signature tune from 'Playschool'. Lindsay's children have borrowed Jumanji *from the video store, the film I saw with the girls the weekend before they died. So many similarities. Alannah's bear, Max, is on temporary loan to Lindsay's daughter, Phoebi, who is six years old. Phoebi has dressed Max in a pink lamé outfit and she calls him Maxine. I give Phoebi one of Lani's rings. Their fingers are the same size. Other songs bring memories. 'We are the Champions', the Queen song used in the film* The Mighty Ducks, *was one of the girls' favourites. I go to the stereo cabinet and choose the* Lion King *CD. I start listening to the 'Circle of Life' and I sing along, but it has lost its meaning.*

It seems every day I have reminders of the time we had together. Yesterday was Mother's Day, 11 May 1997. Mother's Day, already two have passed and I can't believe it. The relentless cycle of yearly events in my life after Netty, Lani and Maddie continues. Birthdays, Christmas, Mother's Day, Father's Day. Eddie Halton asked me to buy boxes of chocolates for all the mothers at the barbeque he had organised. A simple task, but I wasn't buying chocolates for the one mother I wanted to see. Lindsay, Bruce and their children were there in the Hobart park, and lots of friends from the peninsula. Everyone was part of a family, which is a harsh reminder of my current status. Children are running around and playing on the swings. I think what great fun Lani and Maddie would have running around everywhere. The new me is single and alone. Encircled by friends, but without my lifeblood. The three most important people in my life aren't with me.

That night, I read the poems written by Rebekah, who'd been our babysitter in Nubeena. I read the ones she wrote for my three girls. The words, written with such clarity by a young woman of fourteen, trigger the realisation of what I have lost.

NANETTE

Nanette, you were one of a kind,
You always made me laugh
you're so special
no-one could compare . . .

You brought happiness wherever you went
we'll never forget you,
you made sure of that
I started as your babysitter
but I believe we were more than that,
I know that we were friends.

I have so many special memories
ones that'll keep forever
you were so different
but that was your charm

I know you're watching over us, wherever you are.
I love you, Nanette.

ALANNAH

I've shed so many tears
thinking of our memories
you were so happy
full of life
filled with love you wanted to share

You used to run and play
and danced everywhere
we used to sing songs
and play games with your dolls
I can't imagine you not in my life
but I know you'd want me to go on.

I miss you so much
Wherever you are, Larny [sic]
I love you.

MADELINE

When I close my eyes
I can see your beautiful face,
Your cute little curls
and the way you sucked your fingers

Things that seemed so silly
things we didn't think about at the time
now matter, so much

I miss the way that you pronounced my name
do you remember?
you always missed out the 'R'

I want to ask you silly little questions
like do you have a Mama Doll in Heaven?
You called all your dolls Mama Doll

I wish I could have just one last hug
maybe one day I can
I love you, Maddy [sic].

It hits me like a freight train. My heart is seared with pain as I
contemplate holding them for a second and, sitting on the bar stool
in Lindsay's kitchen, I break down and weep for the first time in
nearly a week as Lindsay chops carrots for dinner. I wish they were
still by my side, but now have come to accept that they are, if only
in spirit. I do still love them with every cell in my body and until I
die that will not go away.

In my first months back in Nubeena. I would walk down the street
and people would often not know how to react. They'd turn in the
opposite direction to avoid making contact with me. These were not
just acquaintances, but good customers who I considered good
friends. But, they didn't know what to say to me, so decided it was
better to say nothing at all. In many instances I would chase after
them, turn them towards me and give them a hug. Once this was
done we had acknowledged what had happened and then could
resume the normal day-to-day relationship.

Children's reactions were far more straightforward. The children
from Alannah's school came into the pharmacy to reminisce about
Alannah and Maddie. Some of them cried as they told me of their
memories. I decided to talk to Alannah's class. Many had been to
our house to play or for parties. How did I confront something so
daunting? Then the thought of our pet lamb, Lily, sprang to mind.
Here was something living and special that I could give to the children. The teacher, Suzanne Kingston, agreed. I tied Lily up and

loaded her in the back of the car. Walking into the familiar classroom stirred powerful emotions for me. I was so close to breaking down as I saw all of the despondent faces. I gathered all of my fortitude.

'As you all know, Alannah and Maddie and Nanette are not coming back. I want you to remember all the funny things Alannah would do. I want you all to look after Lily for me and every time you pat her, think of Alannah's smiling face.'

We filed out of the classroom to where Lily was tethered in the courtyard. They all wanted to pat Lily. Even though Lani's closest friends were still crying there was also smiling and laughter. I hoped it would help them come to terms with their death.

In twelve months I have travelled so far and yet I know I have so much more travelling to do. Can someone stop this train? I want to get off.

No matter where I go, there is no escaping the reality of what happened. It hangs like a black cloud above my head. Before all of this, I believed in fate. My lucky number, which I selected in the numerous competitions we entered was 28: Alannah's birthdate. I can't use that number any more. The twenty-eighth of April will be forever branded on my heart.

There were so many people who crossed the path of the gunman that day. And you, Lani and Maddie were killed, Netty. Fate is a strange thing. I think of Gaye and John Fidler and how often they came into contact with the gunman that day, inside the cafe, after they escaped outside and they just missed seeing him the day before the massacre when they visited the same shop in Hobart's Salamanca Place. John even looked into the eyes of the gunman while he was inside the cafe and somehow survived. They are still here and they are so thankful. What would have happened if you had lived, Netty, and our girls had died? Would you have been able to cope? I don't think you would have.

In Lani's baby book, parents are asked to record their first comment after the birth of their child. I read your comment the other day, Netty: 'This is my beautiful daughter and no-one can take her away from me.'

To live without Lani or Maddie would have crucified you. I am left to struggle on.

The inability of people around me to deal with the reality of what has happened to me sets me back time after time. The questions people most often ask: 'How do you go on after something as horrific as this happens in your life? How are you coping?' to which I usually answer: 'All right.'

Lie. It's easier. The other day, arriving at Hobart Airport, a woman approached me. 'I think you've done a really good job standing up to the gun lobby.' I shrug my shoulders and pick up my bag from the conveyor belt. I cannot get used to the public attention.

I know it will always be a problem, especially because I have been so outspoken in the media about gun control, but it's a price I will have to pay. Being a public figure means people will always want to know how I am coping. How would they react if I told them what is really happening? Usually I'm in turmoil. My concentration span is dismal. Thoughts and plans are disjointed. It's hard to get tasks done in a coherent way. Before, doing jobs like paying the accounts or replying to mail were easy. They never fazed me, even if I'd left them to the very last moment. Now, however, it's a different situation. Doing ordinary chores requires more effort than I can muster. Pro-crastination. Something I was never guilty of in the past is now taking over my life. Avoiding things is much easier.

Frequently, I find myself wandering aimlessly through my parents' house. I can't remember why I'm in a particular room. Maybe if I go back to the room where I've just come from, I'll remember. Wrong. It doesn't come back to me. 'Oh well, it couldn't be that important or else I'll remember it again,' is the only way I can reconcile my amnesia. It's so unlike me. In the past I was organised and meticulous. I liked to know where everything was. Now, I lose things continually. I've lost my wallet several times, and my jacket. Once, I left my briefcase and jacket in the middle of a Hobart street after a press conference. Sometimes when I dial a telephone number and someone answers, I don't know who it is I want to speak to. I can't seem to plan for more than the immediate few hours. In the weeks following their deaths, I remember how petrified I became when someone would try to pin me down to an appointment. 'Oh, Friday, I don't know just at the moment. I'll give you a ring when it gets closer.' The return phone call was seldom made. So what is the reason for this state of mind? Pastor Allan Anderson gives me possible answers. He tells me I am trying to process the ramifications of what has happened. I am also having trouble dealing with my predicament. I am functioning in survival mode. Going from day to day. Sometimes I go out and drink to forget. Then, the next day, I feel so vulnerable and alone. I am in another world.

I battled with my life in Nubeena after returning, trying hard to become involved in all of the things that used to bring pleasure. I decided to take part in our local theatre production. It used to be a regular event in the old days with the usual crowd: Eddie, Steve Ireland, Richard Shoobridge and Paul Cooper, the guide from the site who was with me when I heard the news of Nanette and the girls' deaths. They all wrote skits for the production which was held each year in the school hall. I had helped get the productions off the ground. I thought by getting involved again, it might help.

It was a strange sensation getting up on stage. I enjoyed entertaining people, but I felt incredibly guilty about making the audience laugh. I didn't feel like I had a right to do this. With the fake beard and wig, I was well camouflaged when 'Mama Mia' started playing. Underneath it didn't matter if I was sad or crying. The important thing was I could still participate in life and that gave me encouragement. It reminded me that at some point in the future, I could be me again.

In the end, in spite of all the support and caring from friends like Eddie and Steve, I knew I had to leave the peninsula. This was a community that was disintegrating. It could never be as it had been.

Rumours, innuendo, marital breakups and vicious gossip were circulating. It seemed to be affecting everyone. In the months after the shooting, Steve and Pam Ireland's marriage broke up, with Pam remaining in Nubeena and Steve moving up to Hobart. It seemed that a destructive undercurrent was flowing through this small town which was threatening to suck me under.

Back in June, when I returned to Australia from my ten-day trip to New Zealand I found that someone had started a rumour I had committed suicide. My mother fielded phone calls from caller after caller trying to confirm the rumour. At first I laughed, finding it hard to believe such a thing was true, until I discovered how widespread the rumour was. On the peninsula, people seemed surprised to see I was still alive.

Staying in Nubeena was insidiously eating away my soul. What had seemed such a sanctuary less than two years ago had turned into a nightmare from which I had to escape.

FOURTEEN

Expressions of Grief

I am finally beginning to read the pile of bereavement manuals I have been given over the past twelve months. The death of a child and sudden death are given as two major reasons for not being able to resolve grief in a healthy way.

Surely the adjective that is missing is 'violent'. It should read: sudden violent deaths – death of two children and a wife. Does this mean I can never resolve my grief?

My grieving is like a hole in my heart, initially a mortal wound that threatened to take my life. Arterial bleeding pulsating out at a rapid rate. The hole is so big that there is no possibility of stopping it. As time passes, the blood begins to coagulate and the flow lessens slightly. The pain doesn't reduce in intensity and the hole stays the same, but after a long time the bleeding reduces to a trickle. It seems possible that one day the flow may stop altogether but you know instinctively that the hole will always be there. There is a large part of me missing.

Having almost finished writing this book, I am leaving Hobart to return to Melbourne. In one way I want to feel happy because I am setting out to my future life, to my own place again – the house I have bought in Melbourne. A home of my own, no longer a visitor in other people's houses. It is to be a new chapter of life. But I know that my leaving will not erase the horror of what happened at Port Arthur. I am leaving without my beloved family. As I head up the Midlands Highway which bisects Tasmania and links Hobart with Launceston, Eric Clapton's song 'Tears in Heaven' plays on the radio. The lyrics are a tribute to his four-year-old son who fell to his death. I sing the words, but find that the tears come down my face faster than the words come out and I almost have to pull over as my vision blurs. I wish I knew the answer to the same question. Mixed emotions flood my mind. Hurt, anger, frustration, disbelief and, most of all, sadness. Passionate sadness that something like this could ever happen and that it had happened to me. I cling to the fact that I want my grieving and growing to be a tribute to the spirit of my girls.

No-one writing these manuals about how to cope with grief could ever have contemplated that they should include a chapter on what to do in the case of mass slaughter. My grief and the grief of everyone else who lost loved ones in this kind of violent rampage is unique in comparison to other types of grieving. I have met so many people in the past year who have been affected by this horrific incident, whose lives will never be the same. Those who have been physically injured, those who, like me, have lost relatives or friends and those who simply witnessed the horror of it all. In a strange way, they have become my extended family.

Three months after the massacre I decided to visit Carol Loughton, who lived in a Melbourne suburb close to my parents. Carol's only daughter, fifteen-year-old Sarah, was killed in the Broad Arrow Cafe after falling to the floor with her mother. Carol herself was horrifically injured in the back with a ten-centimetre wound, the bullet shattering her shoulderblade, for which she has undergone numerous operations. Sarah died instantly in her arms, the explosion from the shot that killed her daughter shattering Carol's eardrum.

I felt a need to visit the other people who had been affected by the same event, to collect and take on board some of that pain and to spend time with them, to share in our grief. I had already visited John and Gaye Fidler, and read their personal accounts of what happened in the cafe. Their words were almost too difficult to absorb, yet what they witnessed is a horror they have to live with every day. John still has a piece of shrapnel lodged near his lung.

Carol's mother cooked dinner for me. Afterwards, we sat on the couch and talked about things. Carol had recently been discharged from hospital and for most of that time had been on a morphine drip. I was shocked by the extent of her suffering, how her face looked an ashen grey as though her life had been drained away. I discovered that her physical wounds meant she had postponed her grieving for her daughter. She did not realise until the day after the massacre after she came out of surgery that her Sarah had been killed. I was jarred into the realisation of what it must be like having a physical injury to sustain as well as a mental one. For the first time since this dreadful tragedy, I felt almost lucky.

I asked to see a photograph of Sarah. She had to go to the chest in Sarah's bedroom to find one.

'Isn't she gorgeous,' I commented, when she returned with the photo of a young girl with a blonde bob, her hair parted down the centre.

'Yes, she is, but what shall I do with the photo now?' she asked.

'Just talk to her. I talk to my girls all the time and sometimes it helps. You can tell them how you're feeling and how much you miss them.'

'Sarah is all that I've got. I've brought her up on my own. She meant the world to me. She gave my life a purpose and now that purpose has gone.'

When I meet her at the first anniversary, in April, she tells me: 'I don't want to put any more burden on you because you don't need it, but the way I look at it, if you can survive, then I can, too.'

I did not speak my thoughts aloud, but I felt it should be the other way around.

In those lonely months back in Nubeena I read through the letters I've been sent. My bereavement has been such a public affair. It has inadvertently triggered other people's pain, dredged from deep within themselves. Some people don't even know my first name and begin a letter simply 'Dear Mr Mikac'. Strangers confide their darkest thoughts. There is such an outpouring of sadness, sometimes I feel I am almost drowning in it. I need to reply to everyone's messages. They were opening their hearts to me, so I felt obliged to acknowledge every letter I received. I even got a book filled with letters from passengers and the driver of bus No. 43 which operates between Hobart and Dover in the south of Tasmania. On the front of the book is an angel and a brass plaque.

So many of the letters talk about the pain brought on by a loss. Some write about a mother they lost twenty-five years ago, others have lost a child, yet others have had a relative or friend murdered. Some have lost their family in a car accident and others have drowned. These people are describing their own private wounds which are in various stages of healing.

One twenty-five-year-old woman from Brisbane writes of her boyfriend who was murdered:

My whole body was aching from the grief and I thought my heart would attack me and I would die. Two years on, I am crying all through this letter and I'm looking down at the ring finger on my left hand and it's empty. There should be a wedding band there and it should've been put there by him. I miss the babies we would have and should have had together.

Another woman from West Melton near Melbourne experienced three tragedies with her loved ones. Two were victims of murder.

Find a private place where you can scream until you are exhausted. Truly cry and cry and cry; don't let anyone tell you how brave you are by not crying. Some people have no idea about grieving. I have had so many different people advising me who had no idea what they were talking about. They didn't have someone they loved who was murdered. Keep the girls' headbands near you for comfort. One day when you are ready, you will let them go.

I am glad someone is telling me to cry in a society where it's so often considered a sign of weakness. Social conditioning in men has meant that, as adults, they are unable to cry. I know the pituitary gland in the brain releases a narcotic-like substance when you cry, so that's why people say 'you'll feel better after having a good cry'.

It heartens me to see that so many of the letters are from fathers. One is from a forty-three-year-old law enforcement officer who has worked with the Accident Investigation Squad. 'I've had some pretty tough times in this life, but this terrible tragedy simply broke my heart . . . I cried like a baby.'

A man from North Hobart writes:

My wife of thirteen years died in my arms in our bed in February 1996. There was no indication she was ill. She was thirty-five years old. It was a sudden cardiac death, but it was peaceful. She left three young children for me to look after. Her death is completely opposite to that of your family. However, I can understand, in a slight way, how you feel your life and your future has been torn away because that is how I have felt.

Another man from Penguin in Tasmania writes how he has endured the death of his first son.

I understand in some small way, the pain, the anguish, the loneliness, the emptiness you must be experiencing. It is not right that a parent should have to bury their children. Life is not meant to work that way, not in a perfect world anyway.

Some don't even have the comfort of saying goodbye after death. A woman from Melbourne writes about her husband's death in a surf ski accident. It was a week before his body was recovered from the ocean.

He intended to take the surf ski out for just a short paddle and be back within an hour to cook a barbeque tea. Even though we said goodbye earlier that afternoon, it never crosses your mind that it might be the last. I think that's why I find it such a shock, so difficult to accept – as I was never able to see his body, there was no finality.

All those different stories. People who have each been confronted by the finiteness of life. They all have that in common, even though their experiences of grieving may be vastly different. Michael North, who lost his daughter in the Dunblane massacre and his wife to cancer, said that bereaved people can function well if allowed to, but this can be difficult because there are so many preconceptions about bereavement.

There's no one way of dealing with grief and if that's recognised, then perhaps people might understand better, he said.

Allan Anderson commented that, 'Some people use their mourning as a memorial to show the extent of their love for the person.'

Ethnic culture also decrees certain codes of behaviour from the bereaved. My parents felt that they couldn't dance for the prescribed twelve months after the death of my family. My father is the President of the Istrian Australian Social Club in Epping, where they play bocce. Despite my father being there in an official role with work responsibilities, some people clearly thought it was inappropriate for my parents to attend dances at the club even if they weren't dancing.

My choice of happy music at the funeral probably caused some consternation among my parents' generation, although Mum could understand. These people would have felt more at ease with a funeral march. But expressions of grief have changed with time. A hundred years ago, men wore black armbands and women veils for six months as a mark of respect.

All I am able to say about grief is what *I have experienced*. It has been roughly 547,200 minutes since their death. My sleeping hours are dominated by it. So many people tell you to be strong and have courage, but they don't talk about how difficult it is to cope when the person who is grieving *does* show their emotions. I am sure many people feel inadequate. Yet to help a person grieve means doing it without judgement or comment, but allowing them to express how they feel. Whether that takes the form of screaming, talking, hitting an inanimate object or using foul language, it has to be allowed to happen. Only the person grieving knows how they feel.

It was only after the death of my family that my own mother started coming to terms with her mother's death some fifty years ago. A few days after the shooting she told Allan Anderson and everyone in the lounge-room in Nubeena how she had not cried over her mother's death since the day she died. At the age of six, and while growing up, she had been made to feel too ashamed and embarrassed to show her emotions. When her granddaughters and daughter-in-law died, the public nature of her grieving was sometimes distressing. But, she needed to grieve and now she was doing it.

Dad, on the other hand, was more reserved. I knew that he was hurting to the core. He didn't have to say anything for me to sense his anguish. People talk about your heart being broken; well that's precisely the physical distress he encountered. On the Friday night after the shooting he was admitted to the Royal Hobart Hospital with severe chest pains. Despite there being no physical abnormality, the strain of the loss was taking its toll on him. Thankfully he was discharged the next day. I don't know that I could have gone on if I had been faced with any more loss.

I have to confront my grief head on. It is the only way I stand a chance to recover and continue. But I know I have to give it time. I know I am changing from Walter the pharmacist with a wife and children, to Walter who lives in Melbourne with no particular career. I am learning that much of my new life is out of my control and I am learning to accept the changes, but only gradually. Before all this happened I used to thrive on stress. I renovated houses and the pharmacy at Nubeena, ran in three marathons and worked long hours to get ahead. It gave me the adrenalin rush and impetus to complete the most insurmountable tasks. I was invincible – or so I thought.

Tonight I had to drive through Melbourne peak-hour traffic to get to the post office to meet a deadline for my editor. In the past, it would have been a job that had to be done. Now, I feel anxious. I want to ignore the situation and not take any responsibility. The frustration of not being able to cope, as I did in the past, sometimes makes me want to punch the wall. Why can't I get over these handicaps?

I often lose my train of thought and become irritated. I feel like everything is going to collapse around me like a house of cards. I have to keep telling myself that although the progress in grief is slow, I know there is some progress. Their deaths don't continually occupy my thoughts like they did at the beginning, perhaps because I am more accepting now that they are gone. I feel I have the strength to help other people, so I have something to give. I am making plans and continuing with my life. I am going overseas in June for four months with my brother John, visiting Europe, Canada and maybe even Africa. John has given me some glossy brochures on African safaris. Although I have yet to study them, when I feel able, I know I can look at them.

Wanting to continue your life means you are on the right track. I firmly believe that the real test of a person's character is not how they cope with loss but how they are able to live afterwards.

There is, perhaps, another inhibiting factor in my resolution of grief. Because my grief has been so public, I am put on a pedestal which is very daunting. There are moments when I want to fall, descend into the blackness that is so inviting. Withdraw myself from life, cocoon myself in a warm dingy corner away from people's expectations.

I have progressed in my grief from the constant numbness and apathy I felt in those first few weeks where I had no drive to do anything and wanted the world to simply stop. I couldn't believe people were still going to work and continuing their life. My mind was so pre-occupied with my loss that it was hard to focus on anything. I would take twenty minutes to drive to a destination and then I would realise I had been in a trance for fifteen of those twenty minutes.

The day after the massacre, Chris McCann arrived from Melbourne. He looked at me quizzically when I said I wanted to wash the dogs. I was so exhausted and washed out that, at first, Chris found it hard to fathom why I'd bother with such a task. But I needed to do something. Washing the dogs was one of those pleasant jobs that we used to do as a family. Doing it on that day was soothing. Chris later told me that was the longest day he'd ever spent. 'It never seemed to end. Every time I looked at you, I could see the pain in your eyes and face. You would just moan.'

My perception of life has changed forever. Like everyone else involved that day, I know now we are not assured there will be a tomorrow, even though we are taught to assume that there will. Death and loss has an amazing effect on my attitude towards everything. It means having a positive attitude, otherwise I would have been gone ages ago. Often people in shops will ask me, 'Are you having a good day?' To which I reply, 'Well, I'm here, aren't I?' The person often has no idea that I am referring to how fortunate I am to be alive.

I feel more comfortable with people who have been through tragic situations. The fact that they share my changed perceptions is probably why I sought out their counsel in the months following the massacre. They are very clear about what is important about life. Not the weather, the colour of the new car, having the housework done by a certain day or what others think about you. They are concerned with being alive and positive, and about sharing time with friends and family. Eager to help others despite needing help themselves.

* * *

As Alannah's and Madeline's birthdays approached in August, I was becoming increasingly anxious. On 11 August, I went on a skiing trip at Thredbo in New South Wales with my brother Steve. I left with pangs of guilt that I was going somewhere to enjoy myself. I try to find a balance between living life for the moment and thinking of the future – a delicate mix of hedonism tempered with caution. When I let go of common sense, it is as if a huge vacuum cleaner is waiting to suck me up.

Maddie's birthday duly arrived on 15 August, and it required a huge amount of will to drag myself out of bed that morning. I wanted nothing more than to huddle in my bed and dream of holding my precious on her fourth birthday. To feel her golden locks and caress her innocent, soft hands. Getting up on the slopes and skiing seemed pointless, but I did it. I wished that it was tomorrow. That night we had a special dinner to celebrate. We shared a meal, a few wines and a toast to my Maddie.

We called in to a pub opposite the restaurant to listen to a comedian called Gary Who. Within the first five minutes of his routine, I began to feel sick in my stomach.

'What happened at Port Arthur wasn't a massacre, what happened in Hiroshima was a massacre.'

He continued to refer to Port Arthur. I was waiting for someone to pinch me to wake me up, but he kept talking, seeking laughter from a topic where there can never be any humour. It seemed like many minutes ticked by until Steve stood up and threw the contents of his glass of wine at him. Steve motioned to our group that we were leaving. But before my brother could grab my arm, I approached the stage and yelled in a controlled voice: 'You lose your wife and daughters and then laugh about it.'

I now regret not smashing his face in. I'm a lover, not a

fighter, but on that occasion I felt I had good justification for an assault. There is, and can never be, anything funny about the carnage and terror that this person has inflicted on so many lives. He's stolen innocence from our laps and that can *never* be amusing. A moment which changed the psyche of everyone living on this planet.

On 28 August, Alannah's birthday, I was back in Nubeena. The tulips, daffodils and jonquils the girls had planted in April in their own terracotta pots at the bottom of the steps off the verandah were blooming.

I sat down by myself in the lounge-room and watched a video of her last birthday and listened to her squeal as she unwrapped her present. But there is no squealing in this empty house. Only a deathly silence when the video comes to an end.

Now my grief has passed the twelve-month mark, I am realising that to have no limitations to my behaviour is not always a good thing. Gradually, in those early months I started drinking, initially to forget, and then it became a habit and often a weekly event. Not only did the killer take my family but he had also changed the part of me that was confident and carefree before. When I look at photographs in the family albums of how I was before all of this happened, I am staggered by my absolute innocence. I hardly recognise myself. I am a different person. When I look at photo- graphs of my mother and father taken before all of this happened, I see the same carefree spirit that has vanished. Will it ever come back?

In early September, I left Australia for Treble Cone in New Zealand for a skiing trip with my brother John and some friends. One night, I drank a whole bottle of Sambuca. I must have felt the need to do this. I was even beginning to question my sanity. Talking to them in dreams, seeing children who look nearly identical to Lani and

Maddie. Sometimes I would wear Netty's belongings. Often people ask me what aftershave I'm wearing. I don't tell them it's Nanette's perfume. But it makes me feel good. Close to her.

Dealing with the violence of their deaths is enormously difficult. Netty and the girls weren't walking through a war zone – they were having a picnic. I felt let down by society that someone like him had been allowed to infiltrate the mainstream population without any intervention. The system had failed to put safeguards in place to prevent this catastrophe happening.

After returning from the two-week ski trip, I rang the real-estate agent in Nubeena on 14 October. I also rang Barry Axton, the general manager of Fauldings.

'Barry, I've probably said this to you before, but I want to put my pharmacy on the market,' I said on the phone, feeling mixed emotions, a sense of relief that I was soon to be free, but also knowing full well that the pharmacy was far from reaching its potential. I would have loved to have transferred the pharmacy somewhere else.

Within a week, the house was sold to a retired couple from Hobart. The pharmacy was not sold until the end of January, but I knew my locum had expressed an interest. My life in Tasmania was drawing to a close.

Late in the afternoon on the day of my farewell party in mid-November, we went on the old Bundeena ferry which Netty and the girls had taken on their trip to the Isle of the Dead that fateful day. I had Netty's Esprit patent leather shoes that she had worn during her ghost tours. They were in a basket weighted down with concrete and sprinkled with rose petals. We motored out to the middle of Carnarvon Bay.

The ghost tour guides who'd worked with Netty accompanied Steve, John and I on the boat. When we arrived in the middle of the bay, Mandy Hatten, one of the ghost tour guides, read a poem she had written:

ODE TO NANETTE MIKAC

She came into our hearts one day and there Nanette will always stay.
Her lips were always a daring red,
laughter was always the gift that she spread,
Her love of life was what we all admired
and the one thing of which
she never tired
Colourful fashions she loved to wear
not to mention her beautiful hair,
Rich scenting perfumes
she liked to choose
And, of course, who could forget those patent leather shoes
And so, Nanette, we now say, not goodbye but farewell.
For when next we meet
Only time will tell.

And then I cast them to the deep, those beautiful shoes, still shiny and black the way you wanted them.

My farewell party was held that night at the Premaydena Cool Stores, in an insulated room with five-metre-high ceilings. On the invitation, Eddie had written: 'Judging by previous efforts, this night could be awesome.'

Somehow the media had found out about this private function and a television crew had begun to set up equipment outside the venue. Steve, John and I went to speak to them.

'Who's in charge here,' I demanded.

'I am,' the fair-haired reporter answered. 'We were just wondering –'

'This is just not appropriate. This is a quiet farewell for me from the people of the peninsula. I'd appreciate it if you could leave.'

'But we just wanted –'

'Did you have trouble understanding what I said?'

Where the media were concerned I had become more cold-hearted and determined not to allow them to intrude further into my life.

Despite this incident, the party was a great success. A local band played and we all got up and sang. The punch at the farewell was potent. Scooter, one of the teachers at the school, and I ran the 'Nubeena Gift', in our boxer shorts. At 4.30 a.m. eight people ended up in Eddie's spa.

Later on that Sunday, after shedding many tears, I headed up to Hobart. John left to go back to Melbourne, but Steve stayed with me to face what was to be one of the biggest endurance tests I had yet confronted – the court hearing.

FIFTEEN

Inside the Courtroom

I am driving across Hobart's Derwent River towards Bellerive one night late in February. Without realising it, I am in the suburb of Risdon. When I glance to my left, I see the prison sitting on the hill. A chill runs down my spine. I am possibly 500 metres from the pathetic creature who killed my family. Momentarily, I don't know exactly what to do. Stop. Speed up. Throw up. Blow up. It has happened when I least expected it, as if I had been pounced upon by an unseen assailant.

All sorts of crazy thoughts collide in my head. 'My family are not able to do the simple things of life any more, so why should he be able to?'

All sorts of elaborate plans on how to get rid of him – this 'aberration' – filled my head. Then I thought of doing something as a protest. An impressive suicide. Driving my car at breakneck speed over the bridge and then seeing if I could ram through the guard

rail to plummet into the depths below. A spectacular way to go. As
I was thinking this, I remembered the words that my psychiatrist, Ian
Sale, had said to me before the trial. Hired by the prosecution, Ian
had as good a profile of the perpetrator as anyone.

'He's basically a freak of nature. If he was a car that had come
off a production line he would have been rejected straight away.'

I kept driving towards Bellerive.

When I first set eyes on his insipid presence in the courtroom on 19
November, I almost felt sorry for him.

Perversely, it is a beautiful sunny day outside Hobart's Supreme
Court at Salamanca Place, near the wharves. The two-day court
hearing is being held inside this one-storeyed, sandstone besser-
blocked building next to St David's Park, Hobart's first burial
ground.

The hearing followed six weeks of confusion for all those affected
by the massacre, because no-one knew if, at his first court appearance, the gunman was going to plead guilty or not.

I had been thrown onto a rollercoaster of emotions over which I
had no control when, on 30 September, the gunman pleaded 'Not
guilty' to gasps of disbelief from the public gallery.

Six weeks later on 7 November the gunman, with a new lawyer,
changed his plea to guilty.

I had not attended either hearing and was at the Oaks Day races
in Melbourne when I heard he changed his plea. I felt strangely
empty, as if the news was an anti-climax. I gazed from the Members'
Stand at the vista of the racecourse. The beautiful gardens, the roses,
the lavender leading to the mounting yards. The thought of my family's absence turned this vision into black and white, draining it of
all colour.

Mercifully, while I was at the races, I did not know all the facts.
I did not know that as the charges relating to Nanette and the girls
were read out, he stood there smiling, smirking, one hand at his face,
shielding his laughter. I even did a radio interview live to air with

Neil Mitchell from Melbourne radio station 3AW talking about how I felt about the change of plea, still with no knowledge of what had happened inside the court.

I didn't find out until the next day when I read it in the newspaper. I was walking down the side of my parents' house, having collected the paper from the letterbox. I thought, when I saw the first headlines, that it was a case of the media being out of control again, but as I read the differing accounts in the various newspapers, I realised with a sickening feeling that they were not exaggerating.

It was the final straw, the worst possible insult that could be served up to me. As I looked at the photo of the man who harboured so much malevolence, who displayed such acts of irreverence to his victims, the man who had caused me such unbelievable pain, I felt like smashing his face repeatedly against a brick wall. But I was left to use my fists, which I drummed, in a futile gesture of defiance, on the wall of my parents' house.

Revenge is an emotion I have steered away from since the start, a hopeless sentiment that can lead nowhere. For the past seven months I had managed to contain it, to hold it at bay. Nothing that could be done to him could ever bring *them* back. I was sure of that from the moment I saw them lying there.

It would be so much easier if he'd taken his own life like the gunman at Dunblane and most other perpetrators of mass violence. But he *is* still alive, lacking the fortitude to finish the job, protecting himself right up until the end of the siege. After all the horrendous carnage he committed, he sustained only superficial burns. I wish he was *not* alive, but how he dies is not relevant. The constant references to his so-called 'attempted suicides' in the media are offensive.

Inflicting trauma on him may ease the burden for others. Some advocate capital punishment, others want to rip him apart, gouge his eyes out, to try and inflict the same amount of physical pain that he has dealt out. But there is no punishment on earth that fits this crime. When I see others consumed by such futility, I know it is wasted energy.

The following day, I ride my bike to Plenty Gorge in the outer northern suburbs of Melbourne. As I pedal, I am crying for Alannah and Maddie. After the bike ride, I take the dogs for a run and flake into bed at 8 p.m.

All of this was heading towards the climax, even though I didn't want to admit it. I knew I was going to have to face him in court – the worst day I have encountered since the massacre. I know why I'm going in there. I am doing this to represent Netty and the girls. I no longer want to be outside of the courtroom, reading second-hand what was going on inside, especially events dealing with my family. Even though I knew it would hurt and I was scared of the consequences, I knew I had to be there.

I woke up that morning of the hearing at 7.30. By 9 a.m., I was at a conference room in nearby Davey Street, one of Hobart's main streets, around the corner from the court. The room was set up for everyone who was directly affected by the shootings, about ninety people all up. They were all there, the people who had come to play such a large part in my life. Sue and John Burgess, Gaye and John Fidler, Bronwyn and Keith, and Phillip Pears, whose brother was killed after being held hostage at the Seascape Guesthouse. I also met Linda White for the first time and her fiancé Michael Wanders. Her right arm was severely injured during the massacre. It was only later that I learned of the number of operations and the personal trauma she had been through.

I found I was sweating profusely, my hands and armpits clammy with trepidation. I was scared. Scared that this person who I'd never seen would conjure up emotions that were negative and destructive, emotions I had tried so hard to eliminate from my life.

I feared that maybe, enraged by the sight of him, I would launch myself at him and that by doing that he would have some victory and would take even more from me than he had already taken. His pathetic presence deserved no recognition. This was a sentiment echoed again and again by survivors in the cafe as well as relatives of the victims.

Outside the courtroom, camera crews lined the steps, radio microphones at the ready, to approach people entering the court via the cordoned-off area on the steps. Journalists were already filing for early radio bulletins on mobile phones. Despite the sensationalism revolving around the case, there were still seats in the public gallery up until the hearing opened. It seemed he was being treated with the disdain he deserved by fellow Tasmanians.

To avoid the interminable scrutiny, I entered through the side door with Steve. To our annoyance he was later described in newspaper articles as 'John'. After all this time they got it wrong, even though everyone who attended the court that day was named in a list on the door of the courtroom.

A jury anteroom had been set up as a place for relatives and friends of victims where we could all retreat from the bustle of the public foyer and the media.

We were all taken into Court Room Number 7 together. The sixty or so media were allocated to the courtroom next to Number 7 which had a video link to the proceedings. At 9.50 a.m. we went into the court and took our seats. It was a low-ceilinged room made dark with wood panelling and dark carpets lightened by a skylight. I sat between Steve and Bronwyn. I kept wiping my hands on my trousers as the minutes ticked by to 10 a.m. I was becoming increasingly agitated. Shortly after 10 a.m., Justice Cox entered and we all rose.

From a side door to my left a short man with a shaved blond head and light blue suit walked into the room flanked by prison wardens. I was sitting about two metres away from the bullet-proof dock where he sat. Only five people sat between me and the twenty-nine-year-old man. My first impression as I glanced at him was his total lack of presence, how ineffectual he looked, and I found it hard to reconcile the actions of this person with the wimp that stood before me. I prided myself, as I watched him, in not feeling any anger or even aggression towards him.

My spirit buoyed appreciably. He could murder my family, but never ever take my love for them or any space within my consciousness. I felt very gratified that I had decided to come to the court.

But as the first hour passed and the grey-haired and distinguished Damian Bugg QC outlined the case for the prosecution and the brutal deaths of the Martins who ran the guesthouse at Seascape, followed by a description of what had happened within the Broad Arrow Cafe, my feeling of ascendancy fell away. As each injury and indictment was described, the magnitude of what he had done filled my soul and I felt a sinking feeling of despair. At one point during the morning as I watched him, he looked straight at me. It was as if I was looking at something transparent, something that had no substance.

I was still relatively composed at the morning recess when Damian Bugg asked me into his chambers inside the court complex.

'Part of what is to be presented may be something you haven't heard yet,' he said.

'What's that?'

'You may be under the misconception that Alannah was shot from a distance,' he said.

'Well, actually one of the witnesses indicated that to me.'

'That's not correct, I'm afraid. Ballistic evidence shows there were six shots. Two shots were fired which missed Alannah while she was sheltering behind the tree about five and a half metres away from the gunman's car. Alannah was killed behind the tree after the barrel of the gun was held to and pushed against her neck.'

I wilted like a flower being placed outside on a 40 degree day. The sensation was not unlike emptying a sink of water. As a last drop trickled out, I thought my soul could quite easily drift out of my body and not return. This news that I had avoided being confirmed, and how Maddie was shot twice, once in the right shoulder and the second fatal shot in her chest and abdomen, absolutely shocked me. That question I had come to terms with in some way resurfaced. Why? How could anyone do that to a defenceless three- and six-year-old? How could someone do that to my Lani? What on earth could she have done to deserve such terror at her death? A multitude of questions streamed through my mind, through tear-blurred vision. Somehow, I could still hear Damian saying:

'Would you like me to leave the part about Alannah out?'

I said slowly, 'No. It needs to be said the way it was.'

Keith had been asking me whether I wanted all the evidence told in court. I hadn't understood what he'd meant. Now I did.

I was quite clear about my views. 'No, he needs to be seen as the horrific monster he is. I'm not protecting him by leaving his grossest act out. He is a pathetic coward and should be exposed as just that.'

As I walked into the courtroom, I could not face him. It was extremely hard not to imagine the slaughter of my family as it happened. Flashes of each of their deaths as it occurred filled my mind for the rest of the morning session. Admittedly, I found myself thinking many times, 'You fucking bastard', and wanted to let my pain out. However, showing him pain would be giving a little more of me. This thing that should never have been born deserved nothing more in life.

'How could you do this? How could you do that to my babies?' kept recurring in my head. My apprehension grew through lunch as I built myself up for one of the hardest moments in my life. In the afternoon session Damian Bugg took Justice Cox through the sequence of events of 28 April, through each of the 72 counts. Nanette and the girls were counts 50, 51 and 52. As the moment approached, I gripped Bronwyn's and Steve's hands, clutching a hankie at the same time. As the indictment and their names were read, tears swelled to become sobbing and I felt as though I was having an out-of-body experience, viewing what was actually being described. It was a time in my life I truly wished I was dead. As the next indictments were read, my hurt and grief subsided. The sobbing eased and gradually I returned to normality.

I stared at the coat of arms behind the judge and felt a few percent less a person. The charges continued for what seemed like forever.

Leaving the court, I felt a sense of achievement because I had conquered my hardest day since the shooting. I was relatively intact and just wanted to chat to a few friends. A debriefing session had been arranged for all of us back in the conference room at Davey Street.

Within minutes, Gaye Fidler turned to me and said, 'Do you want to stay for this?'

I shook my head, even though I knew I shouldn't leave. I didn't want to describe my feelings to counsellors who were strangers and who had not shared the experience. Instead a group of us headed for our own form of debriefing to the Customs House Hotel opposite Constitution Dock: John and Gaye Fidler with their friends Bev and Peter Kelly, who had also been at the cafe, Peter Grenfell and John Boskovic, two men who, with their wives, had been with Nanette and the girls as they walked up the hill, and my brother Steve. We were later joined by Damian Bugg and his associate, Nick Perks.

As Gaye placed her hand on John's thigh, I felt an increasing sense of melancholy. What I really needed that night was Nanette to hold me, run her fingers through my hair and to care for me as only Nanette could. My heart was empty and, for a few moments, I felt a shattered man.

That night as I lay in bed at Brad and Julia's the visions of my girls being shot kept reverberating through my mind. Sitting on the bed, I just sobbed as Julia rubbed my shoulders and cried with me in an attempt to console me. It helped a little. I left the light on for the first time since the week after it happened. I needed to think of the lamp that stood on the mantelpiece, shining down on the bed and bathing me in light, as being the girls' spirit shining down on me. Somehow allowing me to drift into unconsciousness.

What is happening to me? As the months pass, there's a sort of delayed onset of self-destruction. Perhaps because I have no specific targets in my life, I find myself going out with my brothers or friends and writing myself off. Not caring about what I'm doing to myself. At times, it is as though this feeling is swamping me. I'm at the point of giving in. Ready to surrender – meekly. To be put out of my misery. And yet, I must continue or how else are the girls going to be assured of their place in history? The dark side tells me that I've got no reason to care. Countering this force are the sustaining thoughts of the memories I had with my family. But even while I'm experiencing these positive feelings for them, I am back again at the brick wall of negativity. It would be so easy to join them – a simple cocktail of alcohol and narcotics. No more pain and anguish. No more people trying to tear a strip off you, looking for a way to work out their own problems. What would happen if I wasn't here anyway? The world would continue. It did after their deaths despite me wanting it to stop. But then I think of the consequences on my mum, dad and brothers. How selfish would it be to inflict yet another catastrophe on them, leaving them to feel they had been unable to help me? If I were to leave a will, who would I leave my worldly goods to?

I go to an aerobics 'pump' class and work so hard with the weights that I think I am going to push myself to a cardiac arrest. Singlet soaked and face like a beetroot, I am inflicting pain purposefully. I try to raise my heart rate to the maximum and I feel satisified when I reach 180 per minute.

Near Lindsay's house, after running five kilometres, I run up a 70 degree incline as my grand finale, determined I am going to make it to the top without stopping. I gasp for air with the exhilaration of how far I have physically pushed myself.

I stay out several nights in a row at a nightclub, dancing, seeking a haven, looking for anonymity, to talk to people where I do not need to make a commitment. I do not need to behave in a certain way. There are no conventions.

My emotions are in a straitjacket, constricted by what people expect of me. I am caught between the desire to reveal my inner secrets and a desire to shut myself off.

I know now that life is finite, that time is too precious to be wasted. The motto on my brother John's watch illustrates how I want to live my life – 'Go hard or go home! Make every day count.'

I should be able to do what I want. At a nightclub, I get some release from these constraints. I can go home. Or I can stay till 6 a.m. I can dance or stand around and drink in the dark recesses of the bar without anyone probing too deeply – away from the relentless questions of the curious. Sometimes this frustration cripples me and I don't want to face responsibility. I want to hide from the scrutiny of being constantly under the microscope to somewhere I cannot be found.

I want to avoid sleep. I fear going to bed to face further emptiness and falling into an abyss from which I will never recover. I seek the physical comfort of being with someone, someone to hold, to care for me.

The anger, pain and heartache needs to manifest itself somewhere and often, direct it towards myself, putting myself through a situation that isn't the easiest option. Like doing speeches at gun rallies when I would rather curl up with my hurt away from the limelight. Sitting in front of a barrage of lenses, lights and cameras at a press conference, going to the court case and listening to the graphic detail of how my family came to depart this world. These are the hard options that I choose to put myself through. But then I know that all this suffering pales into insignificance when I think of Nanette. A true hero. She died protecting our children. There can't be any undertaking in this world that could compare to this act of selflessness.

Usually all this consternation leads me back to one positive idea. I've still got a lot to offer this world – notions of how to make this a better place. At the end of the school year, I organise the Mikac Family Perpetual Award at Alannah's school, dedicated to the uniqueness and brilliance of my three beautiful girls. The award goes to the person who is able to make other people happy. 'This doesn't mean being an angel, but doing the simple things that, in the end, benefit the entire community, smiling, caring, loving and being concerned for the fellow people around you.'

By the end of the two-day hearing, I have answers to questions I had been too scared to ask. Questions like what Netty and the girls had been doing in those last hours of their life. These answers had been filtering through since it happened, such as people contacting me to say they had been with the girls as they walked up the hill. A man at the toll booth who saw Nanette and Maddie being shot and described it to me, even though part of me didn't want to know or hear about the girls' distress. I was gradually piecing it all together and the jigsaw was almost in place.

It had become important to me to know these things as I had been through so much agony imagining what might have happened.

I relive those moments in the darkness of my room. The woman who wrote to me about her husband's fatal accident on a surf ski said: 'As my husband fell off his surf ski and realised he had to swim, he would have been pleading for his life, crying, praying and screaming for myself and the girls until hypothermia set in. I don't care if it was two minutes or half an hour, it's that distress he would have been experiencing that causes me pain.'

Likewise for me, Netty, it is the thought of the amount of distress you, Lani and Maddie had to go through in those last few minutes that troubles me.

One woman who was there in those last few minutes before they were shot told me that you died as a heroine protecting our children.

'We're safe now, pumpkin,' you said to Alannah as you walked up the hill along Jetty Road towards the toll booth to what you thought was safety on that dreadful day. You were trying to get out of the place, to escape as far away as possible. And in so doing walked inadvertently into the path of the man who had slaughtered so many of his fellow human beings, who was incapable of any feelings, who was able to kill children in cold blood. What were you thinking when the car stopped and you realised the man in the car was the man who was responsible for the shooting? Why didn't he keep driving? Why did the car stop?

The court was told you approached the car, expecting a chance to escape. John Boskovic, who was fleeing up Jetty Road, approached the car, too. I know now the gunman climbed out of the yellow Volvo and placed his left hand on your shoulder telling you three times to get down to your knees.

'Please don't hurt my babies,' you said to him. Several other

people trying to escape heard you say those words. Those words that will always haunt me.

On the second day of the hearing, Damian Bugg read a statement I had made to the court. He wanted to demonstrate to the judge and everyone in the courtroom the effects on the people left behind. I was but one example.

I can but keep surviving to enshrine their spirit in the world. The incredible, unconditional love, the warmth and freedom, the laughter and dances, the spontaneous cuddling and kissing; they are no longer there. I will, however, proudly endeavour to keep their spirits alive through my life. My love for them will never die and can never be taken.

As the words were spoken I felt as if I'd won the contest with the gunman with a final knockout blow. I had been tense as Damian Bugg began reading the words, but as he continued, I felt myself relax. The gunman could never and would never be allowed to take any more from me than he already had. I had succeeded.

* * *

Two days after the proceedings, on 22 November, the gunman was sentenced to jail for the term of his natural life for the murder of thirty-five and the attempted murder of twenty others. I was back in Melbourne, not needing to be in Hobart any longer to hear the inevitable. I was inside the Channel Nine studios ready to make a prepared public statement, when the news telexes were brought in to me. At 11.04 that morning, the gunman had been sentenced. It also reported that 'Justice Cox said that the court had accepted the medical evidence that the gunman was not criminally insane and that he knew what he was doing when he turned his gun on visitors and workers at Port Arthur.'

The day of my 34th birthday – 29 April 1996. Sitting in the car on the way to see my beloved family who were still lying on the road where they had been killed. Numb, alone and I still haven't had a chance to say goodbye. Compassion is not a word the media comprehend as they set about getting tomorrow's headlines.

AP/AAP

The tears of love. Standing on the steps of St David's Cathedral in Hobart at the state memorial service on 1 May with my brother John (left) and my best friend Chris McCann. I had an incredible sense of déjà vu of my wedding day. The people were outside, but I realised that Netty wasn't next to me. I was saying goodbye to her and my beloved daughters.

Leigh Winburn, *The Mercury* (Hobart)

A celebration of their lives at the Zeltner Hall at Austin Hospital, where Nanette and I met. The colourful coffins are covered in flowers with the girls' artwork pinned on the wall behind. Netty always thought she would be famous, but never in these circumstances. The music of ABBA and Tina Arena was a fitting farewell for my three beautiful girls.

Jason South, *The Age*

The coffin of my three-year-old Maddie being carried out by my cousins, Julie and Gabrielle Mejak (rear), Ruth Cooper and Glenice Foster (front). Somehow society had let us all down. But 'the power of love and creation will always triumph over the power of destruction and revenge', I told the gathering at the funeral.

Jason South, *The Age*

Addressing 3000 people at a Coalition of Gun Control rally in Sydney's Domain at the three-month anniversary. 'There are 35 people who no longer have the ability to improve this country, but have somehow left a candle flickering in every one of us. It becomes a case of considering how we can stand up to represent them.'

News Ltd

The press conference with the Dunblane fathers in Hobart on 14 April 1997 (left to right): John Crozier, Les Morton and Gordon Bounds. During their six-day trip to Tasmania we bonded so well. Les Morton commented: 'I made a vow that if a massacre does happen again, I will be able to look in the mirror and say I did everything I possibly could to prevent that.' This reflected my own feelings.

Leigh Winburn, *The Mercury* (Hobart)

With Eddie Halton, who ran the supermarket at Nubeena and became one of my closest friends on the peninsula, outside my parents' place on the day of the 1996 AFL Grand Final. Eddie and Pam and their children have been a great support to me.

With Jo Winter in my parents' garden. Jo lost her winemaker husband, Jason, in the Broad Arrow Cafe, but her strength and positive attitude to life continues to astound me.

With our good friends Steve and Pam Ireland at my farewell party from the Tasman Peninsula. They were the first two doctors to enter the Broad Arrow Cafe on the day of the shootings.

With my brothers, Steven (left) and John, departing for the Oakes Day races in Melbourne on 7 November 1996 – a day of heart-wrenching emotion, as in Hobart the gunman pleads guilty to all counts, thereby avoiding a trial.

With my family in Hobart as I prepare the wreaths for each of my girls for the first anniversary. My family have been my pillar of strength – there when I need them and thereabouts when I don't. I can't thank them enough for loving me and giving me a reason to go on.

Bruce Miller

*Christmas Day 1996 –
sitting at their grave on
Lani's crocheted rug.
What, for most people, is
a happy day is but a
memory of the excitement
on the children's faces.
Writing about how
wonderful they were
enshrines their memory
and being with them
soothes my soul.*

*Sunrise at the memorial cross at Port Arthur on 27 April 1997.
The anniversary will always be a Sunday for me.*

Leigh Winburn, *The Mercury* (Hobart)

*My family and friends flanking me at Port Arthur on the first anniversary
of Nanette, Lani and Maddie's deaths. Left to right: my brother Steven, Richard
Shoobridge, John's girlfriend, Mary, my mum and dad, my brother John,
Pam Halton, Julia McCance, Eddie Halton.*

Leigh Winburn, *The Mercury* (Hobart)

*The launch in Melbourne of the Alannah and Madeline Foundation, set up
to benefit child victims who suffer due to violence or sudden loss. Foundation patron
Prime Minister John Howard (right) is pictured with Tim O'Shane, the father
of Tjandamurra O'Shane. Tjandamurra was severely burnt after being doused
with petrol in a Cairns schoolyard. He was the first recipient of the Foundation.*

Jason South, *The Age*

At the memorial cross, Port Arthur (from left): John Crozier, whose daughter Emma (aged five) was killed at Dunblane, Sue Burgess, whose daughter Nicole was killed at Port Arthur, Les Morton, whose daughter Emily (aged five) died at Dunblane, Danielle Burgess, Gordon Bounds, whose daughter Aimie Adam survived Dunblane, and myself with arm around John Burgess.

Roger Lovell, *Front Page Photography*

Standing in front of the tree where Alannah died, on the first anniversary of their deaths. I bought three heart-shaped yellow wreaths in proportionate sizes to mark the spot where they died. When this book went to print, there was no permanent memorial to mark the spot.

Jason South, *The Age*

He said the repercussions of the gunman's crimes had been felt across the world and that they fell 'within the worst category of cases and the heaviest penalty should apply'.

With his actions and cold-blooded intent now laid bare for the world to see, I felt he should no longer be allowed to live. This feeling has never left me. If he *must* live, then I hope he is incarcerated until he is 100.

No amount of time is long enough for the man the judge described as 'a pathetic social misfit'.

My public statement was given on behalf of my family, as well as Nanette's:

We are greatly relieved that the public part of our ordeal has been given some finality. Our pain and suffering at such a massive loss will, however, be with us for all of our lives. There can be no appropriate sentence for the perpetrator as we can never have our girls back. I thank all Australians who have shown such immense support and empathy. I just continue to urge Australians to be vigilant in light of our gun law reforms. We owe this to the thirty-five people who so cruelly lost their lives at Port Arthur . . . our debt to them is to make Australia a safer place to live.

SIXTEEN

Intimacy

The letter arrives on 20 January 1997. It's from the Port Arthur Task Force, Tasmania Police.

'Property gathered as evidence': one blue checkered dress, one dark blue jumper, one white singlet.

'Please be advised that certain items of property listed may be soiled or damaged to varying degrees.'

What should I do? That was four months ago and I haven't posted the letter back or ticked any of the options including whether they should be disposed of. I am paralysed with indecision.

The officialness of the letter describing my daughter's clothes, such intimate apparel, in this impersonal way, leaves me confused . . .

Intimacy. It's what I desire most.

One night in February, I am woken gently from a blissful sleep, I can sense fingers running through my hair. Kisses on the nape of my neck. So sensually pleasant that I shiver all over. The hint of body odour is strong. I'm not sure if it's me or my partner, but know that it's in anticipation of what will inevitably occur. A hand brushes past my nipples. Suddenly I sit bolt upright in terror. There is no-one with me. The turmoil wells up inside me. Brutal conflict in knowing what to do now. Feeling insecure and vulnerable, I leave the light on. Maddie's teddy bear is clutched fervently within my arms. The moisture of the tears being my last sensation as I drift back to the lonely state of sleep.

Christmas Eve 1996 arrived and somehow I thought if I could reach just a few days ahead, it would all be over. I go to visit Jacqueline Gillespie and her husband, Iain. In July 1992, Jacqueline's two children, Iddin and Shahirah, were kidnapped by her Malaysian ex-husband. She wrote to me after the massacre and we had met up several times. Telling Jacqueline my feelings gave me some comfort, knowing I was not the only one feeling pain and anguish. In this house also, the thought of Christmas was being contemplated with apprehension.

I went to midnight mass with Mum and Dad. When the priest mentioned those who'd lost loved ones throughout the year and named us specifically, I felt extremely self-conscious. As I stood behind the pew in St Martin's Catholic Church, it was one of the few times I felt trapped and unable to escape. I could not sing one word of a Christmas carol. I knew the carols off by heart; we had all sung them so many times before.

For the past six years, especially since the children arrived, Christmas meant anticipation and love, waking in the early hours of the morning and watching Lani and Maddie opening their presents, tearing the paper open with excitement. This year, I avoided the toy departments when I walked into stores. I usually had my head down so I wouldn't see the decorations and tinsel, preparations for what should be a joyful occasion.

When the congregation was asked by the priest to exchange a sign of friendship and the words 'Merry Christmas' were uttered to me, I couldn't respond. I really wished they were saying, 'Try and have a good day.'

I left the church as quickly as possible through the side door, fearing I would be besieged after the service. It was the last thing I wanted.

I woke on Christmas Day with tears in my eyes. I went to a cupboard at my parents' house and retrieved the photos used for the funeral. I visited the cemetery alone. The headstone still wasn't erected, so I sat next to the mound of dirt and jars containing fresh flowers. The sky above me was dull and overcast with a few showers threatening.

As I placed the Christmas trees and presents I'd bought on the grave, it was so peaceful, I couldn't even hear the sound of birds. I sat on Alannah's multi-coloured crocheted rug. Sometimes, I find the love that fills me for my family is so enormous, I can barely contain it. As I sat there that morning, I felt a deep desire to share a little bit of that with someone, but there is no-one there. No-one who can take on board the enormity of what has happened. I have to deal with it myself.

I open the doors of my car and play the Tina Arena song 'That's the Way a Woman Feels'. Whenever I play it I hear Lani singing, that voice of six-year-old innocence imitating the lyrics perfectly:

When the sky is grey and it looks like rain
Just think of me. I'll come running from wherever I am.
Just as fast as I can.

Gentle rain begins to fall and I feel Netty and the girls are falling down on me. It's a thought I often have when it rains. That the moisture from the rain soaks through the soil and somehow it captures some of them from under the ground, then evaporates up to the sky to fall back down again. It's comforting in some ways and I feel like they're visiting me. Tiny parts of them landing on me.

It's the same sort of feeling I had in those early weeks after returning to Melbourne when I visited the Eltham Leisure Centre and the pool we used to go to. As I got into the water, I felt soothed, thinking of the possibility that there were skin cells from their bodies and I was bathing in it.

As the rain is falling, I pick up the crocheted rug and begin packing up. I tell each of them how much I love them and want to be with them. Departing wasn't easy and yet when I left, I felt tranquil and at peace. The day, at least, would be bearable. Tomorrow, which wasn't far away, would mean Christmas was over.

Later that morning, John, Steve and I went for our traditional Christmas Day run and then visited Uncle Maté for lunch. All of my family were there, as well as my cousins Gabrielle and Julie. We shared a bottle of butterscotch schnapps together. At least I was surrounded by people who loved me – my own family. We had always been close. It was Uncle Maté who told my parents the news that changed them forever.

Mum and Dad had rung our house in Nubeena on that Sunday morning in April.

'They've probably gone on a picnic. We should go for one, too,' my mother thought.

In Mum's last conversation with her eldest granddaughter, Alannah said, 'Maddie and I went with Dad to Mass for Easter. I love you, Bubba.'

It wasn't until 8.30 that night when they were at the Istria Club that someone told them something had happened at Port Arthur.

Dad suggested going home to find out what happened. The phone rang as they walked in the door. It was Uncle Maté, crying his eyes out. My cousin Gabrielle had told him the news.

'My God, has something happened?' Mum said.

'Ring Walter,' he repeated. He couldn't tell her what had happened, he was crying so much.

Finally, he said, 'Nanette and the girls have been shot and Walter might be injured, too.'

Mum screamed in disbelief and couldn't bring herself to do anything. Finally summoning up the courage, at about 10 p.m. she dialled my number.

'Walter, what has happened? Are they dead?'

'Yes, Mum, and I wish I was dead, too.'

My brothers John and Steve had heard something had happened at Port Arthur at about 4.30 in the afternoon on a news flash. They knew Nanette worked night shifts, so they were not concerned.

That evening they went to the Depot as they did regularly on Sunday nights. At about 10.30, there was an announcement in between songs asking Steven to go to the front door. Two police officers were there. He knew immediately it was serious.

My relationship with my family was like the foundations of the building. With the loss of Netty and the girls, some of the structural supports collapsed. What remained had to be strengthened, steel girders put in place in order for us all to survive, bonding us to a depth I could never before have contemplated. The intensity of the bonding sometimes tested us all to the limits.

That first Christmas without Nanette and the girls, lunch was traditional: tagliatella marinara and roast pork, chicken and beef. At 2 p.m., Dad, Steve, John and I collapsed on the recliners in the lounge-room and I sank into a deep sleep.

On Boxing Day, I woke to a feeling that Christmas had passed and I had survived. Most of January was spent at Rye at the beach house. I trained for the Pier-to-Pub race and drank at the Portsea pub, sometimes to oblivion.

'Are you really enjoying yourself?' people would say.

'Hell, no, but I'm a really good actor,' I often felt like replying.

Or, perhaps I should have said, 'What do you want me to do? Go out and bury myself?'

Drinking was a double-edged sword, bringing what I thought was relief, but the following morning my grief was back to haunt me tenfold.

One Sunday morning in January I woke up and felt so bad I couldn't remember what day it was. My mouth felt like someone had emptied a birdcage in it. A brief memory of the cigar I had smoked the night before was obviously the cause. My throat was dry and raspy and my head throbbed. Most of the bodies staying at our beach house were still in bed.

Mum was making coffee in the kitchen.

'How are you this morning, mate? A little bit better than last night?' she asked.

'What do you mean? I was all right last night,' realising full well what she meant.

'Well, when you got home you lay on the concrete outside with your dog, Becky, and gave her a huge cuddle. Do you remember that?'

No, I didn't. In fact, the whole recollection of the previous night was blurry. I hope I didn't say anything inappropriate. Did I behave all right? Perhaps I had descended into one of my morbid states. All these thoughts whizzed past my non-conforming neurons. Mum was silent, also. She was concerned. Concerned at what she saw and had seen on a number of occasions before.

It's on those hungover days that you feel most insecure. Wanting someone to look after you. The way Netty had on New Year's Day the year before. A compulsory stop to be sick on the windy road to Hobart had been met with laughter, but followed with lots of attention. Lots of hair-patting and caressing. What you need most when you're feeling shocking is this kind of devotion.

What is happening to me? There is a deep longing within me that cannot be filled.

Touch. How I long to hold them. Not long after the funeral, I was offered a professional massage by Tanya Flack, a friend of my brother Steve. As I lie on the table and she begins to rub aromatherapy oil into my shoulders, I close my eyes to the delicious sensations of touch. It triggers so many emotions in me. She begins to work on my arm, kneading her fingers on the inside of my forearm, and as she reaches my hand I have a tremendous urge, almost involuntary, to grasp hers. I know I must continue with this therapy as its tangible properties will be invaluable in my healing process.

This sensation of touch reminds me of shortly after the funeral when, I was sitting in our local church in Melbourne behind a lady who was wearing the same top that Nanette had on the day she died, the same deep burgundy, chenille soft to touch. She had similar hair, curly, shoulder-length and an almost identical colour to Nanette's.

I desperately wanted to touch her jumper, to reach forward from my seat and rub my hands over the texture. I knew it was highly inappropriate, even if I'd asked for permission.

After the service we had tea in a hall and somehow I began talking to the woman's husband. I asked him where his wife was and he pointed to a woman inside the hall a few metres away. I told him I would go and introduce myself.

I walked up to her and gave her a kiss on the cheek.

'I've just been talking to your husband and told him I'd come over to give you a hug.'

As I put my arms around her, my hands reached out to touch the jumper to feel what I wanted to have in my arms again. Little did she know of my underlying desire. After the hug, I felt fine, as though I had been fulfilled. I could go on with the rest of my day.

Yesterday was 8 April – Netty's birthday. Like so many of these anniversaries, I wanted the day to be over. We had celebrated this day together for thirteen years. To Netty, birthdays were very special. Days to pamper, give, share, laugh and be together. Consequently, days that should remain in your memory forever. I couldn't muster one iota of happiness being without Netty for the day.

I cut some lovely daisies from my garden to place on the grave. I wanted to be close to her, to touch her. So I did the next best thing and lay on the grave. The hard polished granite enveloped my body as though it were soft. Maybe my body flattened itself out to be close. I'm not sure. Warmth from the sun's rays nearly sent me drifting off to sleep. My eyes, resting on the granite, were red and sore. It was easier to close my eyes than have them open.

Talking to Netty brought no response. I kept thinking of what I would have said to Netty the night before she died, a last goodbye. Netty, have I really made you as happy as you've made me? What are my worst characteristics? I want to at least try to work on some of these. Would you change anything about your life if you could? Would you marry me if we meet again in another life. Am I a good kisser? More importantly, am I a good lover? I'd like to think so after practising so hard with you. Will Alannah and Madeline be able to realise their potential in another world? Will I see you in heaven? Will you love me just as much when I get there?

I certainly wouldn't let Netty sleep. I would talk to and hold her. Keep her talking and hopefully even make love a couple of times. An opportunity to thank her for the good and bad times. The ability to share body and soul with someone. To intuitively know what another human being is feeling for a person. To identify your needs before you even realise them yourself. These are the things I miss. Netty would often say to me, 'I know you better than you know yourself.' 'Go and get changed and go for a run,' she would say and it was exactly what I needed.

'Why don't you go out in the garden for a little while?'

'Why don't you take Keith out for a hit of golf today?'

She could tell just by talking to me or watching me what I really wanted to do. And the non-verbal aspect of sharing with a person. Being at a function or party and sensing that the partner is bored, tired or inebriated or unhappy. Being able to give each other that look that says a thousand words. That look that says I want to be with you forever. The one that says you frustrate me so much, but I know I'd never be without you.

Now I can stand in a room with hundreds of people and feel alone, vulnerable and uncertain. Before, just the sight of Netty in the crowd would make me complete. Secure, strong, knowing that I could take on any challenge the world could offer. I miss that. Is it possible I will ever feel that way again? It could just happen. Although at the moment, I don't think so.

One of the bereavement manuals I read talked about the gender differences in grief. Women usually use verbal communication to achieve intimacy. Men are often left with the belief that intimacy can only be achieved through sex.

I *have* had physical relationships with other women since Nanette died. Some of them seem to be attracted to me, in a perverse way, because of my situation. Nightclubs attract lonely people and I have joined this group. At first, having sex with another woman felt awkward. For so long, I had lived with monogamy. As the past year has progressed I have found the novelty of these relationships has diminished and they have become increasingly futile. I know they are a temporary substitute for the intimacy I've lost and I'm beginning to realise I am raising expectations from these women that I cannot meet, which leads to further complications in my life.

Can you see what I've been doing, Netty? I know you are the best book on the shelf. Can I transfer the love I felt for you to someone else? I am looking, Netty, but I can't find anyone. Some advice I have been given is that no one person can fill the shoes of the loved one who has been killed. It is unrealistic to think that another person or other activities can fill the vacuum in my heart. When I was twenty-three and made the decision to marry you, it was just a case of 'do it'. Now, I conjure up every possible scenario for a relationship not working before it even gets off the ground. The thought of being hurt, of not having control over what eventuates, of freeing my emotions only for them to be dashed against the rocks. The thought of a relationship ending in divorce somehow terrifies me. It still represents a loss and could take a piece of me that I think I no longer have to give.

I'm not yet ready for another relationship and I'm sometimes aware that, through my desire for intimacy, which may be fleeting, and my own fragile recovery process, I may be hurting other people's feelings.

The loss of intimacy is perhaps one of the greatest losses in my life. That closeness to another. The ability to anticipate their behaviour when it's so unpredictable. The person to share your soul. No.

Part of your soul. No-one to tell you you look good in the morning. To tell your anxieties and fears. Those dim, dark secrets that only the closest person will hear. I even miss how my faults used to annoy Netty. My disregard for punctuality drove her nuts. To me it wasn't a priority. Now my watch is continually set fifteen minutes fast so I can get to appointments on time. She'd be proud – I'm even early sometimes.

I have to choose clothes on my own now. After having your guidance for over ten years, I think I'm making judgements you'd approve of, Netty. You'd love my black Hugo Boss suit. I'd never have forked out the money for it before, but now I've got nothing to save for. Today and maybe tomorrow are my only concerns at the moment. So I may as well look resplendent today. I also bought a Boss jumper which you'd love. Mum nearly collapsed when she saw the price. I'm sure you'd commandeer it if you were still here. I sometimes wear your black ghost tour guide parka. I feel strong and close to you when I wear it. Your handwritten 'cheat notes', which gave the prompts for the history of Port Arthur, are still in its pocket.

Every choice I make now is difficult. Before, I'd just go along with most things and take them in my stride. Deciding where to hang pictures in my new home is an effort. I try to think of what you'd say. In a couple of cases I've just put some up anywhere. It only takes a second look to know that you wouldn't approve. I move them.

I have to think about what I'm going to have for dinner. You did such a great job with the cooking. Always something new or different. Could you come back and cook your crispy skin potatoes for me just one more time?

The other day I bought a bronze sculpture from Hobart's Salamanca market. Netty, you'd love it. Bacchus, the god of wine. It will remind me of you. The dinners, bottles of wine, kisses, laughs, hugs, smiles and times we shared. A huge chunk of my life that belongs to you, Netty.

Where is your spirit now? Do you see me all the time and know everything? I sense your presence in quiet moments. Sometimes I expect to see your face when I look at my own reflection, as if you are mirrored in me. In many ways, you were my alter ego. We complemented each other perfectly. Our existence was a partnership. There are times now when I feel you are trying to snatch my spirit from my body – for yourself to still feel complete. I am waiting for you to visit me.

One of your best friends, Karon Oldfield (née Ford), wrote to me from Perth to tell me how she experienced your spirit saying goodbye to her in a dream. She writes:

The dream begins with Greg [Karon's husband] and I and you and Netty seated within a carriage. Like the ones that you see on ferris wheels at the show. This carriage has train wheels and we are moving along the train tracks through magnificent tall trees. The carriage moved at a fast walking pace over the small rises and falls in the landscape. The three of us were dressed in summer clothes, but Netty was how I last saw her. In her wedding dress with striking colours from her make-up.

We were smiling, laughing and talking, then the carriage stopped. When it began to move again, Netty was not with us. There was no more smiling, laughing or talking.

Then we were in a huge hall made of mud bricks and stones with a full-length stained glass window. There was a portrait of a peaceful-looking Nanette hanging on one wall. As we looked at it, bright sunshine through the stained glass window illuminated the image. Nanette then opened her eyes and drifted quickly along the shaft of light towards the stained glass. When she reached the glass, she quickly turned and rushed at us with tremendous speed. I felt her pass through me and envelope me at the same time. This sensation woke me up. I woke up Greg and told him that I felt Netty had just said goodbye to me in her own special way.

Such a wonderful farewell, Netty. Why haven't you and your spirit said goodbye to me? Are you still holding on to me from afar?

Where is my spirit, my sense of inner peace? As I sit here I feel empty inside, like I have lost the meaning of life, that I am like a ball on the pool table bumping against the sides looking for the hole to drop in to. That I have lost touch with myself, lost my own intimacy as well as my innocence.

I write a poem to you and the girls:

You are my memory
You are my hope
My lost existence within your hands
Tears and laughter within your hearts
Life has changed inside me forever.

SEVENTEEN

The Bairns of Dunblane

'What are you crying for, then?' the man with the broad Scottish accent asked. The words were warm and friendly. I had known him for just ten hours.

'Because I want to,' was my reply.

John Crozier needed no more justification. Within minutes I could see tears running down his cheeks. We were sitting on opposite sides of the corridor outside John's room in The Grand Chancellor, Hobart's most upmarket hotel. It was 13 April, two weeks before the first anniversary. Two suit-clad men crying at six in the morning, not touching, not speaking, sharing a bottomless pit of grief.

John's five-year-old daughter, Emma, died at Dunblane in Scotland on 13 March 1996, shot dead by another crazed gunman who let loose in a school gymnasium. John, Les Morton and Gordon Bounds, three of the fathers affected by the tragedy, had travelled across the globe to visit Port Arthur to spread the message that the world would no longer put up with such intolerable acts.

Next to me the plate of toasted ham and cheese sandwiches and chips we'd ordered were going cold. It was the music that triggered the rush of emotion. The woman on the hotel's reception was rather surprised when at 5.30 a.m., John had rung up asking for a CD player to be sent up to his room. There wasn't one in the hotel, so the compromise was to play it over the public address system.

The Bob Dylan song 'Knockin' on Heaven's Door', reworked by Dunblane musician Ted Christopher, and dedicated to the memory of the children of Dunblane, was all that was needed after the hours we'd been drinking, to dredge up the hurt again.

All these guns have caused too much pain,
This town will never be the same again,
So for the bairns of Dunblane
We ask please never again.

So much pain, so much torment that the tears could not wash away. But amongst the pain, the knowledge that we could comfort each other, that there was so much understanding between us.

I wasn't crying for my children, nor even Nanette, but for the fifteen children and their teacher from the other side of the world who I'd never be able to meet and for the parents left behind with all the agony I knew so well.

When I first met John Crozier and Les Morton at Roland and Kate's place in Hobart on the Saturday night, John shook my hand and we gave each other a hug. He and I had spoken on the phone a couple of times, but it crossed my mind that we may not have anything in common, in spite of the fact we were united by such a traumatic event.

'Come and look at this,' he said, taking me through to the kitchen. On the sink stood a terracotta pot wrapped with a tartan ribbon, containing four heather plants.

Then I remembered I'd told him on the phone that during my trip to Scotland in 1984, while visiting Loch Ness, I'd spent ten minutes jumping in the heather.

'You said you wanted to roll in some heather, so here's your wish.' said John with a cheeky smile on his face.

This beginning to our first meeting gave me comfort. John and Les were total strangers and yet we had a connection that went beyond words. (I didn't meet Gordon until the following day as he stayed at his hotel with jetlag.)

The evening progressed through dinner and a few red wines at an inner city restaurant, where it was increasingly obvious we had instant rapport. To be able to share feelings with someone who'd experienced such an incredibly similar loss fuelled my soul. Doctor Bryan Walpole, staff specialist in the Department of Emergency Medicine at the Royal Hobart Hospital, and his wife Kate also attended the dinner. He told me he had seen the bodies of my girls at the hospital.

'The hospital was running a national course in emergency management. We were lucky there were so many specialist people from interstate who'd completed the course and were on hand,' he said. 'There were so many injured with bullet wounds.'

Later, he said to me, 'I don't know how you're able to continue.'

'I've got no choice,' I replied.

We drank more wine and paid the bill.

'What are we going to do now?' John asked.

'Well, how about going for a few more drinks at a nightclub?' I suggested.

'Will you dance then?'

'Yeah, sure. Nanette always loved dancing. And I find it's a kind of release for me. If I do go dancing, I often think of them, too, because they can't do it any more. You'll have to collect me off the dance floor when I collapse.'

John stared at me and said nothing. What I had said clearly stirred something inside him.

'C'mon then, let's get going.'

We danced till 5 a.m. at a local nightclub and it was when we returned to the hotel that we ordered the toasted sandwiches.

The next day he told me he hadn't danced since Emma died thirteen months previously.

My contact with the Dunblane fathers was prompted by a trip Roland Browne and Rebecca Peters were making to the UK in January 1997. They were attending meetings on gun control, and the trip included a visit to Dunblane.

It was at that time that Rebecca asked if I wanted to see some of the information on Dunblane that was on the Internet. Amongst the material was the first newspaper interview the parents had given since the tragedy which appeared in The Sunday Times.

I wasn't quite prepared for the starkness of its content and how much it moved me. How much I identified with so many of the words that were said. They had so many similar experiences – packing up their child's life in boxes, grappling with the memories of life before this all happened, watching videos trying to recapture some of their spirit and bring them back to life again.

Like the family video of five-year-old Charlotte dancing an impromptu Highland fling in a grey school pinafore and sweatshirt. Her father, Martyn Dunn, watched it over and over.

'I filmed this two weeks before she died. I heard her laughing and just grabbed the camera. I'm so glad I did,' he said in the article.

It reminded me of Alannah's Blue Heelers dance which I'd videoed. There were other memories, too, which triggered hurt. Five-year-old Matthew Burnie who had been badly injured, a bullet shearing through his shoulder, greeted his parents with the words: 'You weren't there. Why weren't you there?'

He had lived to be able to ask that question. What would Lani or Maddie have said to me if they'd been injured and lived? How would they have survived with those sorts of memories? One child had even managed to walk out of the gymnasium that morning. Five-year-old

Stuart Weir picked his way through the dead and injured, even though there were two bullet holes in his legs.

How could anyone treat children like this? How could we, as adults, ever give an explanation for what happened?

Gordon Bounds' five-year-old daughter, Aimie, was crippled when a bullet shattered her right leg. She is now in a wheelchair. She also lives with the mental scars of witnessing the gunman kill himself.

Gordon told me, when we met in Hobart, that he and his partner Christine looked after Aimie by themselves. We discussed how she has coped mentally. Gordon tells me that shortly after the shooting, Aimie received counselling from a psychologist.

'He asked her to draw pictures. We went back again and she said: "I don't want to do any more drawings. I'm bored. I want to go to the cemetery to play with my friends".'

'We will all never get over what has happened,' said one mother, Pamela Ross, who lost her daughter, Joanna. 'Each day we live with the loss and nothing in the future will ever allow us to feel that our lives are complete. There will never be a point at which we can say we are coping and everything is fine, because it will never be. We just need the strength to live with it for the rest of our lives.'

These were my sentiments exactly. Life would never be the same again for any of us.

Liz McLennan, who lost her five-year-old daughter, Abigail, said that her other two daughters could not come to terms with it. 'They are scared going to school. They cling together. They even sleep in the same single bed. They're constantly asking "Will it ever happen again?" What can I tell them?'

As I read The Sunday Times *article, I underlined in pink highlighter texta the words that struck a chord. This small act seemed to give me comfort.*

Michael North's now without his wife and child and has only his daughter's cat for company. I understood how important cuddling that animal was. It was his last living connection with his daughter. Wilbur meant the same to me.

Michael says in the article that Sophie's hand-made Father's Day card inscribed 'To the best daddy' still dominated his mantlepiece.

One of Alannah's diaries carried a similar dedication.

I also related to his feeling of disbelief when the events happened. He'd bought tickets to a concert for Sophie and himself an hour after she had been killed, oblivious, as I was when I was playing golf, that such a horrendous thing had happened.

Here, on a page of newsprint, were so many words being expressed that I could understand, words from across the other side of the world, from people who could say with conviction that they knew how I felt. All the platitudes I had been given from wellwishers: 'I know how you feel.' How could anyone know how I felt? Yet, here was a whole group of people who did know exactly how I felt and who were trying to do something to prevent the same thing happening again by lobbying politicians and people in power to control the type of weapons that were allowed to be used in our society.

As a child Michael North said he had never even owned a toy gun and always changed television channels if violence came onto the screen if his daughter was watching. 'I owe it to Sophie and Barbara,' he says of his commitment to changing British gun laws.

The more I read, the more convinced I became that I also had to do something to prevent this happening again. I owed it to Lani, Maddie and Netty.

Kenny Ross, husband of Pamela and father of Joanna, who was killed at Dunblane, asked the then Opposition Leader Tony Blair: 'Do you have a daughter and how old is she?'

'Yes, she's eight years old.'

'Well, I had a daughter. She was five years old and now she's six foot under the ground in a wooden box and she was put there by someone with a legally held handgun.'

The Dunblane gunman had four handguns and enough magazines for 700 rounds. He arrived at the school late, missing assembly by minutes, as he was caught in a traffic jam. In the gymnasium he discharged 105 rounds in less than the time it took to smoke a cigarette.

Michael North said he was not giving up until the gun laws were changed in Britain and guns were not given to anyone.

After reading the newspaper article: I penned my first letter to Scotland – to Michael North.

Dear Mick,

I know exactly some of the emotions that you have felt. I hope that by writing to you, it lets you know that someone in the world can have empathy with some of the things you are feeling. I know that this doesn't ease the incredible desire to hold those bodies again and just be with them for even a millisecond.

I know for me there is sometimes difficulty at finding a reason for being here. But it is at times like these that I think of the love I shared with my three beautiful girls. I hope my letter helps you in even a little, small way.

Lots of love, Walter

I also wrote to all the families – handwritten notes that I hoped they'd understand. I received a reply about three weeks later saying the families had been 'deeply touched'.

Dear parents who lost their children in Dunblane, their friends and families,

I can often be sitting in an armchair and nearly feel the brush of little bodies pushing through or wanting to sit on my lap. The intensity of wanting to feel their hair or hold their little bodies is often overwhelming and brings tears flowing to my eyes.

Being a parent would have to be, in many ways, the ultimate accolade to being alive. When a unique love for your partner is expressed by the creation of life, I feel privileged to have been loved by such a special woman and have two unique children. I am sure many of you have nearly identical feelings to the ones I have experienced.

As a parent, there is a piece of you that has been snatched away.

You know that you have to learn to live without it, but know that it can never be replaced.

I hope that by having each other around brings some comfort and I will think of you all. I am hoping to come to Dunblane later in the year and would dearly love to meet with any of you who might be interested.

God bless.

Lots of love,

Walter Mikac.

My contact with the Dunblane fathers rekindled my desire to prevent a massacre like this ever happening again. As parents, we had never contemplated such a thing could happen to our children. We were living, as Les Morton said, in a developing society which was supposed to go along with civilisation. We were ordinary people and society had let us down.

The children in Dunblane were at school, a public place where they should have been safe. The book *Our Year of Tears*, published in 1997 by the *Sunday Mail*, makes the point: 'They were on their way to a place of fun and laughter; a place where children feel warm and secure, a place of trust.'

As ordinary people, we were determined to take any measures required to change society. Les Morton told me he had made a vow to change the gun laws after meeting Tony Hill, the father of a girl whose daughter was killed at the Hungerford massacre in 1987. He said that he felt guilty at the time that he didn't do something to change the laws more dramatically. Semi-automatic rifles had been banned, but no action was taken on handguns.

Les said if a massacre did happen again, at least he would be able to look in the mirror and say he had done everything possible to prevent that.

Throughout the months ahead, both the Dunblane parents and myself were often accused of being puppets of the anti-gun control lobby by minority groups who wanted less control over guns. Yet these groups ignored the obvious – that we were simply ordinary people who wanted some fundamental rules in our society changed.

The Dunblane parents gained strength from each other. Some had barely known each other before the tragedy and now they were the closest friends. They met every Thursday night for moral support. Even the families of the injured victims met regularly. This was something that wasn't possible for me in Tasmania, as the victims had come from other places, making it harder for the families to give each other this kind of support.

These three fathers had travelled across the globe, far from their place of work and their families, determined to spread their message. The Dunblane parents had already visited the House of Commons in Westminster with a petition containing 428,279 names and had a meeting with Britain's then Prime Minister, John Major. They were to claim a victory in May when Tony Blair, the new British Prime Minister, pledged to the parents to push a total ban on handguns through Parliament.

As the time passed after the massacre, I discovered I could also have a major role in this process. Our great strength as parents lay in the fact that we were not politicians – we had a message that couldn't be polluted from any quarter. We were there to represent our children and our families. We were there because our children couldn't be. And there *was* strength in numbers.

Michael North replied to my letter shortly afterwards.

Dear Walter,

Hearing of your involvement in the anti-gun campaign from friends who have heard you speak at rallies gave me a lot of strength. We have both lost so much but somehow find the energy from within ourselves and from others to do something so important.
With all best wishes,
   Mick.

Rereading some of the letters I'd received after the shooting reminded me that there were many other people out there who shared my convictions. One man from New Zealand wrote:

This world needs someone to be a catalyst for a movement to stop the use of guns in this way. There is no way on this earth that anyone can convince me that people living in a normal modern day existence need to have access to automatic or semi-automatic firearms. And you may be just the man to start or support a movement to ban these types of weapons.

There was also a powerful letter from eleven-year-old Ben Morrison, himself a victim of weapons, who'd been kidnapped in Hobart the year before after watching his parents have a gun held up to their head. He wrote to me in the week following the deaths of Nanette, Lani and Maddie.

Dear Mr Mikac,

I wanted to write to you to let you know that I have not been able to stop thinking about you since I learnt of the terrible tragedy at Port Arthur. I feel so sad that you lost your beautiful wife and your two extra precious daughters. My family and I send you love and tender caring thoughts and prayers and we hope your healing process will one day include some sort of acceptance.

They are so precious in every way and people should not take families for granted. I learnt this lesson well, and so did my family about 18 months ago when two men came into our house and pointed a gun at my Mum and Dad and my little brother and kidnapped me, only leaving a ransom note for my parents. I was tied up with rope around my neck, wrists, thighs and ankles. I had balaclavas pulled over my head so that I couldn't see and was made to get into a little suitcase squashed up like a baby. They put me in the boot of their car and took me some place where they kept me like this for 18 hours. I thought they were going to kill me and I might never get to see my

*parents and family again. I guess I was lucky because they got scared
and let me go.*

*I know this doesn't seem very awful compared to what happened
to you but it helps me understand just a little about how you must
be feeling, knowing you can never see your family again. I wish I
could come and visit and hold you close and hug you till you feel
better but I think, right now, you're probably wondering if you'll
ever feel better.*

*I know, in my heart, that your girls will always be with you in spirit
because when I was scared on my own because of these awful men,
I just knew Mum and Dad were sort of with me . . . if you know what
I mean.*

*I really, really, really hope and pray that one day you will again
find peace and happiness and that the wonderful memories of the
family you lost will warm your heart until that day comes. I will never
forget you and will send you LOVE and LIGHT and prayers forever.*

Ben Morrison and family.

In classrooms throughout the country, the issue of gun control was
being discussed. The children at Grade 4/5 at Princes Street Primary
School in Hobart wrote a series of essays on the topic:

One boy, Robert, had written his own gun laws for Australia:

1. Don't point your gun at innocent people.
2. You can't own a gun if you take drugs.
3. Don't own a gun if you can't control yourself.
4. Put your gun in a safe place.
   But there are more rules about keeping a gun there. I
   wouldn't own a gun because it's a bad habit.
   DON'T KILL PEOPLE.

Lucy from Grade 5 wrote: 'On April 28 1996, a terrible thing
happened in Tasmania. A lunatic went to the Port Arthur Historic
Site armed with a gun, some cans of petrol and handcuffs. He caused
a massacre. When he went to Port Arthur that day, he meant to cause
harm and boy, he did just that.'

The Dunblane fathers held a press conference at Hadley's Hotel in

Hobart on 14 April to reinforce their message about the need for greater gun control. I decided to join them.

Sitting in a cafe before going to the press conference, I felt myself slump into an unexpected depression. The view out the window of the cafe through black steel bars made me feel trapped. I didn't want to move on to the future, but I knew I couldn't return to the past. In so many ways, I had been imprisoned since the events of Port Arthur – in limbo like a prisoner suspended in a time warp with no hope of parole.

But after hearing the moving words of John, Les and Gordon later on that morning, my spirits buoyed. Hearing them speak, I felt relieved that, here at last was a place from which I could draw strength. One thing that Les Morton had said was, 'There is a unique bond between people that have had murder enter their life. It's not a bond that I would recommend be shared by anybody else.'

They had organised a seat up on the stage and I took comfort from the fact that, for once, I wasn't alone in facing the media.

When the press conference finished, I shook hands with John and Les. Gordon was walking towards me to shake my hand. Instead I reached up and kissed him.

When the photo of Gordon and I appeared in the newspaper the next morning, John laughed.

'Look at you two in the paper. You guys should be going to march in that gay law reform demonstration in Hobart today.'

I was discovering that being around these three men was fun. We could joke as well as cry. In the five days we were together, we got to know each other extremely well. It was as if there were no need for pretence, no idle banter. Sitting in a bar, we drank Rusty Nails, (Scotch with Drambuie on ice) and spoke from the heart about what mattered. We shared several meals together and we walked around Constitution Dock where the Sydney–Hobart yacht race ended each year.

Each of them was quite different. Gordon was older than the others, a little more reserved and he often retired earlier than the rest of us.

He had a wry sense of humour which would materialise when it was least expected. I was surprised to find John, who seemed so jocular, was an elder in the 'kirk' (church). Beneath the humour lay a fiery intensity, a deep sense of faith.

'I know the children have gone to heaven and he'll be burning in hell,' he said to me often.

Les was less talkative but underneath this exterior, he held deep convictions. Although he was an atheist, he believed in spirituality. I read some of this book to him, about not having time to say goodbye, and that I had wanted to ask Nanette before she died whether I was a good lover.

'How can you be so honest? I admit that I don't reveal my real feelings to anyone. I just don't feel comfortable sharing them with anyone else.'

Since the shooting, Les had befriended Michael North. Their daughters used to play together, but the two men hardly knew each other. Les remembers when he was told about Emily's death, he was in the classroom looking out the window, and he saw Michael across the quadrangle looking out the window, too.

'I knew what he was being told,' he said. 'And I thought of the degrees of loss.'

He also said that since the shooting he had reassessed his priorities.

'My relationship with Mick probably makes me redefine what I thought in the past were various achievements.'

On the Sunday we had arranged to visit the Port Arthur Historic Site. That morning, after our nightclub outing and only three hours' sleep, John and I attended a service at St David's Cathedral. I felt strangely at peace and soothed by the choral singing, even though when I first walked in, it brought memories of the last time I'd been there – the week after the massacre.

In the car on the way to the historic site, we talked about how often we saw children that looked like ours and for a fleeting moment we believed it was them, at the same time knowing deep down it was not possible.

Les showed me a postcard he had been sent from America. On it were two angels. He produced Emily's photo to show the incredible likeness to one of the angels.

We also talked of how we felt when clinical details were read out about what had happened to our children – details we would all have preferred never to have heard.

Sometimes we sat in silence. To know that I didn't actually have to say anything for them to understand how I felt. And we sometimes shared laughter.

'By the way, Walter, we've coined a phrase that fits the bill when we go out with you,' John Crozier said.

'What's that?' I asked.

'We say we're going to "get Mikaced".'

After parking, we walked round to the historic site via the water instead of going through the toll gates, in case of any unwanted media attention. We were joined by Sue and John Burgess and their remaining daughter, Danielle. I carried Roland and Kate Browne's youngest boy, Asher, in a backpack. Somehow the role of father and protector floated back to me. It was comforting. He felt like a security blanket and I didn't feel so alone.

As we approached the site, I could see the walls of the Broad Arrow Cafe which had been left standing – something I still found hard to believe. My anxiety level escalated as we approached the skeleton of the building. I knew I couldn't walk in there. I knew what had happened in graphic detail, where most of them had been standing or sitting and the sequence of when they had been killed. The court case is still so vivid in my memory. I also find it macabre that if someone could get a detailed map from the court case, they could actually walk through the massacre, step by step. I felt an inner animosity at this fact, as angry as I'll allow myself to get, but at the same time I felt I was in a dream.

When John asked me how I felt, I related this feeling of disbelief.

As we walked around the site, Les commented: 'It's so quiet here. It's very difficult to believe something like this could ever happen here. It's exactly what we thought about our beautiful town of Dunblane.'

We walked around to the memorial cross which stood near the water's edge and laid the wreath from the parents at Dunblane for the victims at Port Arthur: sixteen white roses and thirty-five red roses.

John read out the names of each victim from the top of the cross to the bottom. As he read, I told them as much as I knew about each victim. It took about five minutes. So many people with no reason or no explanation for their deaths.

We took photographs and then had lunch at the tearooms where we met Brigid Cooke, a historic site employee who was injured during the shooting. She had been working in the Broad Arrow Cafe on the day of the massacre and, by going out to warn people outside of the shooting, was shot in the leg.

Then we walked up Jetty Road to place crosses where my girls had been killed. John laid a red rose for Netty and a white one for the girls. It was a very moving moment.

Earlier on, I'd taken a hammer and erected three white crosses on the spots where they'd died. I should have done it ages ago. I knew the road where the girls had been killed was to be replaced when the new Visitors' Centre was built. In the future it would hardly be used and I had a sense of despair at the thought of the area where they'd died simply being forgotten.

I had been waiting for almost a year for the Memorial Committee, who had been appointed after the shooting, to make a decision on a permanent mark of remembrance for those who had died. I had complained to the General Manager of the site, Mr Craig Coombs.

He told me that anything left at the site would only be allowed to stay there for twenty-four hours before being removed. Permanent markers such as crosses or plaques would be put in 'deep archives' for 'future generations' because 'some staff members', including himself, became 'upset' by a permanent reminder of the massacre. Yet apparently this attitude did not translate when it came to the decision to preserve the walls of the cafe.

'What about the current generation who want to remember now?'

I asked. 'Why should we hide what has happened?'

It was as if there was a conspiracy to deny the events of 28 April, just as there had been a conspiracy to cover up the misery and suffering of the convicts. My brother Steve summed it up when he visited the site: 'It's ridiculous. This is a historic site and what they are trying to do is cover up history.'

Even the main cross, where we'd laid the wreath, which had come to represent so much to so many of the bereaved families, was due to be moved – no-one knew where.

I felt like saying that perhaps they should go and drop it offshore in Carnarvon Bay where it would never need to be seen again.

On the way back to Hobart, we visited Nubeena, our old house and the pharmacy. I felt proud to show them where I once lived, the serenity and the beauty of the peninsula. The sun was just setting and it was at its most picturesque. John took a lot of video footage. We were sightseeing, yet there was a poignancy to the occasion that touched us all.

I felt strange asking for permission to visit our old house from the retired couple who had bought it. The man met me at the front gate. There had been many changes. The pond we had taken so long to build had been filled in and the plants pruned to sparseness. The flowers had gone and the enchantment of the garden had vanished with them.

I fell asleep in the car on the trip home, exhausted from the emotional strain of returning to these places which held so much pain, and also happiness, for me.

On the following Tuesday afternoon after the morning launch of the Tasman Conservation Trust where Ted Christopher played 'Knockin' on Heaven's Door', we were walking through the Botanic Gardens.

'Do you guys feel like going to Mt Wellington,' I asked. At 1270 metres high, Mt Wellington had great views of Hobart. Everyone agreed.

As we drove up the hairpin bends to the summit, John asked, 'Is there anywhere we can get a drink up there, mate?'

'No, the only thing up there is a lookout,' I replied.

On the way back down the mountain in the early afternoon, I saw the sign for the tavern at a small village called Fern Tree.

'D'you guys still want to go for that drink?'

It was empty inside the tavern. There was a jukebox in the back room with pool tables in front of it. I ordered some pints of ales and then we began a game of pool. Gordon selected some '70s music: Deep Purple, Led Zeppelin and Queen.

John picked up his video camera and started filming. Gordon and Les grabbed their pool cues and pretended to be playing their guitars. In this relaxed environment, I saw a personal side to the three of them that I hadn't yet observed. We were on our own and we could let our hair down.

John had booked a massage for the two of us back at The Grand Chancellor Hotel, so after an hour or so we reluctantly headed off.

That evening we returned to the Fern Tree Tavern with Ted Christopher and his songwriting partner, Tommy Millar, in tow. Brigid Cooke, Sue and John Burgess, Brian Walpole and his wife, Roland, Kate and a number of other people came too.

We sat around the fire, played pool and sang to the music on the jukebox. The camaraderie was very strong that night. John had has video camera with him and I took some footage of him as he wanted to record a message to his wife, Alison.

'Now you know what we mean, Alison,' John spoke to the camera, 'when we all go out for the night and we say, "Let's 'get Mikaced".'

We were united by such tragic events at the opposite ends of the globe, yet to have seen us that night you might have thought we had known each other for years.

'I was a bit worried when we left home that we were coming to a strange place,' John admitted to me then. 'The wonderful thing is we don't feel like we're foreigners here.'

I have been watching a video called 'Remembering our Children', a documentary of interviews with the Dunblane parents, made by the

ITV Network and screened in Britain to mark the one-year anniversary. It included interviews with Michael North and Les.

As the credits roll, Kareen Turner, whose daughter Megan was killed at Dunblane, reads a verse called 'Little Child Lost' written by Eugene G. Merryman Jr.

I feel the tears running down my cheeks as I hear the words spoken in her soft Scottish accent: how a child can be such a paradox, a little person that generates a conflict of anger and love. The verse is about how we cope with the loss of a little person and how many reminders we have of their existence, how we often hear their voice or catch a glimpse of them out of the corner of our eye and how that child was so much part of our soul. But we should be reassured that even though our loss can never be explained, without our child and other children who have died, there would be no children in heaven. In heaven they are safe and happy.

Towards the end of April I got a call from John Crozier. He had returned to Scotland to be greeted with a present from his wife.

'That's great. What was the present?' I asked.

'It's a pair of booties,' he said, not being able to contain his excitement.

'You're kidding . . .'

'Yeah, Alison's pregnant,' he said.

'Was that your parting gift?'

He laughed and it was as if he was standing there next to me.

EIGHTEEN

Building New Foundations

*O*n the video screen on the wall, a six-year-old boy dressed in a full pressure bodysuit is bending down to pick up a toy. Tears, brought on by the pain of his movements, are running down his face. His face is clear of scars, but his limbs and his head have had skin grafts following massive burns to most of his body. As he finally reaches the toy and stands up again, he stops crying: 'I never even touched the ground, anyway.'

Tjandamurra O'Shane was doused in petrol and set alight in a Cairns school yard in October 1996 by a twenty-seven-year-old man. There was no apparent motive. Like all the children I have come in contact with since the events of my own tragedy, I feel a deep emotional bond.

Today – 30 April 1997 – is the launch of the Alannah and Madeline Foundation, named after my children, and set up to help child victims of violence or sudden loss. The Prime Minister, Mr John Howard, *patron. Tjandamurra is to be first recipient of funds raised by the Foundation and he will travel overseas for a trip of his choice.*

As I stand with the 100 other people on the 35th floor of the Sofitel Hotel (formerly the Regent) in inner-city Melbourne, I can't help but think back to the night eleven and a half years ago when I was here with my bride, our heads full of the promise of a new life.

I realise how much I have aged in those years, how much I have lost my innocence. Back then, my future stretched before me. It never occurred to me that I might not have control over what happened to me. I believed then I had authority over my destiny.

That belief has been shaken to the core by the events of 28 April 1996. At least, I still have a conviction that being positive can make a difference even in the face of adversity.

It is for this reason I am here today – to try to make a contribution in righting the wrongs of our society, to help the suffering of all those children who are innocent parties to violence.

Many people have tears in their eyes when the video of Tjandamurra comes to an end and I find my own are wet with suppressed emotion. His courage reminds me of the courage shown by all of the children with whom I have connections: the injured children from Dunblane, who will, like Tjandamurra, live forever with their memories, and those who died bewildered, like my own two daughters, in the face of unprovoked and incomprehensible violence. Why should these children need to display such courage at such a tender age?

As I look around the room, I can see more suffering. About forty people who were directly affected by the massacre have attended this launch. Linda White, who'd just got married to Michael Wanders, her arms still in a plastic cast from the gunshot wounds, is standing near the window. John and Gaye Fidler are here. So are John and Coralyn Boskovic and Peter and Pauline Grenfell, who walked with Nanette and the girls up the hill moments before they were killed.

They are carrying memories they can never erase. Peter Grenfell was standing helpless near the toll booth as he saw Nanette fall to the ground and then witnessed the gunman firing at Alannah.

Carol Loughton was also there, the week before she went back into hospital for further surgery to fix her shattered shoulderblade.

When it is my turn to address the crowd I tell them that the idea for the Foundation came from another Melbourne father, Phil West, who, just like me, had two daughters. He had been looking at their drawings on the fridge when he thought of the idea of setting up a foundation to help ease the suffering of all these children. He wrote to me in the months that followed the massacre.

I realised that three ordinary fathers had brought about this event today: Tjandamurra's father, Tim, myself and Phil West, all of us wanting the world to be a better place. I referred to this in my speech:

> *To me, this illustrates how an ordinary person can make a difference and it is an ability that is in every one of us. The naming of the Foundation with the names of Alannah and Madeline fills me with pride. Nanette being their mother makes me proudest of all. The choice of Tjandamurra as the first recipient is so fitting. I can relate to those outstanding fighting qualities that I see in him back to my daughters. His courage in the face of ongoing recovery is great to see.*
>
> *Children have a basic fundamental right to live and be safe. This is a right that every Australian should aim for. Whilst our children are our future they are also vulnerable and innocent. They must be protected to ensure their belief in the general good of humanity. And it is to a future of harmony and peace that we should aspire. We must move forward to keep this a wonderful place to live.*

By the end of the launch, there was a strong bond between everyone in the room. A man approached me during the launch, introducing himself as an ambulance driver from Melbourne: 'The amount of therapy that is happening in this room is incredible,' he said.

And I had to agree. After the trauma of the anniversary I felt much more at peace. The knowledge that I could give something back to other people who had suffered was very life-affirming for me.

When Tjandamurra's father, Tim, said to me, 'When I saw you I felt as though you were my brother,' I realised that, once more, love had triumphed over darkness.

The Prime Minister, John Howard, was also touched by the spirit of the occasion. He hugged my mother, Milka – a moment she was to recount to many people afterwards – and told her, 'Your son's very strong. He must be from good stock.'

The first anniversary had taken its toll. I sometimes doubted the strength everyone seems so convinced that I have. The lead-up to the anniversary left me so depleted I felt as if I was running on empty. One of the bereavement manuals mentions that the approach of special dates 'may cause intense pain'. Early in April, perhaps spurred on by the intrusions of the media, I felt I was regressing and more alone than ever. I felt I was not coping, that I could not get back in control of my life, that I would simply lose it and physically collapse – something that had not happened up to this point.

Three days before the anniversary, on Friday 25 April, I woke up to the newspaper headlines: A LETTER FROM THE GUNMAN'S MOTHER: 'A GIFT OF LOVE'. 'Of all people, I weep with you – with your bitter tears, with our suffering tears and with unique, unshareable tears of my own,' she wrote.

What she should have said was: Love cannot restore life.

I felt her words were patronising and unnecessary, that there was nothing she could say and she should have kept her silence.

That same day, Mum was contacted by a radio journalist. She was asked if the letter made her feel any better. She replied: 'No, it doesn't make me feel any better because nothing can bring our girls back. I feel sorry for her as I wouldn't like to be his mother because every mother tries to bring her children up the best they can.'

These were my sentiments exactly.

Port Arthur was back in the news again. Journalists began calling my parents' place three weeks before the anniversary. One note on my message bank was timed 7.23 a.m. Could I ring the journalist back before 8 a.m.? She had a deadline.

Now, when I watch *Frontline*, the comedy satire about the inner workings of the media on the ABC, I see it from a different perspective. I have become one of the 'victims' that the show portrays.

'How are you coping?' journalists ask me. 'What are your plans for the future?'

I tell them my future has been a fragile existence over the past year and my fate is determined by what happens today. The week before the anniversary one television journalist even asked me if I had thought of politics. Perhaps they were running out of questions.

I brief my parents' household on handling calls from the media. I tell them to say that they don't know where I am and to take a message. It has been a steep learning curve, but I have become more assertive.

As the anniversary approached the news crews began to arrive at the Port Arthur Historic Site, some setting up weeks ahead to make sure they had a scoop. They know that, after this anniversary, it wouldn't be a such a major news item again.

But my scars, like the other survivors of that day, are permanent, not a fleeting illusion that can be captured on a television camera or in a photograph. Long after the headlines are gone, all of the victims of the tragedy will still be living with the pain.

There are so many things to keep my mind occupied. Writing the book, the launch of the Foundation, the anniversary. And then, last of all, there's me. I have to stop for a few minutes and ask myself how important all these considerations are. I need to preserve my sanity and that means looking after my health.

As I lie on the massage table, my masseuse, Tanya, says my back is in the worst shape she's ever seen, as if it is a slab of granite. The warmth of the towels and the heat pack on my back and the music by Enya combine to make me feel like I'm levitating. As if I am being embalmed, ready for departing this world. I feel soothed as if I don't have to worry any more about anything. I am accepting of my fate as if death cannot faze me.

On Sunday 27 April, I travelled from Hobart to the Port Arthur Historic Site with Steve, John, their girlfriends Justine and Mary, and my parents. That morning I had taken the family to St David's Cathedral. We realised shortly after we took our seats that we were sitting in the same spot we had been in for the State memorial service. I exchanged looks with John.

We arrived at the historic site about 4 p.m., having stopped at the bakery at the small town of Sorell on the way down, delaying the time we reached the site until after that fateful hour of 1.30 p.m. In the back seat of my car were three heart-shaped wreaths in proportionate sizes, covered in yellow and white flowers.

At almost every point of the day, I had been looking at my watch thinking about what I was doing this time last year. I was wishing all over again, my old 'if onlys' surfacing again. Wishing I had woken up late and not gone to golf, or that we had gone to the Wrest Point Casino in Hobart for the weekend to celebrate my birthday.

There was hardly anyone at the site when we drove through the toll booth. It was an eerie feeling. I knew this would be my last goodbye. The following day everything would be far more public. This was my private time with my family without the intrusion of the media and all the wellwishers.

Pam Ireland told me a few months after the girls' death that my mother had collected some autumn leaves which contained the blood of my daughters when she visited the site the day after they were killed. I only talked to my mother about this recently. She said it gave her comfort to have such a personal memento.

I walked towards the spot that occupies my thoughts so often these days. I bent down and felt the roadside where Nanette had been lying, scraping the bitumen in the hope that under my fingernails I could retrieve some of her blood cells. If there had been no-one else there,

I would have lain down on the ground to feel the vibrations of her spirit.

Unbeknown to me on that Sunday, even in those private moments, a television camera positioned amongst trees about 100 metres away was monitoring my movements. The footage was shown on commercial television that night.

After placing the wreaths I went for a walk around the historic site, retracing my steps along the frantic path I had taken that dreadful Sunday looking for them. The evening was mild in comparison to the previous year, but each step I took brought back memories, that eternal, mistaken belief that they would be okay. That nothing could have happened to them. I still have that sense of disbelief even now, a year later.

That night, my family and I went to Pam Ireland's for dinner and watched some of the videos of recent media footage. I felt drained afterwards. There are days when the emptiness is worse than others. This was one of those days.

When I arrived back at Eddie's house that night I was unable to sleep. My longing for them was so acute. I wanted to cry and talk to the girls, to play some ABBA songs, watch Maddie, dressed in a blue chiffon tutu, playing 'Mama Mia' some twenty times on Anzac Day. Or hear Alannah playing 'Love Me Tender', which she taught herself off the sheet music I had left by the keyboards. Little moments tucked away in time, which were being rekindled by this anniversary.

The day of the first anniversary, Monday 28 April, finally dawned. I was sleeping in Kate's bedroom, one of Pam and Eddie's children. The first thing I saw when I opened my eyes were the shelves full of toys.

As I lay there I knew that it was the Sunday that would hold much more relevance to me. But I still felt anxious. Perhaps I should have spent the day at the cemetery instead.

The ceremony at the old convict church was due to begin at 11 a.m. To pass time I picked up the newspaper, only to read that the memorial cross bearing all the names of the victims was going to be moved. The pain resurfaced when I thought of how hard I had tried to mark the site where the girls had died.

It is 5 June, and I'm in the process of finishing this book. I realise how much I have learnt in the past twelve months. How to deal with the media, to stop being one of its victims. These last two days, I have given interviews to newspapers and television stations about my views on plaques or permanent reminders to mark the spot where my family died at the Port Arthur Historic Site. And today, the Tasmanian government has finally announced that permanent plaques in the shape of an oak leaf will be erected to mark the spot where victims of the tragedy died. It is a lesson to me, as much about the media, as about what makes politicians jump.

Some of the anxiety I was experiencing over the anniversary had been eased by the arrival of the fathers from Dunblane a fortnight before.

One of the first questions I asked them was how they coped on their first anniversary.

'We spent the day quietly with friends,' John said.

'I'm not sure whether to go down to Port Arthur for the service or not,' I said.

'It's going to be a hard day and it should be a hard day, but what you need to remember is that it can't possibly be as bad as what happened on that day last year,' John said.

As I remembered his words, it was as if a veil lifted from my eyes, and I felt a deep sense of relief. They knew exactly how it would be. And they were right.

We drove to the site and parked in the same spot where I'd parked when I'd gone to see their bodies. My immediate family, my brothers' girlfriends, Julia McCance, Eddie and Pam Halton and Richard and Kerrie Shoobridge formed a flank around me.

In the jacket pocket of my suit, I put a corsage of three Dutch

Irises, the same flowers I had carried to the memorial service at St David's after their deaths. My heart was squeezed as if in a vice.

As we walked past the toll booth, three photographers were standing on the side of the road and the motor drives started up.

'Eddie, stay where you are, I'm staying right behind you,' I said, shielding myself from their view.

I hadn't even got to the spot where they'd died and already I was under siege.

As we approached it, I could see there were more flowers and messages now under the trees. I read some of the other cards and tried to concentrate on the words, but I could still picture them lying there, Netty's blood running down the hill, the blood of someone I had loved so much. All I could think of was how much I missed her. My mother went behind the tree where Alannah had been killed. Her anguish as she sobbed cut through the air. Would our pain ever ease?

Afterwards, we all walked across to the convict church for the service. Today, I knew I was going be a public commodity again and I shrank back from the thought. I felt scared and uncomfortable. I suppose I was also scared about coming into contact with other people. Strangers who I didn't know, who for whatever reason wanted to hold me or kiss my hand or give me a hug or tell me that they think I've got great strength.

Tears weren't cascading down my cheeks now. This time the tears were not loud, unstoppable and for the world to see. But they were in many ways stronger. Silent tears that welled deep inside your soul. Tears that swelled with each day I spent without them. I had the girls' headbands inside my jacket pocket and I reached in to touch them, but I didn't put them on.

Whilst being able to fully accept what happened, I know that I can never understand it. My vision has also changed. As I walked into the old church, I watched the changing hues of the trees. On the altar, scarves in autumn colours were covered in leaves from the trees. I watched a large oak leaf gently float to the ground. Things that weren't observed this time last year.

In the church I could see so many familiar faces. Twelve months later the hurt on their faces is no less intense but now it's transformed to the lines on their face, the grey hair and the trembling of their hands. We have all come to share the suffering that has been inflicted on us. Somehow the bond of love and empathy has linked us all. Helped the physical wounds to heal and the psychological scars to fade.

I looked down at the programme that had been handed to me: Port Arthur Anniversary Service 'Moving On'. I felt momentarily annoyed, remembering the words of Les Morton.

'How do you move on? The instinct is to stay where we are. Move on to where exactly? On to the time where my memories of my daughter are less vivid than they are now?'

We took our seats in the front row, at the end of which was the only television camera allowed inside the church. Thirty-five small candles were burning to represent the victims as well as a large one to represent the children killed at Dunblane.

Outside, through the vast empty windows, I was aware of other photographers circling.

Three girls from the peninsula sang a moving song: 'Beautiful in my Eyes'. I put my arm around my mother who had started to sob and I cried, too.

After the service, many people approached my family. Among them was ten-year-old Mary. Mary used to call Nanette 'her other mother'. Her home was about 150 metres down the road from us, but she spent so much time at our house and starred in so many of our videos.

I was struck by how much she'd grown up since I saw her last, almost a year before. As I hugged her, I realised how life has continued in spite of my tragedy. That my girls' age had been stopped so that they will be forever young.

Mary showed me a gold locket.

'Look what I got for Christmas.'

She opened it up and there were colour photographs of Lani and Maddie.

'I never go anywhere without it,' she said.

Her simplicity and innocence were almost too much to bear. Tears rolled down my cheeks as I held her close. She had lost two of her best friends.

Netty, how I wish we had had that third child we were thinking about. I was walking to the cemetery the other day when I passed a lady who was clearly pregnant and was wheeling a stroller with what appeared to be a two-year-old child. There is to me an ethereal appeal about a woman who has had children. Possibly it's that ability to nurture and comfort or maybe it's as simple as the selflessness of the act. Mothering is something that we all need at times. Especially when the situation becomes a little too difficult for us to cope with.

I would have loved to have had a son with you, too, Netty. Little Thomas we would have called him, the fantasy son I used to send postcards to from some of our earlier holidays before we had children. But, imagine if you had been pregnant at the time of the shooting, as you so easily might have been. I couldn't bear that.

I continue to wonder what would have happened if one of you had survived that dreadful day. One of the Dunblane parents said looking after their baby son helped them cope in the first few weeks because they had to get up for him, feed him and to look after him. She said it would have been so easy just to shut the curtains and not answer the door. Perhaps I should have simply closed the curtains anyway, instead of taking such a public stance.

If I had been left one of you, I know my grief would have had a different focus. Instead of relating everything back to me, I would have had someone to care for, someone to focus on, someone to nurture.

Netty, you'd often repeat what Keith had said to you about bringing up children. That a child is like a plant and the parents should be the stake guiding the plant as it grows. It needs to be there to grow straight, but there should be plenty of room for the plant to grow and develop its shape.

After the service, we walked back over to the place where the girls died and Mum, Dad and Lindsay laid down their flowers along the roadside. Bronwyn and Keith were also there and I gave Bronwyn a big cuddle. She is so different to Nanette and I know we will always see things differently. But we were all here to share our grief and I walked with her arm in arm, down to the main cross at the waterside where there was to be a ceremony at 1.30 p.m.

Around the cross, I saw more people I recognised. Lynne, a nurse, and one of the first people to enter the cafe that day, was there. And Brigid Cooke. We talked quietly after the names were read from the cross by the minister and Brigid and I both agreed that what the gunman did that day gave him pleasure and was something he wanted to do. That makes it so much more difficult to live with. Leaving us all in confusion with no reason we can comprehend.

I talked to Michael Beckman and Becky McKenna who were on the ferry that day to the Isle of the Dead. They saw Maddie drop her Port Arthur sticker and heard her ask Netty if they had been good. Becky commented on how beautifully dressed they were.

After the service I placed some flowers in the cafe for Jason Winter on behalf of the girls. I would love to have met him. Through Jo I almost feel I know him.

As we drove out of the site at the end of the day, I noticed that we were being followed by a media car. A television camera was placed close to the toll gates ready to zoom in for a close-up as we passed. I placed a newspaper over my face and as I looked back, I could see the cameraman throwing up his hands in frustration. It was a hollow victory.

Two days after the anniversary, I was back in Melbourne for the launch of the Foundation. At the end of the launch, Neil Mitchell from 3AW handed me a photocopy of an article in a Melbourne newspaper.

Beth and Ashley Mason from Box Hill, an eastern suburb of Melbourne, had named their first baby Courtney Alannah Madeline in memory of my daughters as she was born on the first anniversary of the massacre – a new life in the face of tragedy.

I felt honoured and touched by their gesture and decided to visit them. I took over Maddie's glow-worm soft toy which lights up when you squeeze it.

Courtney's twenty-nine-year-old mother, Beth, told me Courtney will learn the significance of her middle names as she grows up and will be given an explanation of the footnote on her birth notice in the newspaper: 'In honour of those affected by the Port Arthur tragedy'.

'I will let her know she is named after two very precious girls,' she said, and promised to send me progress reports.

As I left their house, I thought of how so many people are concerned about the effect children have on me, whether they should bring their children to visit, or whether I want to be involved in family outings. When my publisher, James Fraser, was in Melbourne he took Lindsay and me to lunch. Lindsay asked him if he had a photograph of his three-year-old daughter, Casey Bell. James quickly replied: 'I wouldn't bring it here.' It's a common sentiment, to avoid mentioning your own children in case it sounds heartless in the face of what has happened to me.

Yet my tragedy can never reflect on the beauty of other children who still retain that wonderful innocence. Children bring joy and heartfelt emotions I often do not experience from adults. I am happy in their company and always will be.

My darling Net, I am in the lounge-room of my new house at the end of May 1997. It is an old Victorian house, built in 1880 for a Presbyterian minister. You would love it. And you are close by, the cemetery only a handful of houses away. I can visit the three of you as often as I like without even getting in my car. From the verandah of the house, I can see Austin Hospital where we met and sometimes, the smoke is billowing out of the chimneys and I can hear your mocking voice saying: 'They're burning the bodies.'

Since I've returned to Melbourne, my visits to you have been almost daily and I come back with renewed faith and a sense of inner peace.

I'm sitting on the kissing couch which I bought to match the period of the house. My only wish is for you to be here with me. To hold me and tell me that everything will be all right one day. I desperately need your reassurance. When Dad came to visit the house, the first thing he said was: 'This was the house Nanette would have wanted.' And you know, he is right. I arrived back from Tasmania last November and the house was up for auction the next day. I decided to act on instinct, the way I always do these days. It was meant to be. I didn't have to decide where I wanted to live, it was presented to me on a plate. Mum and Dad are also only five minutes' drive away.

I have hardly lived here, Netty, even though I bought the house in March, as I spent four months in Tasmania writing this book. I'm glad I opted not to live alone – I have three flatmates, Beth, Narelle and Simone. There is often the smell of cooking on the stove, even if it's not your cooking, Netty. But it helps that I don't come back to an empty house.

Your presence is everywhere, photographs on the mantlepiece, on the walls, your straw hats on the coatstand and the girls' pram in the spare room with their toy box. Familiar items in an unfamiliar setting, yet they give me comfort. In the lounge-room is our couch, the tapestry we bought is on the wall. Alannah's whiteboard with the words she wrote the morning she died is out in the shed and Mr Squiggle is sitting on the couch in the study. Just as I begin to settle into life here, I know in several weeks I will have to leave this new home for my overseas trip. There have been so many changes in my life, I can no longer comprehend another, yet I know I am doing the right thing by getting away.

In the midst of being positive, I am struck sometimes by the meaningless of my existence. Why do I bother having a place that looks good? What does it matter? Who do I have to share it with? I remember the day I moved in, how flat I felt. The feeling that you should have been here to share it with me. Things didn't seem to go right that day. The garage door didn't work, the mirror that was supposed to be moved was still there. Mum went into hospital for observation after feeling faint. She'd been helping me clean all day, but I'm sure the stress of the impending anniversary was taking its toll on her. I could see it in her eyes. There was no motivation. No life. Dad tries to put on a brave face for me, but I know he's hurting, too. How can you not hurt? Life is not and can never be the same again.

I was about to start unpacking the dining room when an INXS song came on the radio. One that we'd danced to many times. The song talks about things staying as they once were. Much as I don't want it to change, everything around me has. There are no constants at the moment. Thank goodness for family who give me an anchor point and thank goodness I have this book and Lindsay to talk to.

Sometimes, I'm worried that what has happened to you will change me, Walter Mikac. I'm scared. Will I become bitter and twisted? Spiteful and wanting revenge? I do feel angry at times. Angry at the rollercoaster ride that I'm on. Fluctuating from survival to wishing dreadfully that I was with you. Anger that one person could create so much hurt. How can it be possible? Is this world still worth being in? Netty, is there an answer?

NINETEEN

The Future Beckons

I opened up the letter and began reading. It was from a doctor whose wife and child were killed in a car accident while they were on a holiday in Eastern Victoria. Although the circumstances of their deaths are different, our loss is comparable. He tells me his life has irrevocably changed:

> Somehow the funeral, the flowers, the sympathy from hundreds of our friends from around the world came and carried me forward. But then it entered a new phase ...
>
> THE FUTURE.
>
> Now it is some time on. I have married again and have a new, absolutely beautiful son. Life is very different, but the past never goes away completely. Whereas for a long time, I thought I could never survive all this pain and loss, somehow I have survived, and even you too can be happy again some day. But I have to tell

you there is no secret formula – just time. And the faith that others have in you. Hang in there. My heart goes out to you, but you know that you are not alone in your torment.

I read the words and gain some comfort, but what he was talking about seemed so far away, elusive, beyond my grasp.

Especially today. I am with Lindsay at my family's grave at War-ringal Cemetery. The three Japanese white pine trees I often think are my three girls stand strong and silent in the cemetery grounds. Warm shafts of sunshine caress our backs as we look at the words etched on the headstone. It is still so difficult to believe the sight in front of us: the identical dates of their death and their names immor-talised in stone.

Both Lindsay and I sense the presence which has been guiding us for these last few months as we have been writing this book. Netty and the girls are with us. Lindsay has sensed it particularly since she arrived in Melbourne this week to finish the last few chapters. Often when I'm sitting here, I feel someone is looking at me, but when I turn around there is no-one to be seen.

Today, I need Netty desperately. I had a housewarming party for my new home last night. I drank too much and finished the night I know not where, waking up with a splitting headache and full of remorse: I had left my own party too early, seeking I knew not what. I know it's not what Netty would have wanted. She knows I am suffering. Even my family and friends are angry at my thoughtless-ness. I can identify with one of my favourite Brett Whiteley paintings, 'Self Loathing', as he sees his reflection in the mirror he holds up. I arrive at the cemetery with a broken spirit. Can you speak to us, Netty? I call. Silence.

It is Lindsay's first time here. I explain to her how coming here recharges my batteries and I know she can sense this. How it turns my despair to hope and shows me light. Lindsay has been patiently listening to my outpouring of feelings nearly every day in recent months. Between us, we have woven those feelings I have experi-enced into what I feel is an accurate portrayal of my life. I thank her for being there. As a support, a loving friend and as someone who was lucky enough to have known Nanette and the girls. It has not been an easy task, as we have both given of our souls, each in a different way, to write this book. Lindsay's gift for the written word, and her encouragement, have made me look at life in a new, more observant way. Conversely, I hope I have been able to give some small inspiration back to her. We sit side by side on the grave, sprinkling the red and pink rose petals from my garden over the slab, spreading our fingers to feel the warmth radiating from the granite beneath us. Lindsay says she would like to spend some time alone with them.

I wish I had my camera with me as I depart. I look back to see her lying on the petal-covered grave, taking in the inspiration of their spirit and bidding her own farewell, the descending sun shining on her back.

I realise over the past twelve months I have changed irrevocably. Physically, I look different. When we watch the 'A Current Affair' tape filmed a year ago, two days after their death, Lindsay says: 'You look so young there. Like an innocent.'

My hair is not cut so short with clippers these days and occasionally I won't shave for a while and leave a goatee. I have put on weight and have gained more muscle from working out at the gym, running, cycling, swimming – all those activities I throw myself into as a way of trying to cope. All these things say I'm not as I was before. Physically, mentally or psychologically.

I have traded our blue Pajero for a red Mercedes, not the sort of car I would have chosen to have with a family. It is almost as if part of me wanted to choose a vehicle that was the antithesis of what I was before.

I have control over how I spend my day and have only myself to consider. I can sleep in if I want or stay up late, go out or stay home. But, in spite of such freedom, I would still trade in all of this for what I had before. Now, I am always alone and can never escape from the memories.

I told the Hobart psychiatrist, Ian Sale, when I visited him before leaving Tasmania, that I was experiencing a rebound of the sensation of how unbelievable it is that this has happened. As I have no explanation for what occurred, there still seems to be the possibility that I will wake from a coma. I will regain consciousness and everything will be as it was. This sense of disbelief still shakes me to the core when I least expect it.

I've changed most in the intensity of emotions I experience. There are moments where I feel strong and yet many times I am vulnerable. One evening I was dining in a crowded Italian restaurant in Melbourne when the passing waiter bumped a tray in my back. My frenzied reaction caught the attention of most people sitting nearby and I felt like retreating to a dark corner. My former carefree attitude to life can never return. There are times when I feel proud of my efforts at continuing life and working to keep Netty and the girls' names remembered. But at other times, I'm starkly aware that I've let my family and friends around me down, but thank them with all my heart for still being there for me. It is healing to be loved and feel wanted. Savouring life to the full after experiencing its fragility, I know, sometimes leads me to be less tolerant of others.

I am still not sure who I really am and whether the person I am now is the result of the grief I experience or other factors in the potpourri of my changing life.

The unjustness of what has happened at Port Arthur means I have surrounded myself with a protective shield. I am more honest in some ways, but so much more guarded in what I tell people. My face has become recognised and I see, time and time again, that look in people's eyes when they recognise who I am. A look that says we know who you are, but we don't know what to say to you.

In the week before I left Hobart, Lindsay and I were eating at a takeaway Asian restaurant. We heard a lady turn to her partner at the door as they were leaving and say, 'Do you recognise that guy? That's Walter Mikac, the guy from Port Arthur.' There's no escaping this factor, particularly as I've been in the media promoting the Alannah and Madeline Foundation and speaking out for stricter gun laws. I could always stay at home and become a hermit, but I know that Netty wouldn't have wanted that. In some ways, I have to be ambivalent about being in public. I gain more strength being surrounded by people who know me and feel comfortable being with me.

So what does the future hold for me, Walter Mikac? I wish I knew.

When people ask about my future plans, what they fail to realise is that when something as traumatic and harrowing as this happens in your life the future loses its relevance and, instead, life becomes a day-to-day existence.

The first few weeks after the death of Netty, Lani and Maddie, I felt like I was in an endless, dark tunnel. No matter how far down the tunnel I walked, it seemed like I was never going to get to the end of it. The only thing that gave me hope was the wonderful memories of times I'd spent together with my family. I had achieved contentment. Happiness. The intangibles that people in modern-day life manically try to attain. Material wealth doesn't always offer a solution. The very simple moments, the ones we often take for granted, are the ones that give life meaning. I still look back on days such as when Alannah and Maddie were born and can feel the pride welling up in me.

I know with conviction that I made Netty happy. What's more, I was so besotted with her that I never doubted I would grow old with her. This is patently obvious to me when I open a box and start reading the cards we sent each other. Like the last one I received from Netty when I turned thirty-four, my last birthday with them:

To my darling husband,
I am so proud of you and what you have achieved. You are my hero and I am full of admiration for you. Just the thought of your nakedness makes me tingle. I love your skin, your smell, your manness. Quite simply, I adore you.
Love always, Nanette.

And the card I wrote four months after we got married:

To my dearest beautiful Netty,

Well, four months have passed since that beautiful day and I am happier than ever. Nothing will make me happier than being able to say that very thing on your 90th birthday.

I love you and will forever.

Happy birthday, bub.

Our love was nurtured over thirteen years so that it was a state of being, a feeling which will stay with me forever. It's so incredibly strong, that often when I'm driving around and I hear one of Netty's favourite songs I get an exhilarating uplift. I watch the last bit of footage still on our video camera of the raft race on the local regatta day at Nubeena. I hear her laughter echo around the room and I can feel her presence so strongly, it's as if I can reach out and touch her.

But I know the future is beckoning. I now have to make decisions on my own.

I have not yet decided whether or not I will return to practising pharmacy. Yet, it's one of the most frequent questions I'm asked.

'Have you been working? Have you still got your pharmacy? What have you been doing?' There are many days when I don't feel like answering. Then I realise it's often the only way in which people can show they are concerned. They don't want to open up old wounds but they do genuinely care.

I do enjoy pharmacy. Dealing with the public is difficult, but it's also extremely rewarding. I have had letters from people who were my customers in Melbourne over ten years ago. I obviously made a strong enough impression for them to remember me and my family. That is very heartening and it is a profession of which I am proud.

Deep down, though, I suspect it is not part of my future. When discussing this with Steve Ireland some months ago, we came to the conclusion that I may move away from pharmacy altogether. Steve advised: 'It's been such a major change in your life that maybe a new career path would also be a good idea.'

Now, twelve months down the track, I think that is a real possibility. I feel the many things I've learned since losing my family will offer me all kinds of opportunities that will challenge me. Areas like counselling or even motivational speaking. I believe I can achieve anything I set my mind to. I always feel inspired by a card sent to me by my close friends Neil and Maryanne:

> *The Winner is always part of the answer*
> *The Loser is always part of the problem . . .*
> *The Winner says: 'It may be difficult but it's possible';*
> *The Loser says: 'It may be possible but it's too difficult.'*

When I started to write this book, initially I didn't think I would have the ability and perseverance to complete such a monumental task. But now I have done it, with Lindsay's help, even though we have used every ounce of energy in our bodies. The book has become a part of me. It's as though my body has been opened up on a dissection table, exposed for all the world to see. The good and the bad. A post-mortem on my life to this point in time.

I realise people will read this book and feel they know everything about me. But life itself is such a complex thing. Words can never fill every crevice in the wall of life. I hope there's enough left of me that is unknown. Allowing myself to be dissected does not mean I will allow myself to feel owned.

There are many parts of me and my personality that are changing and evolving, even now. My humour and love of life, for instance, are as strong as ever. Slowly I know I am recuperating and allowing myself to feel enthusiastic about the future.

Often I think other people can't comprehend how this can be the case. Sometimes I feel it's because they can't conceive being positive in a similar scenario. When people first meet me they grapple with the darkness and negativity of what's happened. I have to live with what has occurred for the rest of my life, but that doesn't mean it has to consume my future as well.

I feel as though I can love more deeply also and appreciate the simple pleasures of life more fully. Sitting in the sun invigorates my body. Exercising helps me feel vibrant and increases my energy levels. But, despite what has happened, I'm not unlike the average person. I love watching the football, walking the dogs, listening to music or reading a newspaper.

One of the other issues facing me in the future is whether I want to have more children. I *would* like to have children. I know what it was like to be a husband and a father and those life experiences can never be taken away from me. I know how satisfying they are and would dearly love to be in that situation again. The main difficulty is it will never be as uncomplicated as last time. Living with another person can be daunting, as you struggle to accept different attitudes, religion, customs and habits. I am thirty-five now. Whilst I have some life experiences behind me, I've always wanted to grow up with my children. To play with them, help them and develop with them. I am a strong believer in grasping as much of life as you're able to. I still live in hope that I'll find someone who will rekindle my love of life. I know full well that there never can or will be another Nanette. I was lucky to have spent some wonderful years of my life with her. I was privileged she was the mother of our beautiful children. I learned from her, was loved by her and am the person I am today because of her.

Adjusting to my new single status is difficult. When Jo Winter came to Melbourne in the weeks leading up to the anniversary to appear with me in a 'Sixty Minutes' programme, I dropped her at the airport. She was filling out her departure card and reached the boxes to be categorised: Married, divorced or widowed?

I sympathised with the pain this request brought. In some ways meeting her again was like meeting an old familiar friend. Words were not necessary. A smile or a look were enough. We both knew the turmoil and hurt we were going through and hope that one day normality will return.

After the television interview, we shared a bottle of champagne and some pasta, talked about our aspirations and hopes and even discussed some of the vivid images from that day. It's difficult to share that with anyone else. We also talked about what had been happening in our personal lives. Being with Jo was comfortable. I didn't have to pretend in any way.

As the book nears completion, I feel a sense of despondency as the source of my entire focus over recent months is disappearing. Where to from here? Do I want to stop thinking about what has happened to me? I feel such uncertainty that I need to sit in front of the laptop, even though nothing is appearing on the screen. It has become a security blanket for me lately.

The phone rings, disturbing me as I stare out the window. It is Pastor Allan Anderson. I haven't spoken to him since well before the anniversary and feel in need of some reassurance. We speak about various issues.

'I watched the anniversary service on television and found it very moving and emotional,' he said. 'Having been intimately involved with so many of the faces in the crowd meant that I knew about parts of their life that nobody else knew.'

I explained to him that I found the reality that they were not coming back hit me hardest after the anniversary.

'You will find that the emptiness you're feeling will last with you for quite some time.'

'I've come to accept that, but it's hard when you get home at night and you know that there's no-one to welcome you and no-one to sleep with,' I confided.

'That will change as you come to turning points in your life. Just as you'll look at their photos and sometimes feel great happiness often sitting alongside sadness.'

'I'm worried that maybe in the future anger will express itself when I don't expect it.'

'Be understanding of yourself if it does happen, but don't be too hard on yourself. From what I've seen you seem to have the skills from your upbringing to diffuse it. You tend to put your anger into action like you've done with the gun issue. Directing energy in that sort of way is more healthy and makes you feel like you're doing something positive with it.'

'Some people I meet don't know what to say to me. They think I walk around in a morbid state without being able to laugh.'

'People's reactions to grief are varied, as many people don't understand it. It's important that they have their grief for you and not your grief for themselves.'

Allan was making sense. Things always seemed to be put back into perspective when I talked to him. Exposing my vulnerable feelings allowed them to be strengthened.

'I've also found some people who were good friends before have gone by the wayside,' I continued.

'Yes, that's often the case. I often tell people who are in the early stages of grieving that they should use a tape recorder to capture some of the ridiculous promises people make shortly after someone's death.'

'I must admit that I feel a more compassionate person and want to bring some good to the world.'

'Well, it's one of those ironic situations where people who have suffered develop a better understanding of life. You are able to see the stars in the sky when it's light, whereas other people can only see them against the backdrop of the night sky. Your perspective on life is unique.'

'But I still really miss not having someone to confide my deepest feelings with. Someone who can accept me for who I am and not for what has happened to me.'

'That will come but remember that you need to build a friendship first where each side is comfortable. Unfortunately our bodies often get in the way of our hearts. That's part of human nature.'

'I still find that sometimes I can be having a good time when something unexpectedly triggers sadness and I shed a tear or two.'

'There's nothing wrong with that. Be comfortable with letting those feelings stand side by side. Let them be together and you'll travel through the peaks and troughs much easier.'

I thanked Allan for his words of reassurance. What he said seemed to put everything back in perspective for me.

'Don't let that brother of yours lead you astray when you go overseas,' he added with a laugh as we said our goodbyes.

I am glad I am going to Europe to take stock of my life and think about where to go in the future. I know I won't have to confront the vexing question of the future immediately. I could never have contemplated in my wildest notions doing what I am doing now just over a year ago. But I *am* looking forward to the anonymity of travelling. Going somewhere where hopefully people don't know me. Where I can maybe resume being me the person and not 'Walter, the person who lost his family at Port Arthur'.

I will visit my friends from Dunblane. John Crozier rings me regularly telling me of golfing outings he's organised. I am looking forward to seeing some of my relatives in Croatia and the beauty of my parents' birthplace, even though I know I will also be sad knowing I never got to take my family there.

In many ways, life has come a full circle. Lindsay reminds me I am going for four months, the same time I spent during my last trip to Europe when I left Netty behind. This time, Netty, it's you who won't be here when I return although I know your spirit and those of the girls will always be with me.

I've travelled so far from the moment I saw you lying on the road, but in travelling that journey, I have sifted through the times we shared with a fine-tooth comb, a chance few people ever get.

I know now, even more than I did at the beginning, that it's my responsibility to carry on your ideals and your attitude to life. Laughter and making people happy was your gift, Netty. Laughter has so often helped elevate me out of the darkness. It's healing and life-giving. Your capacity to love was all-encompassing. For me it was the powerful force which protected me. It kept me focused and gave me the drive to deal with life.

It gives me great comfort to know how secure Alannah and Madeline were in the love we gave them. They were given the freedom to explore, enjoy and relish life. Secure in the love that their parents had for each other and secure in the love that was showered on them.

I hope one day I will dance with you all again, but at least I am secure in the knowledge that what we did when we were together will sustain me till then.

Epilogue

My hands have a blueish tinge and the chill in the air reminds me it is the first day of winter. The sun's rays have lured me outside to prepare my garden for spring. Pruning the roses is a delicate operation. Gloves are needed to protect against the thorns and the cuts must be cleaned. As I bend and snip the spent old canes from the rose bush, I hear children's laughter. Is that Lani and Maddie running around behind my back? Looking at the task before me, I think of the nurturing process. Since writing these last chapters I have wanted to come out into the garden to heal with nature.

While I snip, I think of the wonderful experience of watching a child grow, a product conceived in love with your partner. Witnessing a baby's progress through the unresponsive blob-like stage takes much patience and reassurance, but as visible characteristics appear, it's like a rosebud forming. Seeing an offspring walk, talk or move their hands in a particularly distinctive way is the essence of self-development.

It reminds me of the swelling of the petals inside the rosebud, slowly being nurtured and gaining physical structure. From this point individuality begins to assert itself. The transition from infancy to childhood begins with so many complexities to be learned. We are all introduced to such a gambit of character traits which helps form our own personalities: independence, shyness, intelligence, calmness, dominance – the building blocks of the future.

As the colour of the bud's petals threaten to burst open, its true shade is hidden inside the flower, only to be revealed as the flower blooms. Just as a child's personality develops as skills like reading and writing open up further avenues of self-expression.

While the flower is still a bud, it is in a vulnerable stage of development. A child can act like an adult, but emotionally still be a baby needing ongoing love and commitment. But with tender loving care, the rose can open and display its innate beauty. There is only the initial hint of its fragrance, but its best is yet to come.

This is the point at which I sadly parted from my darling Alannah. She had so much vitality, uniqueness and incredible potential to offer the world.

Maddie didn't even have an opportunity to truly flower. Her independence and character were beginning to assert themselves as she entered infancy. As she looks down on me from the walls and mantlepieces of my house, the innocence of her face arrests me and stops me in my tracks.

My little rosebud, how would you have been, how would you have grown up and why wasn't I allowed to get to know you?

As the sun slides beneath the horizon, I have almost finished my task. I look up from the rose bushes. There's Netty reading on the verandah, her favourite novel open on the wicker lounge. Relaxed and oblivious, she pulls at her ringlets, extending the hair to its full length, sipping from her cup of tea in the other hand. Lani and Maddie run wildly in circles on the large green lawn. Their carefree laughter mixes with delightful fragrance of the last remaining roses that I'm about to prune. The cocktail of sensory pleasure swirls in my head and I gently drift into a euphoric state. For the first time since all this began, I think I have reached a state of peace.

TOMORROW

Life is something we take for granted
something we assume,
but in truth it is fragile
a brief moment in the space of eternity
a flicker in a fire of infinity.

Death doesn't seem real
it is something that happens when we're old
But some aren't so lucky.
For some, life is shattered,
before it has truly begun.

Treasure each moment,
as though it's your last,
cherish those you love,
forgive those you don't,
and do things today,
in case there's no tomorrow.

Note: This poem was written by Rebekah, our babysitter in Nubeena,
after the death of Nanette, Alannah and Madeline.

Acknowledgements

I would like to thank my family for their incredible, unwavering support: my mother Milka, my father Danny and brothers Steven and John.

I would also give deep thanks to Lindsay, who helped me unravel the powerful thoughts and emotions I have experienced in the past twelve months. Without her this book would not have been the same.

I would also like to thank her family, her husband Bruce Miller for his photographs and friendship, and their children Elliot, Phoebi and Oscar.

Thanks also to Nanette's family, the love I was always shown by her late mother Grace and support from her father Keith, and particularly her sister Bronwyn Hibbert and her children, Daniel and Hannah. Also Rodney and Jenny, Peter and Jo, Graeme and Heather and all their children.

Thanks to my Uncle Maté and Auntie Ana and my cousins, Julie, Gabrielle and Andrew, and to my brothers' girlfriends, Mary and Justine, and their families.

To my many friends who have stuck by me through the toughest times: Chris McCann and his wife, Karen, Pam and Steve Ireland, Eddie and Pam Halton, Richard and Kerrie Shoobridge, Maryanne and Neil Taylor, Louise Broughton and Fonz. To my family's parish priest, Father Robinson. And especially to Brad and Julia for their hospitality – and sustenance – while I was in Hobart. To Pastor Allan Anderson, for lifegiving advice, and his wife, Sue.

And to my many new friends: Jo Winter and her brother-in-law, Lester, John and Sue Burgess, Carol Loughton, Linda and Michael Wanders, Gaye and John Fidler and the many others who have suffered as a result of what happened that day at Port Arthur.

To Roland Browne, Co-ordinator for the Tasmanian Coalition for Gun Control, and his wife Kate and their children Asher and Tim; Rebecca Peters, the Chair of the National Coalition for Gun Control; everyone involved in the launch of the CD 'Side by Side', especially Zeljko and Waddie; Tim and Monica Goddard and everyone from Moorilla winery in Hobart for their support for the Alannah and Madeline Foundation, as well as their friendship; Jacqueline Gillespie, who gave me the confidence to write this book; Debbie and Tony Couttie; Heather Wilson for her friendship; Phil West, who gave me the inspiration to set up the Foundation; the Prime Minister, John Howard for being patron, and to Neil Mitchell and Clarke Forbes at Melbourne's 3AW radio station; Tanya Flack for the wonderful massages that helped relieve the stress; and to all at Austin Hospital in Melbourne.

To my fellow Australians and those people from overseas who wrote to me sharing their own personal experiences as well as encouragement and empathy, my heartfelt thanks.

And to John Crozier, Les Morton and Gordon Bounds, the fathers whose children were victims of the Dunblane massacre, there can be no words to describe our bond.

To James Fraser and Amanda Hemmings, my publishers at Pan Macmillan, for their constant support, and to my editor Madonna Duffy for her patience and her unwavering enthusiasm and belief in this book.

While writing the book, several books have been greatly helpful.

The main ones were: *Coping with Grief* by Mal and Dianne Mc-Kissock (ABC Books, 1985), *No Time for Goodbyes* by Janice Harris Lord (Millenium Books, 1988), *Dunblane – Our Year of Tears* by Peter Samson and Alan Crow (Mainstream Publishing, 1997).

W. M.
Melbourne, 1997

I'd like to thank my husband Bruce for his patience while I wrote this book. Thanks also to my three children, Elliot, ten, Phoebi and Oscar, both six, who each displayed such understanding far beyond their years in welcoming Walter as a member of our family. To my mother-in-law Ellen for picking up the pieces on the home front.

And to Walter – the journey has not always been easy but I've found this an incredibly challenging experience and one that has changed my attitude to life. Thank you for the candidness you have shown in sharing your thoughts with me.

Also to Danny and Milka, Steve and John who welcomed me into their family and all of Walter's friends who I have met while writing the book.

To Andiee Paviour for convincing me to do it.

To James Fraser, one of the best publishers in the business, Amanda Hemmings for her support, and our understanding editor Madonna Duffy, who shared so many conversations.

I would also like to thank my agent, Jill Hickson and Associates, in particular, Gaby Naher.

L. S.
Hobart, 1997

The Alannah and Madeline Foundation was formed in February 1997, with the Prime Minister, Mr John Howard as its patron. Its aim is to provide financial or other support to child victims of violent crime or the sudden loss of family.

If you would like to know more about the Foundation or would like to send a donation, write to:

GPO Box 9948
Your Capital City

or telephone:
03 9513 7200